Fun with the Family™ in Alabama

Help Us Keep This Guide Up to Date

Every effort has been made by the author and editors to make this guide as accurate and useful as possible. However, many changes can occur after a guide is published—establishments close, phone numbers change, hiking trails are rerouted, facilities come under new management, etc.

We would love to hear from you concerning your experiences with this guide and how you feel it could be improved and be kept up to date. While we may not be able to respond to all comments and suggestions, we'll take them to heart and we'll make certain to share them with the author. Please send your comments and suggestions to the following address:

The Globe Pequot Press
Reader Response/Editorial Department
P.O. Box 480
Guilford, CT 06437

Or you may e-mail us at: editorial@globe-pequot.com

Thanks for your input, and happy travels!

FUN WITH THE FAMILY™

in ALABAMA

HUNDREDS OF IDEAS
FOR DAY TRIPS WITH THE KIDS
SECOND EDITION

By LYNN GRISARD FULLMAN

The
Globe
Pequot
Press

Guilford, Connecticut

Fun with the Family is a trademark of The Globe Pequot Press.

Cover and text design by Nancy Freeborn
Cover photo by Julie Bidwell
Maps by M.A. Dubé

Library of Congress Cataloging-in-Publication Data
Fullman, Lynn Grisard.
   Fun with the family in Alabama : hundreds of ideas for day trips with the kids / by
Lynn Grisard Fullman.—2nd ed.
       p. cm. — (Fun with the family series)
   Rev. ed. of: Alabama. 1st ed. c1997.
   Includes index.
   ISBN 0-7627-0535-3
   1. Alabama—Guidebooks. 2. Family recreation—Alabama—Guidebooks. I. Fullman,
Lynn Grisard. Alabama. II. Title. III. Series.

F324.3.F85 1999
917.6104'63—dc21
                                                                99-043818

Manufactured in the United States of America
Second Edition/First Printing

Contents

ALABAMA

Acknowledgments

With thanks to wonderful Alabama folks who make this world a better place and who have been untiringly patient with my quests: Ami Simpson, Cameron Reeder, and Russell Nolen with the Alabama Bureau of Tourism and Travel; Georgia Carter Turner with the Alabama Mountain Lakes Tourist Association; Patty Tucker with the DeKalb County Tourist Association; Carol Maner with Calhoun County Convention and Visitors Bureau; Lee Sentell with the Huntsville Convention and Visitors Bureau; Dilcy Hilley with the Greater Birmingham Convention and Visitors Bureau; Debbie Wilson and Alison Stanfield with Florence/Lauderdale Tourism; Lisa Socha with Marshall County Convention and Visitors Bureau; Susann Hamlin with the Colbert County Tourism and Convention Bureau; Squee Bailey and Pam Swanner with Decatur Convention and Visitors Bureau; Robert Ratliff with the Tuscaloosa Convention and Visitors Bureau; Doug Purcell with the Historic Chattahoochee Commission; Lucy Arnold with Mobile Convention and Visitors Corporation; Andy Britton with Montgomery Chamber of Commerce; Lauri S. Cothran with Selma & Dallas County Chamber of Commerce's Tourism Division; Barbara McLaurine with Union Springs/Bullock County Tourism Council; Colette Boehm and Bebe Gauntt with the Alabama Gulf Coast Convention and Visitors Bureau.

Introduction

It took me years to begin looking at Alabama. When I first came here, I looked for friends. Then I looked for roots. When I had both, I began looking at the soil where I had planted myself.

Every day since has been an adventure. I have seen where battles were fought; where trails lead into wildernesses I assumed had vanished; where famous people had their roots; where Civil War and civil rights history was written. The more I see, the more I need to see.

When I travel beyond the state, I am always glad to return home, to a place that is not—thank goodness—all those things that outsiders believe it is. I wonder sometimes if we should let the secret out. Should we tell others about our pleasant year-round climate, our mountains and beaches, our history, and our pride?

I suppose if we were to keep our real selves a secret, few would visit. To keep our region secret, however, would not be typical of our Southern hospitality. We are warm here, not just by climate but with our hearts. While other shovel snow, we watch the first buds of springtime. While others lament growing crime, we polish our silver for pilgrimages into stately, columned homes. While others battle smog, we rub sunscreen on our faces.

To help you explore Alabama, I've divided the state into five areas: Northwest, Northeast, Central, Southwest, and Southeast. Within each region I have listed places I think you will want to visit. Not every town overflows with tourist sites, but, knowing that your travels will lead you down winding roads toward bustling cities, I also have mentioned smaller communities and the sites you and your children might enjoy seeing.

It's a neat place, this adopted state of mine. I've loved every minute of getting to know her better. I trust you will, too.

Please refer to the following guide to determine the cost of establishments in this book:

Rates for Lodging:

$	up to $50
$$	$51 to $75
$$$	$76 to $75
$$$$	$100 and up

Rates for Restaurants:

$	most entrees under $10
$$	most $10 to $15
$$$	most $15 to $20
$$$$	most over $20

Attractions Key

The following is a key to the icons found throughout the text.

 Swimming

 Animal Viewing

 Boating / Boat Tour

 Food

 Historic Site

 Lodging

 Hiking / Walking

 Camping

 Fishing

 Museums

 Biking

 Performing Arts

 Amusement Park

 Sports/Athletic

 Horseback Riding

 Picnicking

 Skiing/Winter Sports

 Playground

 Park

 Shopping

Northwest Alabama

From historic homes to white-water rafting, the northwest corner of Alabama is filled with adventure. Here your family will find nature trails, a national forest, renowned fishing spots, and outdoor dramas. In addition there are homes of noted people, ranging from a jazz great to a war hero, and museums that focus on everything from the Civil War to bugs and Indians. You'll find Indian mounds, a restaurant atop a 300-foot tower, and the nation's original wave pool, which still entices those who seek a reprieve from Alabama's steamy days.

Athens

As you make your way into the state's northern segment, be sure to swing through Athens, which evolved into a center for antebellum planters of the Tennessee Valley after its founding in 1818.

ATHENS STATE UNIVERSITY (ages 8 to 12)

300 North Beaty Street, Athens 35611; (256) 233–8215 or (800) 522–0272; www.athens.edu. The campus is accessible all day, every day. Founder's Hall opens on weekdays at 8:00 A.M. and closes at 6:00 P.M. Monday through Thursday, at 4:30 P.M. on Friday, and at 3:00 P.M. during the summer. It is closed most weekends. Admission is **Free***.*

The university is the state's oldest institution of higher learning, and its campus is picturesque. Don't miss Founders Hall, a noted example of Greek Revival architecture. Dating back to the 1840s, the building originally housed Athens Female College. A small chapel on the second floor contains a hand-carved altar detailing scenes from the New Testament.

Waterloo
Rogersville
Florence
Tuscumbia
Athens
Decatur
Phil Campbell
Haleyville
Double Springs

NORTHWEST

G̲o Fish The Tennessee River in North Alabama offers some of the nation's best largemouth-bass fishing, along with excellent sport fishing for smallmouth, sauger, crappie, bream, spotted bass, stripe, and catfish.

The river presents a mixture of deep drop-offs and shallow banks, narrow tributaries and wide-open spaces, flooded timber, and wave-washed cliffs.

Spring and fall are the best seasons for anglers hunting the lunker.

 HOUSTON MEMORIAL LIBRARY AND MUSEUM (ages 8 to 12)

101 North Houston Street, Athens 35611; (256) 233–8770. The library is open Monday through Friday from 10:00 A.M. to 5:00 P.M. and Saturday from 9:00 A.M. to noon. Open year-round. Admission is 𝐅𝐫𝐞𝐞.

Built in 1835, the former home of George Houston at present holds many items that belonged to the Houston family. An attorney, Houston was a member of the U.S. Senate and twice served as governor of Alabama. Family portraits and the Houston coat-of-arms are among the displays.

A̲nnual Events in Athens

- During the third week in April, Athens hosts a **Dogwood Festival,** which includes several events that your children will enjoy, such as games, crafts, a fishing rodeo, duck races, and a talent show. There is no admission cost but a few small individual charges. Other festival events include a concert in the park and doll, garden, fashion, and car shows.

- Athens State University, on the first full weekend in October, is the setting for the **Tennessee Old Time Fiddlers Convention.** The two-day event includes outdoor competitions among harmonica, banjo, fiddle, mandolin, dulcimer, and guitar players, and buck-dancing sessions. It's a lively time and a chance for your children to hear and see musicians they aren't likely to spot on MTV. (256) 232–2600 or alcc@companet.net.

3

LIMESTONE FLEA MARKET (ages 8 to 12)
30030 U.S. Highway 72 West, Athens 35756; (256) 233–5183. Open Saturday and Sunday.

Your kids can poke around and find all kinds of treasures at this flea market.

Where to Eat

Shoney's. *1402 Highway 72 East, 35611; (256) 233–2330.* Kids five and younger eat **Free** from buffet.

Athens Family Restaurant. *Highway South, 35611; (256) 232–8071.* Kids five and younger eat **Free** from buffet.

Where to Stay

Comfort Inn. *1218 Kelli Drive, Athens 35613; (256) 232–2704 or (800) 725–4056.* The 63-unit hotel has a swimming pool and offers a **Free** continental breakfast and newspaper. $

Hampton Inn. *1488 Thrasher Boulevard, Athens 35611; (256) 232–0030 or (800) 426–7866.* Stays at the 57-unit property include **Free** continental breakfast and newspaper. Families will like the swimming pool and in-room cable television. $

Lucy's Branch Resort and Marina. *6120 Snake Road, Athens 35611; (256) 729–6443 or (800) 242–9284.* Some 15 miles from Athens, via U.S. 72 West, it offers a fully developed campground, 40 rustic family cottages, tennis, miniature golf, swimming pool, picnic and playground areas, and hiking trails. $-$$

For More Information

Athens-Limestone Chamber of Commerce. *101 South Beaty Street (mail: Box 150, Athens 35612); (256)* *232–2600; Web site www. companet.net/cc/Athenscc.html.*

Rogersville

   JOE WHEELER STATE PARK (all ages)
201 McLean Drive, Rogersville 35652; (256) 247–5466 or (800) 544–5639. Open daily year-round. Closed 10:00 P.M. to 5:00 A.M. to those without overnight reservations. $1.00 for adults; 50 cents for children to use the park's day areas, which include tennis courts, beach, shelters, and major playgrounds.

When your family, like thousands of others, descends on Joe Wheeler State Park Resort, you may not realize you are following in the footsteps of a famous Confederate cavalry leader.

Through area meadows, now flooded to create boat basins, and across hillsides, where golf balls have replaced minie balls, the Civil War's "Fighting Joe" Wheeler once led his soldiers toward the Tennessee River, with the Union cavalry at their heels. Almost constantly in battle from the beginning to the end of the Civil War, Wheeler was one of the state's most able Confederate cavalry leaders.

After the war Wheeler returned and settled here. As a resident hero and later an Alabama congressman, he left his name on one of the Tennessee Valley Authority's largest dams, the lake it created, and the state park that has grown up on its banks. He is remembered as a cavalry general at the Battle of Shiloh and for his role in campaigns in Tennessee and Georgia.

Thousands of visitors now follow Wheeler's trails toward the river to find their own refuge at the 2,550-acre resort.

Twenty-five miles east of Florence, the park has a main lodge that is at the end of a winding 4-mile drive off busy U.S. Highway 72 at Rogersville. The park, midway between Florence and Athens, is a water-oriented hideaway created with fishing, swimming, and boating in mind.

Locals often arrive in their boats, tie up at the marina, and then come ashore to eat in the lodge's restaurant. If your family doesn't have a boat, not to worry, the marina will rent you one: Canoes and pontoon and fishing boats are available. If your family isn't into boating, though, you can use the lodge's playgrounds, picnic facilities, or tennis courts, all at no charge.

An eighteen-hole golf course with a pro shop draws golfers from throughout the Southeast. Rustic cabins are available several miles from the main lodge, too.

Grand Golfing Joe Wheeler State Park Golf Course (256-247-9308) is an eighteen-hole, par-72 course that is open year-round. Secluded and serene, it has Bermuda greens with few hazards plus a putting green, driving range, clubhouse, pro shop, and snack bar.

GENERAL JOE WHEELER PLANTATION (ages 8 to 12)
12280 Alabama Highway 20, Hillsboro 35643; (256) 637–8513. Admission is $4.00 for adults, $3.00 for ages 13 to 18, $2.00 for ages 6 to 12, Free *to children under 6. Tours are given on Thursday, Friday, and Saturday from 9:00 A.M. to 4:00 P.M. and on Sunday from 1:00 to 5:00 P.M. (Groups of fifteen or more may arrange tours at other times and with a $1.00-per-person discount.)*

After enjoying the state park, visit the home of the man for whom it is named. You'll find General Joe Wheeler's home filled with many original pieces, including military medals and Civil War memorabilia.

Where to Eat

Joe Wheeler State Park Lodge Restaurant. *4401 McLean Drive, Rogersville 35652; (256) 247–5466 or (800) 544–5639.* $

Where to Stay

Joe Wheeler State Park Lodge and Cabins. *4401 McLean Drive, Rogersville 35652; (256) 247–5461 or (800) 544–5639.* At Joe Wheeler State Park, the 75-room, Alpine-style hotel faces a lagoon where guests may swim, water-ski, or fish. The lodge includes a restaurant, gift shop, pool, and tennis courts. Rooms here book quickly in summer, with weekends going first, so if your family is planning a visit, give yourself enough lead time to avoid disappointment.

Nestled beside First Creek—a half-mile upstream from the main channel of the Tennessee River and about 2 miles upstream from Wheeler Dam—all lodge rooms have balconies with views of the adjoining boat basin and marina. A beach complex is nearby on the main river.

Cottages, a dozen miles away, originally were built for managers who supervised the dam's construction in the early 1930s. Cabins (256-247-0145), which sleep from four to eight, rent year-round.

There is a two-night minimum on weekends and a three-night minimum on holidays.

The campgrounds, open year-round, are among the most popular in the state and include 116 sites plus primitive camping, basketball courts, hiking and nature trails, and a beach complex.

Lodge rates vary by season, but usually are in the $60-per-night range. (Executive suites, which include kitchenettes, range into the low $100s during the peak season.) $

Economy Inn. *Highway 72 (mail: Box 129, Rogersville 35652); (256) 247–5416.* The 60-unit inn offers room service, Free local calls, and cable television. $

Double Head Resort and Lodge.
*145 County Road 314, Town Creek 35672;
(256) 685–9267 or (800) 685–9267.*
This may be the area's best-kept secret.
Kids love this place, with its Indian
theme, outdoor swimming pool, kiddie
pool, wilderness trails, country store,
horseback riding, and watercraft
rentals (canoes, pontoon and fishing
boats, jet skis, and paddleboats). All
cottages have three bedrooms but can
be locked off and rented in various
combinations. Full kitchens have full-
size appliances, trash compactors, and
microwaves. You get your own pier and
hammock and lake-front porch with
rockers. $$$–$$$$

Courtly Castles While in Rogersville, take time for a driving
tour of nearby Courtland, which is listed on the National Register of
Historic Places. More than one hundred homes, buildings, and sites
date from circa 1820 to circa 1938. For details on the town, call Court-
land City Hall, (256) 637-2707.

For More Information

**Alabama Mountain Lakes Tourist
Association.** *25062 North Street,
Mooresville 35649-1075; (256) 350–3500
or (800) 648-5381. Visit the Web site
at www.almtlakes.org or E-Mail to info@
almtlakes.org.*

Tuscumbia

Tuscumbia and the adjoining towns of Florence, Sheffield, and Muscle Shoals
form a quad-city area often called "the Shoals." The region, which sprawls on
both sides of the Tennessee River basin, is rich in culture and history.

Can your kids imagine that a child would be responsible for putting a tiny
north Alabama town on the map? When Helen Keller was born in Tuscumbia
in 1880, few people had heard of this town, not far from the Tennessee bor-
der. Today, however, visitors come by the busload to see the birthplace of a
woman who grew up to influence not just a nation, but the world. Before visit-
ing make certain that your children know the story of Helen Keller.

Born with normal senses, Helen Keller was left deaf and blind by an illness
at nineteen months. Despite her challenges Helen earned a college degree and
became an author and world-renowned advocate for others with disabilities.
The turning point for Helen came when her parents hired a tutor, twenty-year-
old Annie Sullivan, who worked tirelessly to communicate with the half-wild

child. After two weeks with her teacher, the six-year-old had learned a few words. The problem was, the words had no meaning. A remarkable learning breakthrough came one morning at a well pump, where today your family can pause to remember the moment when a child's mind was freed. At the well Helen first understood that a word had meaning. The incident at the water pump was, perhaps, the most dramatic in Helen's life, just as it is the most memorable scene in the William Gibson drama presented each summer at the Keller home.

IVY GREEN (HELEN KELLER'S BIRTHPLACE) (all ages)

300 West North Commons, Tuscumbia 35674; (256) 383–4066. Open Monday through Saturday from 8:30 A.M. to 4:00 P.M. and Sunday from 1:00 to 4:00 P.M. Admission is $3.00 for adults, $1.00 for children 6 to 11, and **Free** *for children under 6.*

Your family can remember this woman of courage at the Keller home, Ivy Green, which is now on the National Register of Historic Places. When you visit, peek through the door of the cottage where Helen was born and see her cradle and toys. In the main house, filled with original furnishings and family portraits, look into the upstairs bedroom shared by Helen and her tutor, Annie Sullivan. Downstairs, notice the parlor where Captain Keller, a newspaper editor, sat to read. One downstairs room is devoted to Helen's personal mementos, including

A Festival Every June thousands of people gather in Tuscumbia for the **Helen Keller Festival,** a three-day event commemorating the accomplishments of the town's most famous native. The celebration includes a parade through downtown, stage entertainment, arts and crafts, an art auction, a tour of historic sites, puppet shows, and sporting events and tournaments.

her Braille typewriter. Don't miss seeing items from the making of the film *The Miracle Worker,* which starred Anne Bancroft as Annie Sullivan and Patty Duke as Helen.

The outdoor drama *The Miracle Worker* is staged on Friday and Saturday evenings from mid-June through mid-July. Reserved seating is $8.00, and reservations are recommended. Ivy Green is 2 miles off Highways 72 and 43 in Colbert County.

A Fullman Family Adventure What Cameron and I most remember about attending the outdoor drama *The Miracle Worker* was the silence as a once-wild Helen knelt at the water pump with her teacher, Annie Sullivan.

In a moment that forever changed her life, Helen felt the water and made the connection between that reality and the words Annie had been spelling into her palm.

Next to us that night was a gray-haired man who could not control his flood of tears in that poignant moment of the drama. Except for the voices of the actors, there was a hushed silence that only the crickets interrupted.

1888 JUDGE ALMON TOUR HOUSE (ages 8 to 12)

201 Almon Avenue, Tuscumbia 35674; (256) 383–1642. Open Monday through Saturday from 9:00 A.M. to 5:00 P.M. and Sunday from 1:00 to 5:00 P.M. Admission is $4.00 for adults, $2.00 for ages 6 to 12, and **Free** *to younger children.*

Across from Ivy Green the 1888 Queen Anne Victorian house, which opened to the public in 1998, is filled with period furnishings and is on the National Register of Historic Places.

ALABAMA MUSIC HALL OF FAME (ages 8 to 12)

U.S. 72 West (mail: Box 709, Tuscumbia 35674); (256) 381–4417 or (800) 239–2643; www.alamhof.org. The museum is open Monday through Saturday from 9:00 A.M. to 5:00 P.M. and Sunday from 1:00 to 5:00 P.M. Admission is $6.00 for adults, $5.00 for ages 13 to 18 and seniors 55 and older, $3.00 for children 6 to 12, and **Free** *for children under 6.*

Four miles from Ivy Green on U.S. 72, 2 miles west of its intersection with U.S. Highway 43, the Alabama Music Hall of Fame honors state music makers from blues to jazz and displays items from musicians and singers such as Erskine Hawkins and Emmylou Harris. Costumes, pencil-written music, musical instruments, and awards are among the items on display. A wax figure of Nat King Cole sits at a piano and seems almost to glare at you as you pass. Among the displays are Elvis Presley's Sun Studios recording contract and outfits worn by Lionel Richie and the Commodores. Children are smitten by the Southern Star, a plush tour bus used by the country-music band ALABAMA.

The hall's final room pays tribute to musicians and producers of the area's studios that claim to be the "hit recording capital of the world," based on the number of chart busters produced here. Be sure your children spot the sound booth, where they can make their own music and carry a copy home to remember the day.

A Fullman Family Adventure

George Lair, museum manager at the Alabama Music Hall of Fame, has been around Tuscumbia long enough to have collected a pocketful of memories about the times famous music makers have been in town recording.

He told us about the time Sonny and Cher were there to record their first solo album—and were spotted late one night at the local Pancake House.

He remembers the early 1980s, when Conway Twitty was in town recording at Muscle Shoals Sound. Twitty and his crew drove through town in a van that had his name on the side, and "a trail of cars was following it like the Pied Piper."

NATCHEZ TRACE PARKWAY (all ages)

To reach the trace from U.S. Highway 72, enter at Mile Marker Six; (800) 344–0783. Open daily, year-round.

If your family is ready to get away from the asphalt jungle, head to the wilderness trail that today is known as the Natchez Trace Parkway. A few dozen miles of the parkway wind through the northwest corner of Colbert and Lauderdale counties.

Built to connect Natchez, Mississippi, with Nashville, Tennessee, the trail originally developed as a major path for Chickasaw and Choctaw Indians. Later it served travelers who had sent their goods down the Mississippi River by raft to New Orleans. At present the trace is a tranquil place to escape the rush of traffic, billboards, and businesses. Trucks and buses are prohibited, so you will find a leisurely haven with Indian mounds, historic landmarks, walking trails, picnic areas, and rural landscapes.

Lace up your hiking shoes and take the short trail leading to Buzzard Roost Spring (at the trace entrance in Cherokee). You'll feel like a true adventurer when you walk this pristine land, where sunlight filters through trees and the roar of automobiles is missing.

Amazing Alabama Facts You'll learn these facts when visiting the Alabama Music Hall of Fame:

- Sandy Posey is from Jasper, Alabama.

- Tuskegee proclaimed July 25, 1977 "Commodores Day."

- Bobby Goldsboro attended Auburn University.

- The Music Mill Studio was the first in the Muscle Shoals area to concentrate on country music.

COON DOG CEMETERY (all ages)

Coon Dog Road, Cherokee 35646; (800) 344–0783 or (256) 383–0783. Open daily. Admission is **Free**.

Chances are no one in your family has seen a dog cemetery. Not many other people had either, until 1937, when Key Underwood picked this tree-shaded place to bury his fifteen-year-old coon dog, Troop. The site is where Key and Troop made their final hunt together. Coon Dog Cemetery is now filled with dozens of graves, and it is interesting to read the varied markers. Nothing much happens here throughout the year, but if your family visits on Labor Day, you'll find dog owners trading tales and sprucing up graves. The get-together, which includes music, barbecue, and buck dancing, is an annual event that marks the anniversary of the graveyard's founding. A picnic pavilion makes a good spot for a meal. Both visiting the cemetery and using the picnic pavilion are **Free**. The graveyard is open daily during daylight hours. (To get there, go 7 miles west of Tuscumbia on U.S. Highway 72; turn left onto Alabama Highway 247 and go 12 miles. Turn right onto Coon Dog Road and follow the signs 5 miles.)

Barbecue Man L. O. Bishop, now in his sixth decade, has lived all his life on a farm about 1 mile off Natchez Trace. He and his family raise hogs, corn, and soybeans—and prepare and distribute Bishop's Barbecue. Look for it in local grocery stores.

The Alabama native is known for being community-minded—and for helping those in need. He once stopped to offer a hitchhiker a ride; when their routes didn't overlap, he handed the transient a $50 bill. Now that's Southern hospitality.

Colbert County Courthouse

Colbert County Courthouse The Colbert County Courthouse was built in 1881, gutted by fire in 1908, and rebuilt in 1909.

On Main Street in Tuscumbia, the courthouse is reminiscent of the grand days of the Old South, as is the surrounding neighborhood, which is on the National Register of Historic Districts.

Where to Eat

Barnacle Bill's Crabhouse. *624 East Second Street, Sheffield 35660; (256) 314–6733.* Huge murals make guests feel as though they're beside the sea at this eatery, known for its salads, pasta, and seafood choices such as shrimp, salmon, and crab legs, which are an unexpected find this far from the coast. It's closed on Sunday. $$

Claunch Cafe. *400 South Main Street, Tuscumbia 35674; (256) 386–0222.* In an old house with wooden floors and filled with wooden tables and chairs, this cafe, in Spring Park, offers families a homey feel and daily specials. Especially popular are pecan-chicken salad, fresh vegetables, home-baked breads, and a killer banana pudding. $

Ivy House Restaurant. *107 East Sixth Street, Tuscumbia 35674; (256) 383–9300.* A lunch buffet means plenty of choices for the entire family. Specials are catfish, chicken, and salads—and there is a children's menu. $–$$

Old Rocking Chair Restaurant and Country Store. *800 U.S. 72 West, Tuscumbia 35674; (256) 381–6105.* Downhome cooking is the trademark, and, for diners who overeat, there are front-porch wooden rockers for after-meal rests. Don't miss the catfish and fried pies. $

Chuck E. Cheese's Pizza Restaurant. *4700 Hatch Boulevard, Sheffield 35662; (256) 383–3836.* Your kids will love the games and entertainment while you savor the pizza. $

Where Are We Now?

Where Are We Now? The Shoals area—which includes Muscle Shoals, Sheffield, Tuscumbia, and surrounding areas—is 48 miles west of Decatur, 70 miles west of Huntsville, and 120 miles northwest of Birmingham.

Where to Stay

Holiday Inn. *4900 Hatch Boulevard, Sheffield 35660; (256) 381–4710.* The 200-room hotel has plenty of things to make a family's visit comfortable—a fitness center, an outdoor swimming pool, a hot tub, and a restaurant. Guest rooms have irons, ironing boards, coffeemakers, blow dryers, and teleports (in case someone wants to sneak in a few minutes of work). $

Key West Inn–Shoals. *1800 U.S. 73 West, Tuscumbia 35674; (256) 383–0700.* The two-story inn, with 41 guest rooms, offers a **Free** continental breakfast and in-room refrigerators, both wise ways to stretch a traveler's dollars. A coin laundry makes this an efficient pit stop for families. $

Sharlotte's House Bed and Breakfast. *105 East North Commons, Tuscumbia 35674; (256) 386–7269.* Two blocks from Helen Keller's birthplace, the stately Victorian home, with 3 guest rooms, has been renovated and redecorated by owner/operators Coy and Sharlotte Roper. The couple, who have nine grandchildren, welcome children of all ages—and even have toys and videos to share. The house is smoke-free and alcohol-free. $

For More Information

Colbert County Tourism and Convention Bureau. *Highway 72 West (mail: Box 440, Tuscumbia 35674); (256) 383–0783 or (800) 344–0783; Web site www.shoals-tourism.org or E-mail shoalstourism@worldnet.att.net.*

Florence

Originally settled as a trading post, Florence later drew industry to the area, thanks to affordable TVA power, the by-product of the Tennessee River and Wilson Dam. A number of attractions, including an Indian mound and the home of W. C. Handy, make this city well worth a visit.

INDIAN MOUND AND MUSEUM (all ages)

1026 South Court Street, Florence 35630; (256) 760–6427; www.flo-tour.org. Admission is $2.00 for adults and 50 cents for student-age children. Hours are Monday through Saturday from 10:00 A.M. to 4:00 P.M.

The museum holds all kinds of displays, including fluted points (projectile points for spears that pre-date the use of arrowheads) and very old pottery. At one time an Indian ceremonial mound, the site has arrowheads and Indian bones. Displays are well marked, too, so even young guests can roam the museum and learn about the area's early residents. After touring the museum head outside to scale the mound, which has seventy-two steps and a handrail. Although it's a straight shot up, reassure your family that the steps are small and not too tough. If you pause to catch your breath, take a look at the nearby Tennessee River. Once you reach the top of the mound, you'll find benches and a single picnic table; so if everyone was game enough to lug along some grub, you're now at a unique picnic spot. Historians believe the mound was used as a chief's house or ceremonial temple.

Salute To Its Namesake On the fourth weekend in October, Florence salutes its ties to Florence, Italy, by highlighting the twelfth through sixteenth centuries and playing medieval games.

The **Renaissance Faire,** held on the corner of Tuscaloosa Street and Wood Avenue, has crafts, music, plenty of food, and dueling knights. (256) 740–4141 or (888) 356–8687.

POPE'S TAVERN (all ages)

203 Hermitage Drive, Florence 35630; (256) 760–6439; www.flo-tour.org. Admission is $2.00 for adults and 50 cents for school-age children. Hours are Monday through Saturday from 10:00 A.M. to 4:00 P.M.

At first glance Pope's Tavern might not seem like a kid kind of place. Give this restored stagecoach stopover and tavern a closer look, though. It showcases area history, which could seem stuffy, but it's also a very real kind of place. One of the town's earliest structures (dating back to about 1830), the tavern is filled with antiques and engravings that depict the area's ties to Andrew Jackson. You and your children can imagine what it must have been like when the inn was used as a hospital for both Union and Confederate soldiers during the Civil War.

Climb the stairs to the low-ceilinged second story, where you'll see a model of a wounded soldier lying on a makeshift pallet. The soldier is what kids most remember about this stop, even though it's a look-don't-touch place. The old dolls and toys are another favorite with kids, who usually end a tour wanting to buy one of the gift shop's Civil War puzzles, coloring books, swords, or hats.

WILSON DAM (ages 8 to 12)

Alabama 133 South, Florence; (256) 740–4141; www.flo-tour.org. The dam can be seen daily, but there are no guided tours.

The dam was begun in 1918 as a power-supply center for munitions plants in World War I. Later, it became the cornerstone of the Tennessee Valley Authority. Wilson Lock is one of the largest single-lift locks in the world. Although tours are not offered, you and your family can walk around. If your timing is right, you can watch boats and barges pass through the locks, a process that usually takes from ninety minutes to two hours.

RENAISSANCE TOWER (all ages)

1 Hightower Place, Florence 35630; (256) 764–5900; www.flo-tour.org. The tower is open Monday through Saturday from 10:00 A.M. to 5:00 P.M. and Sunday from 11:00 A.M. to 5:00 P.M. It is closed on Thanksgiving and Christmas. Admission to the lower-level exhibits is $4.00 for adults, $3.00 for seniors 65 and older, $2.50 for student groups, and $2.00 for children under age 6. For visitors wanting to go to the top of the tower, cost is $1.00 per person. (Diners in the tower-top restaurant do not have to pay $1.00.)

If your family wants to see Wilson Dam and the Tennessee River from another vantage point, visit Renaissance Tower on the north bank of the river. The state's tallest tourist attraction rises some 300 feet above the dam. On a clear day you can see for a few dozen miles from the tower.

Be sure to point out to your children the outside wildflower garden, filled with more than 200 varieties of native plants and wildflowers. The Shoals Aquarium and Nature Center, on a lower level of the tower, has more than one hundred exhibits, which include aquariums and small animals and birds from around the world.

W. C. HANDY HOME, MUSEUM, AND LIBRARY (ages 8 to 12)

620 West College Street, Florence 35630; (256) 760–6434; www.flo-tour.org. Admission is $2.00 for adults and 50 cents for school-age children. Hours are Monday through Saturday from 10:00 A.M. to 4:00 P.M. The site is closed on major holidays.

One of Florence's most popular sites is the W. C. Handy Home, Museum, and Library. It includes the log cabin birthplace of Handy, who has been called "Father of the Blues." An adjoining museum has personal items, including Handy's trumpet, letters, photographs, awards, and the piano he used to compose his famous "Saint Louis Blues." Kids can sit at Handy's piano and play a tune, which should help them appreciate what he faced when composing. Children are allowed to play the piano, but they are discouraged from pounding on it and abusing it.

Children also are often drawn to Handy's Braille watch and Braille music, items he needed for the last fifteen years of his life after losing his sight at age seventy. Despite the blindness, Handy, who died in 1958, continued composing and performing, leaving a legend not just of musical greatness but of determination.

After your kids have played the piano to their hearts' content, head across a ramp that connects the museum with a third log cabin used as a library. Filled with abundant resources on African-American history, the library also has books for kids and plenty of places to sit and read.

Handy Festival Each August, Florence is the setting for a week-long W. C. Handy Music Festival, which includes parades, jam sessions, runs, a picnic-and-jazz evening on the banks of the Tennessee River, a Street Strut (a parade with no vehicles involved), and a concert led by noted jazz musicians. The event is especially intriguing for children with musical aspirations. (256) 740–4141 or (888) 356–8687.

Where to Eat

Court Street Cafe. *201 North Seminary Street, Florence 35630; (256) 767–4300.* In an old brick building in historic downtown Florence, the cafe has a children's menu and offers kids crayons and balloons. $–$$

Renaissance Grille. *1 Hightower Place, Florence 35630; (256) 718–0092.* Atop Renaissance Tower and with a grand view of Wilson Dam, the restaurant, which has a children's menu, is a good place to top off a day in Florence. Ask for a table with a view of the river. $–$$$.

Ricatoni's Italian Grill. *107 North Court Street Florence 35630; (256) 718–1002.* In the historic district of downtown Florence, bold colors of the Italian flag are painted over old, red brick on the outside of the restaurant. Baked in a wood-burning oven, pizzas are favorites with young diners. A signature item is pepperoni bread made from pepperoni and Parmesan and mozzarella cheeses folded into pocketed, braided, and baked pizza dough and served with tomato sauce. $

Famous Folks Who Have Visited Limestone Manor Built

in 1915 from blocks of local limestone, Limestone Manor has been visited by automotive pioneer Henry Ford, inventor Thomas Edison, and screen star Humphrey Bogart. Ford is said to have been in North Alabama in 1921 to visit Wilson Dam.

Where to Stay

Hampton Inn. *2281 Florence Boulevard, Florence 35630; (256) 764–8888.* An outdoor swimming pool and **Free** continental breakfast and afternoon cookies and juice make this a favorite place with traveling families. $

Jameson Inn. *115 Ana Drive, Florence 35630; (256) 764–5326.* Convenient to shopping malls and restaurants, the inn has an outdoor swimming pool and offers **Free** continental breakfast. $

Limestone Manor Bed & Breakfast. *601 North Wood Avenue, Florence 35630; (256) 765–0314;* *www.bbonline.com/al/limestone/; E-mail: ellisons@HiWAAY.net.* The Georgian Revival–style home offers visitors a video library, a book exchange, and a selection of board games. Rooms have private baths and queen-size beds. The Thomas Edison Suite, filled with white wicker and lace, has an adjoining sitting room, suitable for two additional guests. Proprietors Bud and Lois Ellison serve a candelit breakfast at a time of guests' choosing, allowing traveling families to tailor mornings to their individual schedules. $–$$

For More Information

Florence/Lauderdale Tourism.
One Hightower Place, Florence 35630;
(256) 740–4141 or (888) 356–8687;
Web site www.flo-tour.org;
E-mail dwilson@floweb.com.

Rule of Our Roads Unless otherwise marked, Alabama's max-

imum speed limit is 70 miles per hour on specified rural interstates, 65 miles per hour on highways with four or more lanes, 55 miles per hour on other open highways, and 45 miles per hour on county roads.

Waterloo

Indians who were relocated to Oklahoma and western reservations often came through Waterloo, where they were held in camps to await transfer to boats headed west. Many of the Indians died along the way. At the end of Main Street, a marker stands beside the Tennessee River and recognizes the suffering that American Indians endured in the 1830s.

For overnight stays and dining out, visitors typically wind up in nearby Florence.

EDITH NEWMAN CULVER MEMORIAL MUSEUM
(ages 8 to 12)

Main Street (mail: Box 99, Waterloo 35677); (256) 767–6081. The museum is open Friday, Saturday, and Sunday from 1:00 to 4:00 P.M. Admission is $2.00 for adults; $1.00 for student groups, seniors 65-plus, and children ages 6 to 18; and **free** *to younger children.*

Filled with period antiques and Civil War and Native American items, the museum opened in 1995 in a home dating back to 1870. Ms. Culver donated her ancestral home to the town in 1995. Waterloo town fathers made repairs and converted the two-story frame house into a museum. When the museum opened later that year, it was big news for a town that rarely had reasons for outsiders to visit.

The museum collection includes old photographs, paintings, kitchen items, and Indian artifacts sure to be hits with your children. (Arrowheads probably top the list of favorite Indian items.) In a room highlighting the Newman family, your kids may sit in an old barber chair used by the late Clark Newman when he cut people's hair on the front porch of the home-turned-museum. There's also an old organ that your children can use, provided they know how to play and don't abuse the instrument.

For More Information

Florence/Lauderdale Tourism.
One Hightower Place, Florence 35630;
(256) 740–4141 or (888) 356–8687;
Web site www.flo-tour.org.;
E-mail dwilson@floweb.com.

Phil Campbell

DISMALS CANYON (all ages)

901 County Road 8, Phil Campbell 35581; (205) 993–4559. The site is open daily from Memorial Day through Labor Day from 10:00 A.M. to 5:30 P.M.; on Friday, Saturday, and Sunday from March 1 to Memorial Day and Labor Day through November 1. Admission is $8.00 for adults, $6.00 for children ages 3 to 11, and **Free** *for younger children.*

The canyon retreat is a bit of wilderness in a busy state. In the past a ceremonial ground for Indians and a refuge for outlaws, the site, designated a national landmark, is a cluster of geological formations filled with plants, waterfalls, cliffs, towering trees, and intriguing rock formations.

You can explore by hiking limestone trails through sky-reaching boulders, passing thundering waterfalls, and heading into a secret world of mossy green filled with ferns and giant trees. After sunset look closely and you'll see glowing dismalites (worms) that cling to canyon rocks. This is the place to explore mysterious sanctuaries where Indians held secret rituals. Don't miss swimming in the natural pool carved out of solid rock by the rushing waters of Dismals Creek.

> **A Hiding Place** After killing Alexander Hamilton in a duel in 1804, former U.S. Vice President Aaron Burr hid for months at an ancient Indian campsite at The Dismals. As you explore the Dismals with your children, try to imagine just where Burr might have taken refuge. The options are plentiful.

If your family wants some real adventure, canoe down Bear Creek the way the Indians did. You can lie on secluded beaches, fish in clear waters, or drift aimlessly under gigantic rock cliffs. Vacationers wanting more adventure will find Class I through Class IV rapids at the upper end of the creek.

This area is one of the oldest untouched tracts of forest east of the Mississippi River. The attraction, with a small museum and gift shop, has cabins with kitchens, fireplaces, and a couple of bedrooms each. There also is great rustic camping if you aren't hung up on needing modern kitchens and baths. In summer it might get hot here, but you won't find mosquitoes, flies, or poison oak.

Canoes rent for $45 for a whole day and $32 for a half day. Depending on the month and the day of the week, cabin rentals range typically from $120 to $165 nightly for up to six people. (Two additional people may be added for an additional cost. A one-time clean-up fee, starting at $50 for two people, is charged.) Each of the site's two cabins has a stone fireplace, a kitchen with dishwasher and microwave, a master bedroom with a queen-size bed and access to an 8-foot deck, and a second bedroom with four bunk beds. Cabins are furnished down to the firewood and linens.

Hamilton

An agricultural town, Hamilton was originally called Toll Gate because it was a stop for stage coaches. At present it remains a quiet place, giving little hint of the time when soldiers carved out a passage here on their return from defeating the British at New Orleans.

JERRY BROWN'S POTTERY (all ages)

Alabama Highway 81, 1 mile north of Alabama Highway 17 (Route 4, Box 66, Hamilton 35570); (205) 921–9483. Brown's retail store is open Monday through Saturday from 8:30 A.M. to 4:30 P.M. Admission is **Free**.

This is the place where your children can learn about talent and family traditions. Jerry Brown, a ninth-generation potter, has been honored as a National Heritage Fellow, recognizing the tradition and excellence of his craft. Brown, who digs his own local clay and processes it with a mule-powered pug mill, specializes in a full line of folk pottery and face jugs prized by collectors. If your family is lucky, on weekdays, especially in the mornings, you're likely to find the craftsman at work and willing to allow you to look over his shoulder as he creates.

Where to Stay

Best Western Hamilton. *2031 Military Street South, Hamilton 35570; (205) 921–7831.* Near shopping, the 80-room hotel has a swimming pool, cable television, **Free** cribs, and coin laundry. Ask about AAA discount. $

A **Fullman Family Adventure** When Jerry Brown's pottery was shown on the television shopping network QVC, 2,500 of his pieces sold in two minutes, a fact that still makes him marvel.

On a crisp fall day, as clay clung to his fingers and smudges peppered his face, Brown leaned over his potter's wheel and crafted a jug from what minutes earlier had been nothing more than a glob of wet clay.

"Nothing bothered my Dad more than somebody making something shoddy. I guess that lesson is what distinguishes what I do. I put my heart and soul into each and every piece I make," he told us.

For More Information

Hamilton Area Chamber of Commerce. *110 Railroad Street, Hamilton 35570; (205) 921–7786.*

M **ule Day** If you're in the area on the fourth Saturday in September, don't miss the fun in nearby Winfield, which annually hosts **Mule Day.** On this day mules are the stars, pulling wagons in a parade and giving rides to visiting youngsters. The event includes a flea market, an old car show, and mule judging. For details call Winfield's City Hall, (205) 487–4337.

Natural Bridge

NATURAL BRIDGE OF ALABAMA (all ages)

U.S. Highway 278 (mail: Box 342, Natural Bridge, 35577); (205) 486–5330; www.almtlakes.org. Natural Bridge is open daily from 8:00 A.M. until sunset. Admission is $2.50 for adults, $1.50 for children 6 to 12, and Free for children under 6.

Natural Bridge of Alabama is an attraction with plenty of space for little legs to run and cavort. The double-span sandstone arch stretches 148 feet wide and stands 60 feet high. The bridge has been called the longest natural bridge east of the Rockies. With hiking trails and picnic and concession areas, the setting is ideal for a family outing. There's also a gravel-covered trail that's less than 1 mile long. The trail, with some ups and downs, is mostly easy going; but there are a few high steps where you'll need to help very young children. Beside the gift shop, which is about 100 yards from the bridge, there is an artesian well. The water is tested monthly and always passes health inspections, so feel free to sample. To hike the trail and explore the bridge takes most families about one hour, but you can extend a stay by picnicking. The bridge is south of Haleyville on U.S. Highway 278 at Alabama Highway 5.

Where to Stay

Imperial Inn. *Highway 5 South, Haleyville 35565; (256) 486–5205.* The 65-room inn has a restaurant and non-smoking rooms. $

For More Information

Haleyville Area Chamber of Commerce. *1200 Twenty-first Street (Box 634), Haleyville 35565; (256) 486–4611.*

Symbols of Alabama

- State Bird: Yellowhammer
- State Flower: Camellia
- State Tree: Southern pine

Double Springs

Double Springs, in the Winston County portion of the William B. Bankhead National Forest, is the place to learn a surprising fact about Alabamians: Some were staunch Unionists during the Civil War. The area's mixed loyalties are evident when you spot a statue outside the Winston County Courthouse. There stands the replica of a Civil War soldier flanked by both Confederate and Union flags. As your family looks at the statue and the two flags, you can explain loyalties, war, and brotherhood to your youngsters.

Highway 278 in Winston County—beginning at the Marion County line and traveling to the Cullman County line—has been designated "Looney's Tavern Parkway." It was a logical name when you consider the important role the former tavern played here.

LOONEY'S TAVERN AMPHITHEATER (all ages)

Box 70, Double Springs 35553; (205) 489–5000 or (800) 566–6397. The outdoor drama, on selected dates beginning in mid-June, begins at 8:15 P.M. Tickets to the drama are $12.00 for adults and $6.00 for children 12 and under. Tickets can be held at the box office.

The tavern's tale and influence are detailed at a modern-day structure, Looney's Tavern Amphitheater, which is the setting for an outdoor musical drama. The story, detailing Winston County's struggle during the Civil War, captivates children, who are entertained as they learn about the Civil War and its effects on the country. The drama reveals the role that Looney's Tavern played in the attempted 1861 secession of the "The Free State of Winston" from Alabama.

Presented under a starry sky while crickets fill the night with their songs, the drama crescendos to a climax of spectacular fireworks.

Although the play begins at dusk, your family will want to arrive early enough to play miniature golf on adjacent grounds, to browse the large gift shop, and to savor a Southern buffet, complete with fried chicken and biscuits, at Sister Sarah's Kitchen. The buffet dinner is $8.00 for adults and

In Case of Rain Summer showers are scattered and isolated and thus rarely prevent production at Looney's Tavern. Rain checks are offered only if a production is canceled before intermission.

$5.00 for children 12 and under. The restaurant, amphitheater, gift shop, and miniature golf course are within easy walking distance of one another, so you can park once and spend the day.

The amphitheater is 7 miles east of Double Springs and 30 miles off Interstate 65 on U.S. Highway 278.

A special treat is a sightseeing trip aboard *The Free State Lady*, a replica riverboat that docks about a mile from the amphitheater and plows Smith Lake. Narrated, two-hour trips include captivating tales— some believable, some not, but all enjoyable. The storyteller (often Neal Shipman, who started this whole hilltop attraction) tells ghost stories and talks about the works and antics of early settlers. Somehow you get the feeling that his tall stories are part legend, part history, part just fun. The boat stops occasionally so that you can get a closer look at certain rock formations, including one that looks amazingly like an Indian head. Then, it's back to the waters, the tales, and occasional corny jokes that make passengers groan and laugh all at once. Soft drinks are sold on board, and restrooms are available. In fall, when the hillsides have turned all sorts of reds, yellows, and oranges, boat rides are incredibly beautiful.

Riverboat rides, at 3:15 P.M. during show dates, are $12.00 for adults, $5.00 for children 3 to 12, and **Free** for younger children. Dinner cruises, beginning at 5:30 P.M. on show dates, are $22.00 for adults and $15.00 for children. Reservations are required for both dinner and excursion cruises.

A Fullman Family Adventure

Cameron was just sure she'd never manage to sit through the entire drama without wiggling and squirming.

I think even she was surprised that intermission came—and her mind had not once wandered. The outdoor drama is that mesmerizing.

BANKHEAD NATIONAL FOREST (all ages)

Mail to: District Ranger, Box 278, Double Springs 35553; (205) 489–5111. Open year-round. Picnic area closes at 10:00 P.M. daily.

Sprawling over some 181,000 acres, the state's largest virgin hardwood forest is the place for picnics, hikes, camping, and canoeing. If your family has had a long day of travels, this is also the place to stretch legs and roam free. Just don't let anyone get too far out of sight because the forest stretches over half of Lawrence County and a big chunk of Winston County.

The park's Sipsey Wilderness area is scenic but rustic. Hiking here can be fun but comes with some precautions. Beware of rocky and steep areas that might be too demanding for young hikers in your group.

Take time to note the small plants, mosses, flowers, and ferns. Read a map with your kids' help and outline a path to the Bee Branch trail, where you'll see the largest yellow poplar tree in the eastern United States (it measures 80 inches in diameter). While in the wilderness, remember that you are not allowed to cut or chop any live plants or trees.

The national forest includes the Corinth Recreation Area, with seventy campsites, each with a picnic table, grill, lantern pole, camping pad, and trash container. Along a swimming beach there are bathhouses, where you can cool off after a tough day hiking. The recreation area is open from April through October, but the season often is extended when weather permits.

The Sipsey River, which races through the forest, is rapidly gaining nationwide fame among canoeing enthusiasts. Each year thousands of canoe devotees make the white-water journey from Sipsey River picnic grounds to Low-Water Bridge. The float trip, which takes about seven hours, passes rock canyons and overhanging bluffs. The water here is so clear that you can see every fish that swims past. The best times to canoe are in the spring and fall or after a heavy summer rain.

Houston Recreation Area is a quiet, secluded place to pitch a tent, picnic in the shade of century-old trees, or drop a line into Smith Lake.

Adjacent to Smith Lake, Clear Creek Recreation Area, open from spring through early fall, has picnic sites, a white-sand beach, a swimming area, bathhouses, and a bike trail that parallels the lake and crosses two bridges.

Brushy Lake Recreation Area is ideal for spending an entire day—or several days, if your kids don't need lots of city-dude creature comforts—hiking trails, fishing, boating, or camping.

Tips For Forest Visitors

When visiting Bankhead National Forest, follow these precautions:

- Don't drink the water even though it may look clear and inviting. The water can make you sick—even up to two weeks after you drink it.

- Beware of poisonous snakes, high cliffs, gorges, and the potential for flash floods.

- To avoid straying off beaten paths, study maps before setting out.

- Before hiking, let someone know your travel route.

For More Information

Alabama Mountain Lakes Tourist Association. *25062 North Street, Mooresville 35649–1075; (256) 350– 3500 or (800) 648–5381; Web site www.almtlakes.org; E-mail info@almtlakes.org.*

Town of Double Springs. *(205) 489–5447.*

Northwest Budget-Minded Suggestions For an affordable getaway visit area attractions that do not charge admission. Among them are:

- Cook's Natural Science Museum
- Coon Dog Cemetery
- Jerry Brown's Pottery
- Old State Bank
- Wheeler National Wildlife Refuge

Decatur

Chances are that after your kids have visited Decatur, they will remember it as the town with bugs and waves. That's because this city has both.

Begin your tour at the Decatur Visitors' Center, housed in a Victorian house on U.S. Highway 31. The two-story building, at 719 Sixth Avenue Southeast, is the place to find friendly faces and loads of information about where to visit. Abundant brochures are available, so grab a few if you need details on area sites. The office is open weekdays from 8:00 A.M. to 5:00 P.M., Saturday from 9:00 A.M. to 5:00 P.M., and Sunday from 1:00 to 5:00 P.M.

Historic Districts While in Decatur, don't miss driving through the Old Decatur and New Albany Historic Districts, which are on the National Register of Historic Places. The 115-acre Old Decatur District is one of the state's most intact Victorian neighborhoods. The New Albany District, with more than one hundred homes, dates back to the late nineteenth century.

In December Decatur hosts a **Holiday Tour,** with homes in both districts open for evening tours. Call (800) 524–6181 to find out the dates.

COOK'S NATURAL SCIENCE MUSEUM (all ages)
412 Thirteenth Street Southeast, Decatur 35601; (256) 350–9347. The museum is open Monday through Saturday from 9:00 A.M. to noon and from 1:00 to 5:00 P.M. Sunday hours are from 2:00 to 5:00 P.M. Admission is Free.

Your family will enjoy the displays of bugs, mounted wildlife, birds, rocks, minerals, and seashells at a museum that was started to showcase critters to children of Cook's Pest Control employees. The museum has been called one of the South's best displays of its kind. Be sure to see the rock and mineral collections and the extensive collection of exotic insects. Talking exhibits intrigue kids but probably not as much as getting to touch a snake.

POINT MALLARD (all ages)

1800 Point Mallard Drive Southeast, Decatur 35601; (256) 350–3000 or (800) 669–9283. Hours are seasonal, with the water park open from mid-May through Labor Day. Water park admission is $10.00 for adults, $6.50 for children ages 5 to 11, and **Free** *to younger children.*

Now to the waves at Point Mallard, a sprawling park east of Decatur. When the pool opened in 1970, it was the first of its kind in the nation. (Since then, it has been joined by some three dozen others across the country.) The original wave pool is 180 feet long and 75 feet wide at the deepest end and 150 feet wide at the carpeted beach area. The 3-foot-high waves give kids and adults a fun ride.

The aquatic complex includes an Olympic diving pool and a diving tower, a kiddie pool, a squirt factory, a sky pond, a three-flume water slide, as well as a picnic ground, playground, and sand beach.

The 750-acre park has year-round recreational facilities including tennis, campgrounds, hiking trails, a miniature golf course, and an eighteen-hole golf course that skirts the Tennessee River.

Civil War Walking Tour Make the Civil War come to life for your children by taking a walking tour of Decatur's war-related sites. Ask for a brochure at the Visitors' Center (719 Sixth Avenue Southeast), Old State Bank, or from merchants along Bank Street. It's a **Free** and educational outing.

OLD STATE BANK (all ages)

925 Bank Street Northeast, Decatur 35601; (256) 350–5060. Hours are weekdays from 9:30 A.M. to noon and 1:00 to 4:30 P.M. Call for weekend tours. Admission is **Free***.*

Your kids will love visiting Old State Bank, which was founded during Andrew Jackson's presidency. Built in 1833, this pre–Greek Revival structure is Alabama's oldest bank. Don't miss visiting upstairs, where the head cashier lived with his family. For most children the fun is seeing the thick vault on the main level just behind the tellers' cages. One of Decatur's few structures to survive the Civil War, the bank was used as a hospital for wounded soldiers. Before leaving notice the war-era graffiti still visible on the outside walls.

*S*pecial Events

- Point Mallard on Memorial Day Weekend hosts the **Alabama Jubilee Hot Air Balloon Classic,** the mid-South's largest such competition. Plan to arrive early to watch the balloons inflate, then float into the sky. Be sure to take your camera to this colorful affair. Admission is *Free*. For details call (205) 350-2028 or (800) 524-6181.

- On the Fourth of July weekend, Point Mallard hosts the **Spirit of America Festival** (800-524-6181) that offers children's parades, sports tournaments, games, entertainment, and fireworks. It's a colorful tribute to the nation's birthday and a fun event for families.

- On Labor Day weekend Point Mallard is the setting for a **Civil War Reenactment** (800-524-6181), with camps, battles, and skirmishes. Candlelight tours and living-history camps and battles give a close view of military history and help children to understand that infamous war.

- In late September the area hosts the **Racking Horse World Competition.** The ten-night event which honors the state's official horse, draws thousands of horses that strut for honors.

- On the third weekend in November, Calhoun Community College, north of Decatur on U.S. Highway 31, hosts the **Southern Wildlife Festival** with artists, including duck-decoy carvers, painters, and wildfowl photographers. For details call (800) 524-6181 or (205) 353-7243.

HARTSELLE ANTIQUE DEALER (ages 8 to 12)
(256) 773-0933. Open Monday through Saturday.
This cluster of thirty shops sells antiques and arts and crafts and gift items. Kids like the old-fashioned toys.

WHEELER NATIONAL WILDLIFE REFUGE (all ages)

2700 Refuge Headquarters Road, Decatur 35603; (256) 350–6639. The Visitors' Center is open March through September, Wednesday through Sunday from 10:00 A.M. to 5:00 P.M. Hours the rest of the year are daily from 10:00 A.M. to 5:00 P.M. Admission is **Free.**

East of Decatur, the state's largest wildlife refuge—with 34,500 acres—has the state's largest concentration of ducks and Canada geese during winter.

When you arrive at the refuge, your first stop should be the Wildlife Visitor Center, which is filled with displays explaining the site's purpose. Be sure your kids pick up a bird checklist. Informative and easy to use, the list includes 285 species of birds that have been spotted here. Listings are coded so that you'll know in which seasons the birds appear, whether or not they are rare, and how common they are here. Nature films are shown on weekends at the refuge, which has walking trails, picnic areas, a wildlife observation building, a waterfowl observation platform, and a boardwalk that juts into a swamp.

The Hunt At Wheeler Wildlife Refuge managed hunts are held for squirrel, rabbit, raccoon, opossum, and white-tailed deer. Fishing is permitted, so take your fishing gear if you'd like.

In fall thousands of Canada geese, snow geese, mallards, widgeons, gadwalls, black ducks, shovelers, canvasbacks, and a host of other ducks migrate to the refuge from northern nesting grounds.

Although the refuge attracts thousands of wintering waterfowl, there are other creatures here, including 115 species of fish, seventy-four species of reptiles and amphibians, forty-seven species of mammals, and 285 species of songbirds. In spring you'll most likely spot mallards, the most common waterfowl found here.

By traipsing out to the observation building, you can look across woodlands and calm waters. As you stand in a glass-enclosed structure, an intercom brings outdoor sounds indoors, where several telescopes help you to take a closer look.

Water and fluctuating water levels influence the birds' arrival time, but you can be sure of spotting something whenever you visit. During January waterfowl numbers are at their peak. The population begins to decline in February and ebbs even more in March, when turtles come out to sun themselves and crappie fishing is at its best. April brings abundant wildflowers and more migrating birds, including warblers and vireos. Broods of wood ducks arrive in May, along with mallards and black ducks. May is also the time for young songbirds and rabbits.

In June, with migration at its end, only resident birds and mammals are here. In July waterfowl activity is at its lowest, but you should be able to spot young songbirds in the woods and fields. August is when songbirds begin their fall migration, with purple martins bunching for their move south. In September blue-wing teal migration peaks, shorebirds and swallows begin moving through, and the first incoming geese arrive. During October, as waterfowl continue arriving, sport fishing is at its best. In November songbird migration is at an end, and waterfowl numbers continue to rise. This also is the time to spot great blue herons and red-tailed and marsh hawks. In late December waterfowl numbers reach their peak, and, on occasion, you can spot bald and golden eagles.

To reach the refuge take exit 334 off Interstate 65 and follow the signs.

An Olympic Hero Olympic track great Jesse Owens, who won four gold medals in the 1936 Berlin Olympics, is honored in his hometown of Oakville with a memorial park. The park includes a visitors' center, picnic pavilions, a bronze statue, a replica of Owens' home, a ballfield, a museum, and a gift shop. Museum and visitors' center hours are Tuesday through Saturday from 11:00 A.M. to 3:00 P.M. and Sunday from 1:00 to 5:00 P.M. Call (256) 974–3636.

Where to Eat

Big Bob Gibson's Bar-B-Q. *1715 Sixth Avenue SE South, Decatur 35602; (256) 350–6969.* Open daily, the landmark is operated by Don McLemore, who carries on the enterprise begun in 1925 by his grandfather. Barbecue pork, beef, chicken ribs, and barbecue potatoes and homemade pies (don't miss the chocolate) are specialties. $

Simp McGhee's. *725 Bank Street, Decatur 35601; (256) 353–6284.* The upstairs dining rooms in this restaurant

which is housed in a turn-of-the-century building, have cloth-covered tables and a feeling of elegance. Specialties are steaks, seafood, pastas, and chicken. $$–$$$

Classical Fruits & BBQ. *8831 Alabama Highway 157, Moulton 35650; (256) 974–8813. Open daily.* Kids love having a gift shop to explore before and after meals. Try the loaded baked potato—and expect to be tempted by the showcase of fudge. $

Where to Stay

Country Inn and Suites. *807 Bank Street, Decatur 35601; (256) 355–6800.* Adjacent to Old State Bank and convenient to downtown shops and restaurants, the all-suites property gives families plenty of space to spread out. Suites have coffeemakers, small refrigerators, and microwaves. Children under age 18 stay **Free** in their parents' suites. $–$$.

Holiday Inn Downtown. *11061 Sixth Avenue, Decatur 35601; (256) 355–3150.* The 225-room property offers some suites with two televisions, microwaves, and refrigerators. Children under age 18 stay **Free** with their parents, and kids under age 12 eat **Free**. $–$$$

For More Information

Decatur Convention and Visitors Bureau. *719 Sixth Avenue SE (Box 2349), Decatur 35602; (256) 350–2028 or (800) 524–6181; Web site www.decaturcvb.org.*

Author's Top Picks

- Civil War Walking Tour, Decatur (256–350–2028 or 800–524–6181)

- Coon Dog Cemetery, Cherokee (800–344–0783 or 256–0783)

- Cook's Natural Science Museum, Decatur (256–350–9347)

- Dismals Canyon, Phil Campbell (205–993–4559)

- Indian Mound and Museum, Florence (256–760–6427)

- Ivy Green, Tuscumbia (256–383–4066)

- Jerry Brown's Pottery, Hamilton (205–921–9483)

- Looney's Tavern Amphitheater, Double Springs (205–489–5000 or 800–566–6397)

- Natural Bridge of Alabama, Natural Bridge (205–486–5330)

- Point Mallard, Decatur (256–350–3000 or 800–669–9283)

Northeast Alabama

The old and the new are one in northeast Alabama, where the most visited attraction is a space-and-rocket center filled with towering earthbound rockets. There also are bargains at an outlet mecca, waters rife with wildlife, and hillsides boasting—would you believe?—a dude ranch and a ski resort. Both musical greats and Civil War heroes have made this land their home and have given travelers added reasons to explore this region, where the Appalachian Mountains come to rest in Alabama.

Mooresville

Your children may not have heard of Mooresville, but they will be interested to know that Painted Fences productions in 1995 used Mooresville for the town scenes of Hannibal, Missouri, in the feature film *Tom Sawyer.* Jonathan Taylor Thomas of TV's *Home Improvement* and Brad Renfroe, who starred in *The Client,* were featured in the movie. Set in 1845, the tale was well suited to Mooresville, the second-oldest town in Alabama, where nothing much has changed since that same era. For filming, sets were built to depict Hannibal's commercial and residential districts, and some facades and porches were constructed.

Mooresville, between Huntsville and Decatur, never grew because early residents refused to allow the railroad to come through it. Although there are no amusement parks in Mooresville, the 1-square-mile town is worth a stop, if for no other reason than to see a place that time seems to have forgotten. A walking tour, which can be accomplished in short order, is the best way to see Mooresville and to let your children burn energy.

When your family visits, look for Broad Street, which leads to the old Mooresville Cemetery, where Union and Confederate soldiers are buried. From

NORTHEAST

Bridgeport
Stevenson
Huntsville
Scottsboro
Mooresville
Woodville
Mentone
Valley Head
Fort Payne
Arab
Guntersville
Cullman
Boaz
Gadsden
Oneonta
Warrior

the south end of Market Street, you can reach the spring that gave the town its original water supply. A tailor shop once owned by Joseph Sloss is on the southwest corner of Piney and Market Streets. Sloss's specialty was the Prince Albert–style coat: a man's double-breasted coat, with a full skirt reaching to the knees. A young Andrew Johnson, who later became the nation's seventeenth president, was in Mooresville sometime between 1826 and 1835 to study under Sloss.

The tiny Mooresville's 1840s post office intrigues youngsters, who love to see how mail was posted into slots. The postmistress is friendly, patient, and glad to answer questions.

A Walking Tour Festival is held in May of odd-numbered years (next one is 2001).

Mooresville doesn't have any overnight spots. Best bets are to get back in the car and head ten minutes away to Madison or twenty minutes to Huntsville, where options are plentiful.

Where to Eat

Mr. Prime's Family Restaurant.
5700 Mooresville Road, Belle Mina 35615; (256) 340–0999. Known for sandwiches, chicken, steak, and daily specials, this full-service restaurant has a children's menu (all items under $6.00), with choices such as a child-size top sirloin, chicken nuggets, hamburger, and fried fish. $

For More Information

Alabama Mountain Lakes Tourist Association. *25062 North Street, Mooresville, 35649–1075; (256) 350–3500 or (800) 648–5381; Web site www.almtlakes.org.*

North Alabama State Parks

North Alabama has four state parks:

- DeSoto State Park, on Lookout Mountain

- Joe Wheeler State Park, on Wheeler Lake

- Lake Guntersville State Park, on a 500-foot bluff overlooking Lake Guntersville

- Monte Sano State Park, overlooking Huntsville

Huntsville

Huntsville gained international fame when Redstone Arsenal sprang from thousands of acres of cotton fields and began producing munitions and chemical weapons during World War II. Following the war the site's usefulness was in question until the U.S. Army lured Dr. Wernher von Braun and his team of German rocket scientists, who developed the nation's first rockets. Their rockets put astronauts on the moon.

U.S. SPACE AND ROCKET CENTER (all ages)

1 Tranquility Base, Huntsville 35805; (256) 837–3400 or (800) 63–SPACE; www.ussrc.com. Open daily except Christmas Day and Thanksgiving Day. Hours: Memorial Day through Labor Day from 9:00 A.M. to 5:00 P.M. and Labor Day through Memorial Day from 9:00 A.M. to 6:00 P.M. Adult admission to the museum, film, and a bus ride to NASA's Space Flight Center is $14.00; $10.95 for children under 13; Free *for children under 3. The center is on Interstate 565 at exit 15.*

Thanks to a team of German scientists, much of the nation's space history was written in Huntsville, where the U.S. Space and Rocket Center remains one of the state's most popular attractions. Here your children can push levers, touch spacecraft, and feel they are a part of the nation's space program.

The museum has an abundance of hands-on exhibits that make exploring especially fun for youngsters, who too often find themselves in hands-off places. They can climb aboard an Apollo command module, stack cubes with a robotic arm, fire a model rocket engine, and take the controls of a space-shuttle simulator.

Kids can see a huge collection of rockets developed by Huntsville scientists and engineers. They will be drawn like magnets to the full-size

High above Huntsville The Saturn V rocket west of downtown Huntsville looks as if it is about to blast off any minute.

Towering forty-two stories above Interstate 565, the rocket replica is the world's only Saturn V standing upright. The Saturn V displayed behind the space museum was the first ever built and is a National Historic Landmark. (The second and third actual Saturn Vs are in Florida and Houston.)

space shuttle *Pathfinder,* complete with two solid-rocket boosters. Kids seem to gravitate to the *Apollo 16* capsule, a full-size replica of the Hubble Space Telescope, Skylab, and an actual Saturn V rocket. Be sure you see the exhibits focusing on the early scientists who pioneered the nation's space program.

A highlight is a movie shown in the Omnimax theater that creates feelings so authentic you sometimes have to close your eyes to ward off twinges of motion sickness.

Space Shot is a thrill ride that takes you on a 4G, 45 mile-per-hour trip straight up a 180-foot tower. Before your children climb aboard, explain that they will be placed in a seat with a shoulder restraint and lap bar. Using compressed air, the ride launches the twelve-passenger vehicle up the tower using more G-force than that experienced by astronauts during a typical space-shuttle launch. Passengers experience about two seconds of weightlessness at the top of the tower as they literally are lifted out of their seats. Next, they are forced down by compressed air faster than a free fall. They bounce about halfway up the tower again before slowly descending to the ground. The entire experience takes about thirty seconds.

If the ride leaves your family needing a more tranquil experience, board a bus for a tour inside the National Air and Space Administration's Marshall Space Flight Center. Giant Saturn rockets and boosters were developed at this NASA facility, and astronauts have trained for space walks here, too.

If the center strikes your children's fancy, don't leave without gathering information about U.S. Space Camp. Designed to entice a new generation into space and to satisfy longings of older participants, the camps draw adults and children from around the world.

ALABAMA CONSTITUTION VILLAGE (all ages)

404 Madison Street, Huntsville 35801; (256) 535–6565 or (800) 678–1819; www.earlyworks.com. Hours are Monday through Saturday from 9:00 A.M. to 5:00 P.M., with final tours beginning at 4:00 P.M. Admission is $6.00 for adults, $3.50 for children ages 6 to 18, $5.00 for seniors ages 55+, and **Free** *to children under 6. (You can save with joint tickets. For adults village and depot is $10; for EarlyWorks and one other tour, $12; for EarlyWorks and two other tours, $13.)*

After your family explores space, bring them back to earth with a visit to Alabama Constitution Village, one of the Southeast's few full-time living-history museums. Standing on the site where statehood was granted to Alabama in 1819, this is where your family can spend time with villagers who are busy with their daily tasks and seemingly unaware that nearly two centuries have come and gone. Among the more than a dozen structures are a cabinet shop, a land office that sold the first tracts of northern Alabama land to settlers, and the city's first newspaper and print shop.

You'll enter through a picket-fence gate to smell baking bread, hear the whir of a spinning wheel in motion, and observe a carpenter shaping a table leg. In the print shop don't miss seeing tiny letters held in wooden cases, with capitals stored in the "upper case" and other letters in the "lower case," an arrangement that resulted in the names we know of uppercase and lowercase letters. Depending on the weather you might see interpreters tending the orchard and grapevines, planting or weeding the garden, quilting, weaving baskets, making candles, or spinning.

After you've toured the village, head to the confectionery shop at the entrance, where you can buy home-baked goodies and Alabama crafts.

EARLYWORKS (all ages)

404 Madison Street, Huntsville 35801; (800) 678–1819; Fax (256) 564–8151; www.earlyworks.com. Open Monday through Saturday from 9:00 A.M. to 5:00 P.M. Cost is $6.00 for adults, $5.00 for seniors 55+, $3.50 for children ages 6 to 18, and ℱ𝓇ℯℯ *to children 5 and younger.*

EarlyWorks will take your family back to a time before the Heart of Dixie became a booming space capital, before cotton became king, even before Alabama became a state. You'll journey to the nineteenth century at the state's only hands-on history center. Across the street from Alabama Constitution Village in downtown Huntsville, EarlyWorks is the place to learn about Alabama's past and the South's rich heritage.

In an eighty-seat theater you'll get started on your journey with the video *Alabama: From Territory to Statehood,* narrated by Alabama football hero Bo Jackson.

EarlyWorks is a collection of Alabama's early history experiences and includes names, dates, stories, events, and customs that put visitors in charge of "making history happen." EarlyWorks is not just a vacation stop; it is also a wonderful learning tool. Your kids will listen as a 16-foot-tall robotlike tree spins tales and legends. On a sprawling map of Alabama painted on the floor, your family will be challenged to stand their ground and touch the original twenty-two counties, Alabama's major rivers, the regions, and the five capitals. Log cabin, Federal and Victorian–style houses and a general store give you a glimpse into the architecture and lifestyles of the early 1800s.

Your kids will probably most like walking the plank to board a 46-foot-long keelboat set in the river-transportation area. In the cotton area they can turn the handle on the miniature cotton gin to separate seed from cotton and read about the impact of cotton on Alabama's economy.

Alabama's Seal First adopted in 1819, the state seal has an Alabama map that shows the state's rivers and bordering states.

The rivers served as important shipping routes when Alabama had few good roads. Today, the rivers are important to the state as sources of hydroelectric power.

HARRISON BROTHERS HARDWARE (all ages)
124 South Side Square, Huntsville, 35801; (256) 536–3631; www.huntsvilleal. com/hbhs. Open weekdays from 9:00 A.M. to 5:00 P.M. and Saturday from 10:00 A.M. to 2:00 P.M.

A stroll away from EarlyWorks is Harrison Brothers Hardware, the state's oldest hardware store, which will captivate both you and your children. Better than a museum, it is stocked from floorboards to high ceilings. Some items are kept in tiny, numbered drawers. Items stored up high are reached from tall, rolling ladders. The store also has a rope elevator, which must be hand operated, and a pot-bellied stove, warms the store on cold days. On a tall desk there is an untidy mound of old invoices, catalogs, and calendars, remaining just the way the final Harrison brother left them in 1983.

Kids will notice the massive, hand-cranked cash register that still rings up sales of everything from cotton throws, colorful tins, and oak rocking chairs to garden gadgets, bird feeders, and cast-iron cookware. Like generations before them, your children likely will be quick to notice the antique biscuit jars filled with candies.

TWICKENHAM HISTORIC DISTRICT (all ages)
(256) 551–2230.

The nearby historic district is the state's largest district of antebellum homes. A living museum of nineteenth-century architecture, Twickenham hosts a pilgrimage to allow you to look inside these stately homes on a late April weekend each year.

A no-hassle way to get an overview of Huntsville's historic district is to take a narrated trolley ride (256-535-6565). If you opt for a walking tour, ask the conductor to point out where to begin your trek among Twickenham's antebellum homes. You can leave the blue trolley at any attraction and board again at no extra charge. The trolley-looking bus, which departs from Depot Museum, circles on the hour and half-hour and takes a 12:30-to-1:30 P.M. lunch break. Trolley rides cost $2.00 for adults and $1.00 for children under 13. Infants ride for **Free**.

HUNTSVILLE DEPOT MUSEUM (all ages)

320 Church Street, Huntsville 35801; (256) 535–6565 or (800) 678–1819; www.earlyworks.com. Open Monday through Saturday from 9:00 A.M. to 5:00 P.M. Closed Sunday and some major holidays. Admission is $6.00 for adults, $3.50 for children ages 6 to 18, $5.00 for seniors ages 55+, and **Free** *to children under 6.*

At the renovated depot, tours, led by guides outfitted in railroad clothes, begin with a short audiovisual presentation focusing on the city's early years. After that the pace quickens in the wood-floored depot, where animated characters tell about life in a 1912 ticket office. You and your children will be taken with the still-visible messages scrawled on depot walls by Civil War prisoners and soldiers. Upstairs, where exhibits highlight early Huntsville, you'll find a diorama of the depot during the Civil War. For a look at what life was like when steam was king in the 1800s, watch as scale-model trains sweep through detailed miniature landscapes, pass stores and farmhouses, then chug past tree-covered hills.

If souvenirs are on your list, this is the place. The Train and Trolley Shop has spikes, conductor caps, watercolor prints, T-shirts, toy trains, stuffed animals, and books telling about America's love affair with the locomotive. Outside, train engines and cars make a good backdrop for a family photo. The depot is on Church Street at exit 19-C (Washington Street) off Interstate 565.

THE HUNTSVILLE–MADISON COUNTY BOTANICAL GARDEN (all ages)

4747 Bob Wallace Avenue, Huntsville 35805; (256) 830–4447;www.hsvbg. org. Open Monday through Saturday from 9:00 A.M. to 5:00 P.M. and Sunday from 1:00 to 5:00 P.M. Admission is $4.00 for adults, $3.00 for seniors 55+, and $2.00 for students.

The garden makes a fun and leisurely stop. You'll know you've arrived when you see the stone columns that herald the gardens. The fluted structures are from the old Madison County Courthouse. Save time to walk woodland paths, to explore the grassy meadows, and to smell the roses. One of the best times to visit the garden is the first Saturday in October, when a special event includes ghost stories, hayrides, a plant sale, a flower show, and a children's "creepy corner". The gift shop has loads of fascinating items that will intrigue kids with money burning a hole in their pockets.

(To reach the garden from the Space and Rocket Center, follow the access road and keep east on Bob Wallace.)

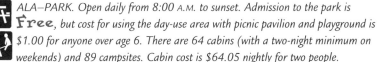

Shopping Kids popping to shop? Take them to **Madison Square Mall,** the largest retail center in North Alabama. On U.S. 72 West at Rideout Road, the mall has department stores, record stores, candy shops, and arcade centers.

Children also like what they find at **Temptations,** a high-end specialty clothing store at 7531 B Bailey Cove Road, (256-882-1150).

The Purple Peanut, 102 Longwood Drive, (256-534-5767), is known for children's specialty clothes, beginning with infant sizes and going to a boy's size seven and a girl's sixteen. Look for brands such as Zoodles and Sweet Potatoes.

MONTE SANO STATE PARK (all ages)

5105 Nolen Avenue, Huntsville 35801; (256) 534–3757 or (800) ALA–PARK. Open daily from 8:00 A.M. to sunset. Admission to the park is **Free***, but cost for using the day-use area with picnic pavilion and playground is $1.00 for anyone over age 6. There are 64 cabins (with a two-night minimum on weekends) and 89 campsites. Cabin cost is $64.05 nightly for two people.*

If your family appreciates the beauty of state parks, you won't want to miss Monte Sano State Park atop Monte Sano Mountain, which towers 1,000 feet higher than the eastern edge of Huntsville. Open since 1935, the park, built by the Civilian Conservation Corps, has a recreation area, picnic spots, scenic overlooks, nature trails, a Japanese garden and teahouse, and rustic cabins available for overnight rentals.

While on this mountaintop, be sure to take the park trail that leads to the site of the O'Shaughnessy home. Although all is lush here now, after the Civil War the mountaintop was a shamble of ruined buildings. The site's original home, with its arches and cedar floors and steps, was among the casualties. Rebirth on the mountain crept slowly along until the Space and Rocket Center ushered in a new era, prompting the addition of an RV park, a planetarium, and a Japanese garden.

BURRITT MUSEUM (all ages)

3101 Burritt Drive, Huntsville 35801; (256) 536–2882; Fax (256) 532–1784; www.huntsville.org/things/att.html. Buildings are open from 10:00 A.M. to 4:00 P.M. Tuesday through Saturday and from noon to 4:00 P.M. on Sunday. The site is closed from mid-December through February. There is no admission charge for the mansion, nature trails, and picnic area. Admission cost to the historic park is $3.00 for adults, $1.00 for children 18 and under, and $2.00 for seniors 55+.

While you're on the mountain, don't miss Burritt Museum, centered by the former home of one of the city's wealthy physicians, William Burritt. (Despite three marriages, the doctor died childless and left his mansion and surrounding acreage to the City of Huntsville to become the city's first museum.) For your children the most fascinating exhibits most likely will be the Indian pottery fragments, gems, and minerals. At the driveway leading to the basement garage, notice the two concrete tire paths aimed at the garage entrance. Because dense winter fog made driving a car difficult, Dr. Burritt designed trough-shaped channels to guide the driver's side tires into the garage. When the guides failed to work, the doctor filled them with concrete.

The land behind the house at one time was part of a farm where fruits and vegetables grew and where goats were raised. Today there are walking trails and a living-history site of nineteenth-century buildings that have been moved here from the surrounding area for historic preservation. Your family will have fun exploring the log houses, barn, frame church, sorghum mill, boiling furnace, springhouse, smokehouse, dogtrot house, and blacksmith shop. During museum hours there are living-history interpreters in period clothing doing daily chores from the era.

Annual Events at the Burritt Museum The Burritt Museum hosts an **Earth Day Celebration** in April, a **Fall Sorghum Festival** in September, an Indian Heritage Festival in October, and a **Candlelight Christmas** event. Call the museum for details.

Trails at the Burritt site lead to Monte Sano State Park. This is a several-hour hike, but if you persevere, you will see along the way a pit-cave called The Natural Well. Although you cannot go into the cave, look from the entrance and understand why for years the pit was considered to be bottomless. It actually stretches through a 196-foot vertical shaft, slants down a slope to the floor 245 feet below ground, and it then opens into a Cathedral Hall with a 100-foot-high ceiling.

Trails atop the mountain lead you past mountain streams, cascading wet-weather waterfalls, and nineteenth-century coal mines. You can step off the boardwalk and walk on the gravel path to get a bit closer to some of the caves. Stand a few minutes and feel the cool air blowing from the cave, where temperatures year-round are 57 degrees. You also can walk along the 1840s Big Cove Turnpike, site of the Confederate surrender in Madison County in 1865. A handicap-accessible nature trail is filled with wildflowers in spring.

To reach Monte Sano Mountain, go east on U.S. Highway 431 up the mountain. From there signs show the way.

Space Camp Barbie During her four decades as one of the world's most popular dolls, Barbie has had many careers, ranging from dentistry to computer whiz. In the summer of 1999, Barbie launched a new career when Mattel, Inc. unveiled a Space Camp Counselor Barbie.

The new Barbie is tied to the U.S. Space and Rocket Center, which makes no money from the doll's new career but saw the link as a new way to interest girls in the space program.

The doll's debut coincided with the thirtieth anniversary of the first man landing on the moon.

SOUTHERN ADVENTURES FAMILY ENTERTAINMENT CENTER (all ages)

2150 Leeman Ferry Circle, Huntsville, 35801; (256) 880–6599 or (256) 382–PARK. There is no admission charged to the pay-as-you-go park. The water park ($12 for ages 13 and up and $10 for ages 12 and under), is open May through September. The park is open year-round and hours vary by seasons. Miniature golf is $5.25 for adults, $3.75 for children 4 to 12, and Free *for children under 3 when accompanied by a paying adult. To ride a cart alone, children must be at least 52 inches tall; those who are shorter may ride with an adult. Cart fee is $5.25 for one rider and $6.25 for an adult accompanied by one small child. The best deal is a Family Pack of tickets, thirty for $20 or one hundred for $60.*

When your kids get an urge to run, scream, and yell, take them to Southern Adventures. Two eighteen-hole miniature golf courses are complete with life-size replicas of exotic animals, caves, and waterfalls. There also are video and pinball machines, which cost from 25 cents to $1.00, and a water park with a swimming pool and three open flumes each more than 320 feet long, one enclosed tube, two rides, and an interactive water-play area where parents and kids can play together. Batting cages offer 40-, 50-, 60-, and 70-miles per hour baseball and slow pitch softball. The folks here claim that their quarter-mile go-cart track is the fastest in Huntsville. There's food here, too; kidstuff like hamburgers, hot dogs, pizza (made on site, fresh daily), and nachos. So plan to make a day of it. (The park is behind Joe Davis Stadium.)

Rule of Our Roads Alabama allows right turn on red after making a full stop and determining the way is clear, unless a sign forbidding such turns is posted.

MUNICIPAL ICEPLEX (all ages)

3185 Leeman Ferry Road, Huntsville 35801; (256) 883–3774. Open daily. Hours are seasonal. Closed some holidays. Admission is $4.50.

If your youngsters still have an abundance of energy, head to the city-owned Municipal Iceplex, a twin-rink ice-skating facility. The schedule changes daily, so call before going. Arcade games and a concession stand are offered, too. Skate rental is $1.00 per person, but ask about a discount for a family with three or more.

NORTH ALABAMA RAILROAD MUSEUM (all ages)

694 Chase Road NE, 35815–4163; (256) 851–6276; www.suncompsvc. com/narm. The museum is open April through October on Wednesdays and Saturdays from 9:30 A.M. to 2:00 P.M. Museum admission is **Free**. *Excursions run on selected dates, typically April through December. Cost for regular train excursions is $8.00 for adults and $4.00 for children under 12. Lap babies may ride* **Free**.

Have your children ever ridden a steam-powered train? If not, they will have their chance in Huntsville. Regular train trips run just more than an hour. Geared to kids ten and younger, children's specials, typically some forty minutes long, include The Goblin on Halloween and a Santa Train on a December weekend. You'll ride in an air-conditioned coach originally built for the Pennsylvania Railroad, and during your ride you may visit a remodeled baggage car for sightseeing. So that your children won't be disappointed, remember to make advance reservations for train rides.

The museum holds the country's smallest union station, a walk-through passenger train, and the excitement of a real operating railroad. Some thirty pieces of antique railroad equipment are on display. In addition, the Chase Depot—complete with a waiting room, a ticket window, an agent's office, and a freight room—has been restored. Outside is a watchman's hut, a display train, and the excursion train. All aboard!

S**lugger Hugger** The wonderful image of baseball slugger Mark McGwire hugging his son after breaking the homerun record in 1998 has special meaning for baseball fans in Huntsville. McGwire played for the Huntsville Stars minor league team in 1986, and his son was born that season in Huntsville.

Where to Eat

Bubba's. *109 Washington Street, Huntsville 35801; (256) 534–3133.* Bubba's offers favorites ranging from ribs to sushi in a historic building. Tables in the rear overlook a courtyard. $

Clementine's. *525 Madison Street, Huntsville 35801; (256) 533–4438.* Salads and gourmet sandwiches are served in an old house 1 block from Early-Works history museum. Local artwork is displayed on the walls. $

Eunice's Country Kitchen. *1006 Andrew Jackson Way, Huntsville 35801; (256) 534–9550.* Aunt Eunice Merrill has been serving country ham and biscuits for breakfast and hugging customers—young and old—in this location for a half century. Walls are lined with autographed photos of entertainers, astronauts, and politicians who've eaten here. $

Lunch Pad. *Space and Rocket Center, 1 Tranquility Base, Huntsville 35805; (256) 837–3400 or (800) 63–SPACE.* Buffet line offers value-priced sandwiches, salads, and burgers. You can eat and watch activities either in the Rocket Park outside or the Space Camp training center inside. $

Annual Events

Annual Events Each April, the town sponsors the **Huntsville Pilgrimage.** Your children will get a kick out of **Cemetery Stroll.** Held in conjunction with Pilgrimage, it has costumed spirits that linger at appropriate grave sites and tell the story of the person buried there. Among the characters are several nineteenth-century Alabama governors, an early Huntsville madam, and the wife of an Alabama governor, who reportedly still is seated in her favorite rocking chair in her tomb. Visitors to Cemetery Stroll also learn that the late actress Tallulah Bankhead is said to visit the grave of her mother, who died two days after Tallullah's birth.

Rocket City, as Huntsville is called, has a spring art festival that puts children front and center. Students' artwork and performances highlight the **Panoply Festival of Art** (256-533-6565), which the Huntsville Arts Council stages the last weekend each April at downtown's Big Spring Park.

Each September Big Spring Park hosts the city's other major festival, the **Big Spring Jam.** A children's stage presents performing personalities from Sesame Street, Nickelodeon, and the Disney Channel. Meanwhile, adults enjoy rhythm and blues, rock, jazz, and country performers on half a dozen other stages. Call (256) 551-2230 for a schedule of performers.

Nightly, from Thanksgiving through New Year's Eve, the Huntsville-Madison County Botanical Garden hosts **Galaxy of Lights**, with more than a quarter million lights creating botanical and holiday scenes. (Admission is per carload, so load up the whole gang for this event.)

One special Christmas event in the Huntsville area is the **Parade of Lights,** held at Ditto Landing (256-882-1057) on the Tennessee River, several miles south of downtown. As darkness falls, boats go to Hobbs Island and head to Whitesburg Bridge before returning to the dock.

Where to Stay

Country Inn & Suites. *4880 University Drive, Huntsville 35816; (256) 837–4070 or (800) 456–4000; Fax: (256) 837–4535.* Here you get a refrigerator in your room and a **Free** activity packet for kids under 13. Better yet, you're within striking distance of University Drive's "restaurant row." $-$$

Days Inn–West. *102 Arlington, Highway 20 West, Madison 35758; (256) 772–9550 or (800) 329–7466.* Convenient to the airport, the 143-room property has a swimming pool and appealing pricing. $

Executive Lodge Suite. *1535 Sparkman Drive, Huntsville 35816; (256) 830–8600 or (800) 248–4722; Fax: (256) 830–8899.* Convenient to the Space Center, the 308-room property has especially large rooms, a swimming pool, a restaurant, and **free** continental breakfast. Ask about their all-inclusive package that includes Space Center tickets. $-$$$

Holiday Inn–Research Park. *5903 University Drive, Huntsville 35816; (256) 830–0600 or (800) 845–7275.* In the parking lot of Madison Square Mall, the 200-room hotel has a hot tub and both indoor and outdoor swimming pools. $-$$

Huntsville Hilton. *401 Williams Avenue, Huntsville 35816; (256) 533–1400 or (800) 445–8667; Fax: (256) 534–4581.* In Huntsville's historic district the 227-room hotel is within walking distance of several museums. $-$$

Huntsville Marriott. *5 Tranquility Base, Huntsville 35805; (256) 830–2222 or (800) 228–9290.* On the grounds of

the U.S. Space and Rocket Center, the 290-room hotel is ideal for families with space-camp kids. Other features are indoor and outdoor swimming pools, a hot tub, and a restaurant. $-$$

La Quinta Inn–Huntsville Research Park. *4870 University Drive NW, Huntsville 35816–1847; (256) 830–2070 or (800) NU–ROOMS; www.laquinta.com.* You'll like the upscale amenities not typically found at mid-priced hotels. Offers 25-inch televisions with Nintendo game systems, in-room coffeemaker, **free** local telephone calls, and **free** "First Light" breakfast. Children under 18 stay **free** with parents. $

La Quinta Inn–Huntsville Space Center. *3141 University Drive NW (Highway 72), Huntsville 35816–3137; (256) 533–0756.* **Free** breakfast, **free** local calls, in-room coffee, and 25-inch televisions with Nintendo game systems. Kids under 18 stay **free** with parents. $

For More Information

Huntsville/Madison County Convention & Visitors Bureau. *700 Monroe Street, Huntsville 35801–5570; (256) 551–2223 or (800) SPACE–4–U; Fax (256) 551–2324; Web site www.huntsville.org.*

Alabama Mountain Lakes Tourist Association. *25062 North Street, Mooresville, 35649–1075; (256) 350–3500 or (800) 648–5381; Web site www.almtlakes.org.*

S **tatehood** Alabama officially became a state on December 14, 1819.

Woodville

OLD MACDONALD'S PETTING ZOO (all ages)

7826 U.S. Highway 72, Woodville 75776; (256) 776–4332; www.geocities.com/Heartland/Ranch/3123. The zoo closes at the end of November and reopens in mid-March. From mid-March to late August, it is open Monday, Tuesday, Thursday, and Friday from 9:00 A.M. to 2:00 P.M. (closed Wednesday). Saturday hours are from 9:00 A.M. to 4:00 P.M., and Sunday hours are from noon to 4:00 P.M. After Labor Day and until late November, the zoo is open Monday, Tuesday, and Wednesday from 9:00 A.M. to 2:00 P.M.; Saturday from 9:00 A.M. to 4:00 P.M., and Sunday from noon to 4:00 P.M. (in those months the zoo is closed on Thursday and Friday). Admission is $4.00 per person, with children 2 and under admitted **Free***.*

Between Huntsville and Scottsboro in Woodville, Old MacDonald's Petting Zoo offers children lots of room to roam. Your family will discover domestic, exotic, and unusual animals, many of which you may pet and feed. There are ducks, swans, peafowl, pheasants, a Siberian lynx, porcupines, exotic chickens, pigeons, a llama, and an emu. Owner Sherry Lewis, who lives at the site, even has her own lamb named, of course, Lamb Chop.

Here, children may pet the animals, something they can't always do in larger zoos.

You'll find walk-in cages filled with gentle animals such as sheep and donkeys, a playground, a pond, and a nature trail. If your crew gets hungry, a small snack bar sells prepackaged foods such as candy, popcorn, and crackers. If you need something heftier, pack your own picnic and take advantage of the picnic tables. If you're looking for a memento of the day, there's a children's toy shop.

The zoo is 25 miles east of Huntsville, near Mile Marker 122 on U.S. Highway 72 East.

Scottsboro

JACKSON COUNTY/SCOTTSBORO HERITAGE CENTER (ages 8 to 12)

208 South Houston Street, Scottsboro 35768; (256) 259–2122. Open Tuesday through Friday from 11:00 A.M. to 4:00 P.M. Pioneer village is accessible anytime at no charge. Museum admission is $2.00 for adults and $1.00 for school-age children.

In downtown Scottsboro the Jackson County/Scottsboro Heritage Center is an entertaining and educational stop where some visitors do genealogical research while others enjoy the displays of Indian tools and weapons.

The really fun part of the visit is out back. Behind the 1880s house-turned-museum are pioneer log structures that re-create life in early north Alabama. The collection of buildings is called Sagetown, the name originally given to the town. Your children especially will enjoy the old schoolhouse and the blacksmith shop. To get the most from a tour, you should make arrangements ahead of time and specify which tour your family wants. You can choose the two-and-a-half-hour general tour, which begins with Native American life in the area and concludes with the Depression Era; a one-hour tour of the pioneer town; or a one-hour Native American tour that includes demonstrations of tools and weapons.

What a Deal, What a Day

Show your children good old-time bargaining in downtown Scottsboro at one of the region's oldest and largest trade days. The bartering, haggling, and swapping of goods dates back to the mid-1850s, when the circuit court met here on the first Monday of each month. A blend of antiques shows, craft fairs, and rummage sales, Trade Day is held year-round, morning until night, still on the first Monday of the month and also on the Sunday before. There is no admission cost.

UNCLAIMED BAGGAGE CENTER (ages 8 to 12)
509 West Willow Street, Scottsboro 35768; (256) 259–1525. Open Monday through Friday from 9:00 A.M. to 6:00 P.M. and Saturday from 8:00 A.M. to 6:00 P.M. Admission is **Free**.

If your kids are old enough to enjoy browsing and bargain hunting, head to Unclaimed Baggage Center. The store sells everything from books and cameras to clothes and jewelry at a fraction of their original costs. If you're a careful shopper, you can find some really good bargains here. Items are neatly arranged and are grouped by sizes and sometimes by colors. Pricing indicates that personnel are onto name brands and mark those up accordingly. (One recent find was a two-piece silk outfit for $25.)

The center has had a load of attention since it was featured on the *Oprah* show, when the daytime television maven proclaimed it one of the country's best-kept shopping secrets.

GOOSE POND COLONY (all ages)

417 Ed Hembree Drive, Scottsboro 35769; (256) 259–2884 or (800) 268–2884; www.goosepond.org. Open daily. Admission to the park is **Free**.

Owned by the City of Scottsboro, Goose Pond Colony is the place to golf, fish, swim, boat, and escape. The 360-acre peninsula park sprawls on the west bank of the Tennessee River and brims with activity year-round.

Except for a few very cold winter days, golf is played all year on the par 72, George Cobb–designed eighteen-hole course.

Fees for golf and overnight stays are nominal, especially when you consider that the golf course has been called "one of the best golf courses in the Southeast." Water comes into play on half the holes.

If the water calls, you can rent a pontoon boat either for a half or whole day and head into placid Lake Guntersville. This makes a fun, daylong outing that's peaceful and provides the chance to learn about nature, fishing, and, most likely, your family. Just remember to save time for the hiking and walking trails at the park. One trail begins at the water's edge adjacent to the cottages, so you can even trek a chunk of the pine-straw-strewn walkway at dusk. While on the trails, look for the Japanese magnolias and the dogwood trees, which have abundant pink and white blossoms in spring.

A Fullman Family Adventure When we visited Goose Pond Colony, General Manager Joe Reed Brumley talked about the abundant geese that are the park's namesake. The geese can play havoc with golf greens, but they also can make for some laughs.

Reed recalled when a goose appeared to have an arrow through his neck. "That critter would turn this way and that to avoid getting caught by bushes, and we just couldn't figure out what that arrow was," he said. When some sympathetic golfers figured out a way to catch the goose, they discovered that the arrow had sliced through a neck band placed there by conservationists. The goose was not harmed, only aggravated by his burden. The golfers removed the hunter's wayward arrow and returned the goose to its flock.

Each July Fourth the complex's amphitheater is the setting for an elaborate fireworks display that draws thousands of spectators.

You can grab a hot dog or hamburger in the poolside restaurant, get a morning sausage biscuit in the pro shop's snack bar, and save up for a feast at Crawdaddy's Too. The pro shop snack bar has everything from breakfast items to BLTs and tuna-fish-salad sandwiches. (Goose Pond also has meeting rooms, a civic center, and 105 camping sites.)

Where to Eat

Crawdaddy's Too. *417 Ed Hembree Drive, Scottsboro 35768; (256) 574–3071.* At Goose Pond Colony, eat in the screened-porch dining area and watch activity on the adjacent pier. Seafood is the specialty. Hours vary by seasons; call before going. $–$$

Payne's Restaurant. *101 East Laurel Street, Scottsboro 35768; (256) 574–2140.* In a former pharmacy on the town square, the eatery has an old soda fountain where your family can sit for lunch and watch as servers blend and stir carbonated drinks. On special occasions servers wear poodle skirts. $

Where to Stay

Goose Pond Colony. *417 Ed Hembree Drive, Scottsboro 35769; (256) 259–2884 or (800) 268–2884.* One- and two-story, two-bedroom, two-bath cedar cottages, each with living room, central heat and air conditioning, grill, docking pier, and decks and screened porches that overlook Lake Guntersville. A large living area and kitchen divide the two bedrooms. Your family will love having an entire home, and you'll love the chance to save some eating-out dollars by using the furnished kitchen or cooking on an outdoor grill that overlooks the lake. Plan to linger on the screened porch. If you plan to golf, ask about a golf package. $$–$$$

Hampton Inn. *46 Micah Way (Highway 72), Scottsboro 35769; (256) 259–4300 or (800) HAMPTON.* Save here with **Free** continental breakfast, **Free** newspaper, and no extra charge for kids staying with their parents. If you've been a while on the road, you'll like the coin-laundry facilities. $

Jameson Inn. *208 Micah Way, Scottsboro 35768; (256) 574–6666 or (800) JAMESON.* Kids stay **Free** with their parents, and you get **Free** extended continental breakfast. There's an outdoor swimming pool and a fitness center. $

For More Information

Scottsboro-Jackson County Chamber of Commerce. *407 East Willow Street (Box 973), Scottsboro 35768; (256) 259–5500 or (800) 259–5508; Fax (256) 259–4447; Web site www.sjcchamber.org.*

Alabama Mountain Lakes Tourist Association. *25062 North Street, Mooresville 35649–1075; (256) 350–3500 or (800) 648–5381; Web site www. almtlakes.org.*

Stevenson

STEVENSON RAILROAD DEPOT MUSEUM (all ages)

Main Street (Box 894), Stevenson 35772; (256) 437–3012. Hours December through March are Monday through Friday from 9:00 A.M. to 5:00 P.M. Hours April until Thanksgiving are Monday through Saturday from 9:00 A.M. to 5:00 P.M. Admission is **free**.

In downtown Stevenson the museum has displays relating to railway history, Indian heritage, the Civil War, and the town's history.

Annual Event During the first week of June, the Stevenson Railroad Depot Museum hosts **Depot Days.** You can expect activities to focus on the depot, which was an important junction during the Civil War. The festival includes wagon rides to a Civil War fort, square dancing, clogging, storytelling contests, big-band entertainment, and ice-cream socials.

Where to Stay

Budget Inn. *42973 U.S. Highway 72, Stevenson 35772; (256) 437–2215.* The 30-unit motel allows pets and has non-smoking rooms. $

Crow Creek Cottage. *361 County Road 287, Stevenson 35772; (256) 437–2535.* You won't have to worry about your kids making too much noise when staying at Charles Loyd's secluded cottage which is accessible only through his farmland. There's a dock for fishing, and he'll even loan you fishing gear. (Expect to reel in bass and crappie.) The two-bedroom cottage, which sleeps six, has a fully equipped kitchen, a screened front porch, and a wrap-around deck. $–$$

For More Information

Alabama Mountain Lakes Tourist Association. *25062 North Street, Mooresville, 35649–1075; (256)* *350–3500 or (800) 648–5381; Web site www.almtlakes.org.*

Bridgeport

Bridgeport is where Spanish explorer Hernando De Soto, heading south in 1540, entered the territory now known as Alabama.

RUSSELL CAVE NATIONAL MONUMENT (ages 8 to 12)

3729 County Road 98, Bridgeport 35740; (256) 495–2672; Fax (256) 495–9220; www.nps.gov/ruca. Opens daily at 8:00 A.M. Closing is at 5:00 P.M. except in winter months, when closing is at 4:30 P.M. Closed Thanksgiving Day and December 25. Admission is Free.

Seven miles northeast of Bridgeport, the cave is one of the country's earliest documented shelters for prehistoric humans. It is the state's only national historic site.

Part of a larger cavern stretching some 7 miles into a mountain, the overhanging cave shelter is where archaeologists have unearthed tools, pottery, weapons, bones, campfire remnants, and other evidence of pre-historic people. Their findings verified that cave dwellers were here from 7000 B.C. to about A.D. 1000. Kind of mind-boggling, isn't it?

The attention focused on the cave is a lesson in the power of the press. The site remained relatively unknown until an excavation by the Smithsonian Institution and the National Geographic Society was begun during the 1950s. Newspaper and magazine articles that followed the diggings generated interest in the 310-acre site. After work was com-pleted in 1961, the area was donated to the state.

To better understand Russell Cave, begin your visit by looking at the exhibits in the visitors center. After viewing objects dug from the site, head next to the mouth of the cave. Don't be disappointed to discover, though, that you are not allowed deep into the cave, which is cordoned off. Despite the limited access, from the mouth of the cave you can look beyond the fencing to see how the cave was excavated and get some idea of what life must have been like for Alabama cave dwellers.

The cave is administered by the National Park Service. Ranger-led guided tours—along with demonstrations, audiovisual programs, and museum exhibits—tell the story of how small family bands of prehistoric Indians, long before the time of Columbus, fed, clothed, and protected themselves.

Valley Head

SEQUOYAH CAVERNS (all ages)

1438 County Road 731, Valley Head 35989; (256) 635–0024 or (800) 843–5098; www.hsv.tis.net/~dekbtour. Open March through November from 8:30 A.M. to 5:00 P.M. daily. Open December through February only on weekends from 8:30 A.M. to 5:00 P.M. Cave admission cost is $7.00 for adults, $4.00 for children 4 to 12, and Free *for children 3 and younger.*

Sequoyah Caverns, 6 miles north of Valley Head, is a fun family place named for the Indian chief who invented the Cherokee alphabet. The highlight of your visit will be touring the multiroom cave that stretches almost one-quarter mile inside the base of Sand Mountain. Filled with still pools of mineral water, the cave has several intriguing sections, including one where the water seems to flow upward; if you take a closer look, however, you'll realize that you are looking at a motionless reflection. Although the hike into the cave is level, it is a long and winding path that is probably not a desirable undertaking for anyone who has trouble walking. The in-cave temperature year-round is cool, so your family may want to take sweaters or sweatshirts.

After touring the cave you are welcome to spread a picnic on the grounds, roam the acreage, or play volleyball. There's also an RV park with a swimming pool for registered guests. To get to the caverns, follow signs off Interstate 59 to U.S. Highway 11.

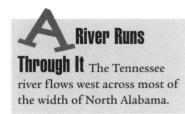

A River Runs Through It The Tennessee river flows west across most of the width of North Alabama.

Where to Eat

Tiger's Inn. *132 Commerce Avenue, Valley Head 35989; (256) 635–6855.* Known for country cooking and lunch and dinner specials that include drinks and dessert. $

Where to Stay

Winston Place. *353 Railroad Avenue (Box 165), Valley Head 35989; (256) 635-6381 or (888) 494-6786.* Dating from the 1830s, this columned house was built by William Winston, a wealthy man who assembled master craftsmen to create sweeping verandas and mighty columns. During the Civil War, Union officers used the house for their headquarters, and troops camped on surrounding acreage. From here they headed to Chickamauga, Georgia, for one of the war's bloodiest battles. Win-ston Place is 1 block off Alabama Highway 117. Owners prefer that children be at least age 6 or older, but they are willing to make arrangements because the house is large enough to keep possible noisemakers separated from guests who may not enjoy children's voices. If you're traveling with an entourage of folks, you may want to rent the entire house. That way, you can sleep from eighteen to twenty five and have the run of the place for $650 per night. $$$

For More Information

Alabama Mountain Lakes Tourist Association. *25062 North Street, Mooresville, 35649–1075; (256) 350–3500 or (800) 648–5381; Web site www.almtlakes.org.*

Mentone

Near the Georgia state line, Mentone is intriguing, small, and a great place to escape the world. In this town, whose name means "musical mountain spring," the narrow, twisting streets are filled with shops, restaurants, and craft places, many housed in historic buildings. One of the things that fascinates shoppers are the dolls crafted from gourds. The "gourdies" are "dressed" for numerous occasions, including in graduation gowns, wedding dresses, and tuxedos.

Annual Event An ideal time to visit Mentone is the third weekend in October during **Fall Colorfest,** when leaves on Lookout Mountain Parkway turn red, orange, and yellow, and temperatures have moderated. Sponsored by the Mentone Area Preservation Association (256-634-4664), Colorfest includes storytelling, craft demonstrations, country music, and barbecue. There is no admission charge.

CLOUDMONT SKI AND GOLF RESORT AND SHADY GROVE DUDE RANCH (all ages)

89 County Road 614, Lookout Mountain Parkway (Box 435), Mentone 35984; (256) 634-4344; www.cloudmont.com. Dude ranch and resort at Cloudmont are open year-round. Golf, horseback trails, and fishing available typically April through December. Snowmaking is limited to colder months, which in Alabama can vary year to year, usually January and February.

Cowhands and snow lovers will find mutual ground at this resort and ranch on Lookout Mountain Parkway. Cloudmont, the state's only ski resort, sits atop Lookout Mountain in 1,000 wooded acres filled with trails and waterfalls.

Cloudmont Ski and Golf Resort offers golf that is both affordable and spectacular, with the first tee perched atop a 30-foot rock. When temperatures drop to 28 degrees, man-made snow is blown from machines to blanket two slopes that have vertical drops of 150 feet. The unlikely Alabama spectacle is ideal for those who want to practice skiing before heading to greater heights elsewhere.

The state's only dude ranch, Shady Grove Ranch, has a stagecoach, buckboard wagons, hayrides (for groups of eight or more), and daily trail rides for drive-in and overnight guests. Lodge accommodations, swimming, nature trails, and fishing are also offered. The ranch has more than 100 miles of hiking trails and has miles of river and wilderness adventure. Some really colorful characters work here, so don't miss getting to know the staff. Be sure to have your picture taken astride the wood horse and get a signed certificate from ranch owner Jack Jones. Jones fell in love with this mountaintop when he came from Florida to attend summer camp. He vowed he'd buy the land one day, and he did just that, creating a place that's just right for the family looking for adventure in Alabama.

Where to Eat

Caldwell's Restaurant. *Highway 117, Mentone 35984; (256) 634–4040.* This family restaurant pleases everyone, with the chef's famous chicken, Caesar salad, sandwiches, and homemade cakes and pies. $

The Cliffs Restaurant. *15861 County Road 89, Mentone 35984; (256) 634–3040.* Scores of wall clocks fill the lobby, and the mountain view is spectacular. $–$$

Cragsmere Manna Restaurant. *17871 Lookout Mountain Parkway, Mentone 35984; (256) 634–4677.* You'll find good food Friday and Saturday nights, 5:00 to 9:00, in one of Lookout Mountain's oldest remaining structures. $–$$

Dessie's Kountry Chef. *5951 Alabama Highway 117 South, Mentone 35984; (256) 634–4232.* You can't go wrong eating foods prepared by Dessie Newberry, voted "Best Cook in DeKalb County." $

Dish. *6081 Alabama Highway 117, Mentone 35984; (256) 634–3669.* This restaurant is ideal for parents sneaking away without the kids. Menu changes daily with limited, and yummy, options. Housed at the rear of a downtown Mentone antiques store, it has indoor seating for seventeen; outdoor, for ten. Reservations are advised. Hours are limited and change seasonally. (Call before going.) Expect breads baked fresh daily and choices such as black-bean burrito, chicken curry, pot roast, or mushroom moussaka. If you do take the kids, ask about kids' foods, not shown on the menu. $

Log Cabin Deli. *Highway 117 (Route 1, Box 300) Mentone 35984; (256) 634–4560.* Housed in a structure dating from around 1800, Log Cabin Deli serves drinks in fruit jars; a specialty is a great cabin cooler, a secret mixture that resembles sweet spice tea and Sprite. Soups usually are made from locally produced vegetables. Try the homemade fudge cake and ask to sit on the screened porch. $

Where to Stay

Raven Haven. *651 County Road 644, Mentone 35984; (256) 634–4310.* Owners Tony and Eleanor Teverino are gracious hosts, and Lookout Mountain is the backdrop for this rock home with a wide front porch filled with rocking chairs. You'll be served a full gourmet breakfast. Children over 14 only. Two-night minimum April through October. Tea, hot chocolate, a selection of coffees and home-baked snacks are left out overnight. $-$$

Shady Grove Dude Ranch. *89 County Road 614, Lookout Mountain Parkway (Box 435) Mentone 35984; (256) 634–4344.* Nine units and the chance to be a cowboy for a night. Fishing, hiking, and horseback riding are available. $

Stone's Throw Cottage. *16106 County Road 89, Mentone 35984; (256) 634–4849.* Cottage with central heat/air, wood-burning stove, kitchen, baby crib, toys, and games. On the scenic Lookout Mountain Parkway, named by *Reader's Digest* as one of America's Most Scenic Drives. $

Valhalla Luxury Cottages. *County Road 626, Mentone 35984; (256) 634–4006.* Four cottages nestled in the forest along Serenity Pond. Each has kitchen, gas-log fireplaces, TV/VCR, stereo, and screened-in porches. On-property, eight-person hot tub available. $$

For More Information

DeKalb County Tourist Association. *P.O. Box 681165, Fort Payne 35968;* *(256) 845–3957; web site www.hsv.tis.net/ ~dekbtour or www.mentone.com/tourist.*

Fort Payne

Fort Payne, known as the sock capital of the world because of the huge number of socks produced here, has more to showcase than socks. In fact, none of the sock mills are open routinely for tours, but there's plenty more to do.

The city has become a household word thanks to "the boys," the name locals give to members of the country music group ALABAMA.

 ### ALABAMA FAN CLUB AND MUSEUM (ages 8 to 12)
101 Glenn Boulevard SW (Box 680529), Fort Payne 35967; (256) 845–1646; www.wildcountry.com. Open Monday through Saturday from 8:00 A.M. to 5:00 P.M. and Sunday noon to 4:00 P.M. Museum admission is $1.00 per person; children under 6 Free.

The museum is filled with personal items belonging to band members. Most kids who pass through the museum can't resist bouncing around as they listen to the sounds of the band playing softly in the background, setting the tour's tone. Each of the band's members has a glass-enclosed exhibit filled with items he chose to include. There also is a collection of police badges, patches, and awards; all favorites with children.

 ### FORT PAYNE DEPOT MUSEUM (ages 8 to 12)
105 Fifth Street NE (Box 681420), Fort Payne 35968–1615; (256) 845–5714; www.hsv.tis.net/~dekbtour. Open Monday, Wednesday, and Friday from 10:00 A.M. to 4:00 P.M. and Sunday from 2:00 to 4:00 P.M. Admission is Free.

Your family shouldn't come this far without seeing the Fort Payne Depot. Dating from before the turn of the century, the old depot has found its destiny as a museum displaying early farm equipment, pottery, Civil War artifacts, and Indian items. Adjacent to the museum and worth seeing are the dioramas, which were once part of a traveling show.

Did You Know? DeKalb County was formed from land ceded by the Cherokee Nation after the signing of the Treaty of New Echota. The treaty, which called for the forced removal of Native Americans from their homeland, mandated a march to the West, which became known as the Trail of Tears.

DESOTO STATE PARK (all ages)

13883 County Road 89, Fort Payne 35967; (256) 845–5380 or (800) ALA–PARK; Fax (256) 845–8286; www.mentone.com/desoto. Open daily from dawn to dusk. Park admission is **Free**.

DeSoto State Park, 7 miles northeast of Fort Payne off Alabama Highway 35 on Highway 176, has plenty of reasons you'll want to visit. Cabins, with handmade furniture, are scattered far enough apart to let you feel as though you're really on a great wilderness adventure in the mountains of north Alabama. DeSoto sprawls over some 5,000 acres along the ridge of Lookout Mountain. A falls and canyon are the park's main attractions, but the park also offers hiking and nature trails.

Lonely River Situated atop Lookout Mountain, Little River is the only river in the United States that runs its entire course on the top of a mountain.

The Little River, which appears on top of the mountain, plunges 100 feet over DeSoto Falls before continuing south and dropping another 60 feet over Little River Falls. Your family can see the canyon by driving the scenic parkway dotted with overlooks.

Expect to hear some "oohs" and "aahs" from the backseat when you approach Little River Canyon, visible from 20 miles of paved scenic drives that follow the west rim. The canyon is the heart of a 15,000-acre national preserve that encompasses the state park and a nearby wildlife management area. Sometimes called the Grand Canyon of the East, Little River Canyon has an average depth of 500 feet and at one point dips to 800 feet. Be sure to keep little ones in tow at these picturesque sites.

The park includes a couple dozen guest rooms at a lodge where three meals are served daily. Chalets and rustic cabins book quickly, so be sure your family plans ahead.

SALLIE HOWARD MEMORIAL CHAPEL (ages 8 to 12)

County Road 165, just off Lookout Mountain Parkway (mail: 218 Parker Avenue SE, Rainsville 35986); (256) 845–1986. Open daily, twenty-four hours. "Come-as-you-are" Sunday service at 10:00 A.M. Admission is **Free**.

The chapel's huge boulder, which serves as its rear wall, will fascinate your kids.

Be sure they know the chapel's story. It was built in 1937 by Colonel Milford Wriarson Howard, with help from the Civilian Conservation Corps, as a memorial to his late wife, who had been buried in California. According to his final wishes, Colonel Howard was cremated so that his ashes could be placed inside the giant rock of the memorial chapel.

Words from Sally's last letter to him are printed on a huge beam inside the chapel. They are: "God has all ways been as good to me as I would let Him be." Howard added a single word above hers. His, simply, is: "Immortality." Read these inscriptions with your older children, and you should have plenty to talk about as you drive away. (Note that even though the mailing address reads Rainsville, the chapel is just off Lookout Mountain Parkway, some 7 miles from downtown Mentone and adjacent to DeSoto State Park.)

 COLLINSVILLE TRADE DAY (ages 8 to 12)
(mail: Box 256, Collinsville 35961); (256) 524–2536. Held every Saturday from 5:30 A.M. until mid-afternoon.

Dating from 1955, the weekly affair sprawls over more than forty acres with more things than you might imagine. You can find arts and crafts, antiques, junk and collectibles, farm equipment as well as farm animals, and, yes, even the kitchen sink.

Where to Shop

Big Mill Antique Mall. *105 Fifth Street, Fort Payne 35967; (256) 845–3380.* You never know what you'll discover in his converted hosiery mill, but count on plenty of antiques plus toys, books, pottery, and quilts.

CJ's Wholesale Socks, Inc. *504 Gault Avenue North, Fort Payne 35967; (256) 845–7986. Closed Sundays.* Don't miss the chance to stock up on socks for the whole family—and at huge discounts.

Where to Eat

Burger King. *Interstate 59 at Highway 35 South, Fort Payne 35967; (256) 845–7200.* Operated by local franchise owners Stafford and Kristie Rastall, this is the place for a quick and affordable meal. $

Mountain Inn Restaurant (DeSoto State Park's Dining Room). *13903*

County Road 89, Fort Payne 35967; (256) 845–5380 or (800) ALA–PARK. The view's as good as the food here. $–$$

Quincy's Family Steak House. *Interstate 59 at Highway 35, Fort Payne 35967; (256) 845–0033.* The hot bar should have something to satisfy everyone, and there's a weekend breakfast bar. $

Shoney's. *Interstate 59 at Highway 35, Fort Payne 35967; (256) 845–3881.* Great salad and breakfast bars. $

Taco Bell. *610 Glenn Boulevard, Fort Payne 35967; (256) 845–7512.* Quick place for an affordable meal. $

Western Sizzler. *2200 Gault Avenue North, Fort Payne 35967; (256) 845–6111.* Wide variety of foods and great lunch and dinner specials. $

Where to Stay

Days Inn. *Glenn Boulevard SW, Fort Payne 35967; (256) 845–2085.* At Highway 35 and Interstate 59, Days Inn offers Free continental breakfast, Free local calls, and some suites. $

DeSoto State Park Lodge. *13883 County Road 89, Fort Payne 35967; (256) 845–5380 or (800) ALA–PARK.* This 25-room lodge has all the amenities of a chain hotel with the bonus of park activities nearby. Children under twelve stay Free. Also cabins and chalets. $

Holiday Inn Express. *112 Airport Road, Fort Payne 35967; (256) 997–1020.* Just off Highway 35 and Interstate 59 in south Fort Payne, it offers suites, in-room refrigerators, and Free continental breakfast $

Knotty Pine Resort. *1492 County Road 618, Fort Payne 35967; (256) 845-5293).* Cabins and campgrounds are shaded by pine trees. Plenty of places to romp and play. $

Quality Inn. *1412 Glen Boulevard (Highway 35 and Interstate 59) (Box 680986), Fort Payne 35968–0986; (256) 845–4013 or (800) 228–5151.* With 79 units the inn has a swimming pool with kiddie pool, restaurant, Free local calls, Free extended continental breakfast, guest laundry, picnic area, and large outdoor swimming pool. $

Travelodge. *1828 Gault Avenue North, Fort Payne 35967; (256) 845–0481 or (800) 255–3050.* The 68-unit property has a swimming pool, restaurant, and king rooms with work desks. $

For More Information

DeKalb County Tourist Association. *P.O. Box 1165, Fort Payne 35967; (256)* *845–3957; Web site www.hsv.tis.net/ ~dekbtour.*

Sock It To Me Alabama's sock manufacturers are concentrated in DeKalb County. Hosiery mills in Fort Payne produce an average of 120 million pairs of socks each week. The mills have a weekly payroll of more than $1 million.

Grove Oak

BUCK'S POCKET (ages 8 to 12)

393 County Road 174, Grove Oak 35975; (256) 659–2000 or (800) ALA–PARK. Open year-round Sunday through Thursday 8:00 A.M. to 4:00 P.M., Friday and Saturday 8:00 A.M. to 5:30 P.M. Admission is Free.

Head west if your tribe is game for a roughing-it kind of overnight in a virtually undisturbed area. If so, they'll like Buck's Pocket, which sprawls across a couple thousand acres in DeKalb, Jackson, and Marshall counties.

The park is heralded by a sign posted at the entrance. It is also called a "haven for defeated politicians," a reference to a time when former governor "Big Jim" Folsom lost a senate race and announced his plan to go to Buck's Pocket to "lick his wounds." Folsom invited other defeated candidates to join him at his favorite retreat. Being here makes it clear why you could lose yourself and the world's cares in the midst of the natural wonderland.

Camping is strictly rustic in this pocket of the Appalachian Mountain chain; from your sleeping bag, though, you'll have incredible mountain vistas. In addition to fifty-five improved and forty-five primitive sites, there are picnic grounds, a boat ramp, a fishing area, a playground, and hiking trails.

An Indian legend gave Buck's Pocket its name. It is said that when Cherokee Indians lived in the area, they once trapped a big buck deer on a high ledge. To avoid capture the deer jumped to his death on the rocks below.

Later the site was used for a mill that cut, dried, and shipped hardwood lumber. Many of the old ox trails are used today as hiking trails.

If you have time for only one trail, hike to Point Rock, a 2-mile walk that's not too difficult but rewards you with a view of the canyon some 400 feet below. Make sure you see the abundance of wildflowers and ferns and note the geologic formations. Another choice that is fairly easy to walk is Indian House Trail, which leads to an overhanging rock where Cherokee Indians are said to have taken shelter.

The best seasons in which to visit are spring, when wildflowers are abundant, and fall, when leaves are changing colors.

Guntersville

Being outdoors is the best reason to visit Guntersville, where Lake Guntersville is the leading lady and a state park is the supporting cast.

LAKE GUNTERSVILLE STATE PARK (all ages)

1155 Lodge Drive, Guntersville 35976; (256) 571–5444 or (800) 548–4553. Park is open daily, twenty-four hours. Park admission is **Free**.

The Alabama State Park system's motto, "Something for everyone," is aptly illustrated at Lake Guntersville State Park, filled with mountains, lakes, hillsides, beaches, and hardwood and pine forests.

A healthy deer herd wanders freely in the 6,000-acre park, where guided hikes are available anytime. If your family heads out with a guide, specify what you want to see: the eagle places, turkey roosting trees, beaver dams, old home sites, or pioneer cemeteries.

Stays here are an adventure, with access to golf, fishing, boating, and hiking. There also are tennis courts, a playground, and a swimming pool. The park has a lodge that looks rustic but isn't, plus cabins and chalets that have kitchens and all the creature comforts you'll need.

The campground has a fascinating display of natural wonders, including bird nests, turtle eggs, fossils, Indian artifacts, and insect collections. Park naturalists, on duty daily, help kids with science projects and can answer all kinds of questions. If you have one of those kids who can't quit asking questions, this is the place to go. On Friday and Saturday nights, programs vary from slide shows and movies to live music and dancing. Guest speakers include bluebird experts, archaeologists, and forest rangers.

If your family visits from January through early March, you might see eagles. Special Eagle Awareness weekends offer information and guides, or you can hunt on your own. Keep in mind, however, that the supervised eagle outings require early-morning departures; so be certain your children are game for getting up in the dark. Take plenty of clothes for these winter outings, too, because it's most often cold, especially before sunup. The lodge's coffee shop and restaurant have excellent food, making it possible to remain at the park during your entire visit.

BEACH MOUNTAIN GOLF AND ARCADE (all ages)

Wyeth Drive (mail: Box 446), Albertville 35950; (256) 582–4653. Open Monday through Saturday from 10 A.M. to midnight. Costs vary.

When you're ready to leave the wilderness behind, take your children to Beach Mountain Golf and Arcade . The thirty-six-hole miniature golf course has cascading waterfalls, streams, and beautiful landscaping. There's also an arcade.

Where to Eat

Covington's. *524 Gunter Avenue, Guntersville 35976; (256) 582–5377.* In the 1933 Hotel Glover, Covington's serves only lunch ("soups, salads, and such") and has a faithful following. $

Lake Guntersville State Park Lodge. *1155 Lodge Drive, Guntersville 35976; (256) 571–5440 or (800) 548–4553.* A restaurant and coffee shop offer a range of choices and excellent food. Convenient for those staying at the park. $–$$

Where to Stay

Lake Guntersville Holiday Inn Resort Hotel. *2140 Gunter Avenue, Guntersville 35976; (256) 582–2220 or (800) 579–5464.* The 100-unit hotel offers in-room coffee, and has a restaurant and rooms with kitchenettes. $

Lake Guntersville State Park Lodge. *1155 Lodge Drive, Guntersville 35976; (256) 571–5440 or (800) 548–4553.* Lodge rooms have all the conveniences of a chain hotel, plus balconies with mountain views. Also

chalets and cabins, ideal for extended stays. $–$$

Mac's Landing Motel. *7001 Val-Monte Drive, Guntersville 35976; (256) 581–1000.* **Free** continental breakfast. $–$$$

Super 8 Motel. *4740 Highway 431 South, Guntersville 35975; (256) 582–8435 or (800) 800–8000.* Thirty-eight affordable units, plus nonsmoking rooms. $

For More Information

Lake Guntersville Chamber of Commerce. *200 Gunter Avenue (Box 577), Guntersville 35976; (256) 582–3612 or (800) 869–LAKE; Web site www.lakeguntersville.org.*

Marshall County Convention and Visitors Bureau. *200 Gunter Avenue (Box 711), Guntersville 35976; (256) 58–7015 or (800) 582–6282; Web site mccvb@mindspring.com.*

Arab

Before you begin exploring Arab (pronounced Ay-rab), explain to your children how the town got its name. It's a good lesson in honest mistakes. Asked for three name choices, settler Tuttle Thompson submitted possibilities, including his son's name, Arad. In Washington, D.C., officials misread Thompson's handwriting and, in 1882, named the town Arab. Knowing the cumbersome red tape that would be needed to rectify the mistake, Thompson left the name.

A walking- or driving-tour brochure is the best tool for exploring this small town atop Brindlee Mountain. If you don't get a brochure in advance, ask for one at the Chamber of Commerce downtown on Main Street. "Just ask anybody who lives here," one local explained, "and they'll know where the Chamber is."

A walking- or driving-tour brochure gives insight into a couple dozen structures. Among them is the Methodist Church Cemetery, where settler Thompson is buried. Also on the walking tour are sites with lengthy histories but modern-day occupants such as dry cleaners and car dealerships.

Poor Man's Greens Each year, usually at the end of April or early May, Arab is the setting for a tribute to "poke salat," the large, wild, purple-stalked plant that has been called the "poor man's greens."

Most children wouldn't care to try these, but the annual **Poke Salat Festival** draws plenty of merrymakers, some of whom compete for the best recipe using the leafy plant. The event, held on Brindlee Mountain, was started by a group of men who religiously meet at downtown's L-Rancho Club, which serves the likes of turnip greens and corn bread. The men just thought it'd be fun, and it has been, especially for a community that is fairly isolated and has to make its own merriment.

ARAB'S HISTORIC COMPLEX (all ages)
Arab City Park; (256) 582–7015 or (800) 582–6282. Guided tours are by appointment. Admission is Free.

Arab's Historic Complex includes a 1935 school, 1912 church, country store, and museum. Dating from the 1880s, the complex's structures have been preserved with authentic furnishings. It's a great place to step back in time.

Where to Stay

Jameson Inn. *706 North Brindlee Mountain Parkway (Highway 231), Arab 35016; (256) 586–5777 or (800) 526–3766.*

𝕱𝖗𝖊𝖊 continental breakfast; some kitchenettes. $

For More Information

Arab Chamber of Commerce. *1157 North Main Street, Arab 35016; (256) 586–3138 or (888) 403–2722.*

Marshall County Convention and Visitors Bureau. *200 Gunter Avenue (Box 711), Guntersville 35976; (256) 582–7015 or (800) 582–6282; Web site mccvb@mindspring.com.*

Cullman

Cullman, founded by German immigrant Colonel John Cullmann, still displays a heavy influence from Deutschland. (Cullmann dropped the second "n" from his name when naming this northeast Alabama city.)

 CULLMAN COUNTY MUSEUM (ages 8 to 12)
211 Second Avenue Northeast, Cullman 35055; (256) 739–1258; Fax (256) 737–8782. Open Monday, Tuesday, Wednesday, and Friday from 9:00 A.M. to noon and from 1:00 to 4:00 P.M. Thursday hours are from 9:00 A.M. to noon. Sunday hours are from 1:30 to 4:30 P.M. Museum admission cost is $2.00 for adults and $1.00 for children under 12.

The best place to quickly uncover the town's German heritage is at Cullman County Museum, a replica of the founding father's home, which was destroyed by fire in 1912. Opened in 1973 during the town's centennial, the museum has eight rooms, each with a theme focusing on the city's roots and early years. The archaeological room has displays of Indian artifacts and a 7-foot-tall carving of an Indian warrior that always attracts the kids' attention.

If your children lose interest in the displays of china and jewelry, direct them to the school bell, which the director is willing to sound. (Just remember to cover your ears because this bell makes one heck of a noise.) The beer wagon and fainting couches also leave an impression on youngsters, as does the re-creation of Colonel Cullmann's room, complete with his rocking chair, bed, and sofa.

AVE MARIA GROTTO (ages 6 to 12)

St. Bernard Abbey, 1600 St. Bernard Drive SE, Cullman 35055; (256) 734–4110; Fax (256) 734–2925; www.sbabbeyprep.org. Open daily (except December 25) from 7:00 A.M. until sunset. Admission is $4.50 for adults, $3.00 for children 6 to 12, and **Free** *for children under 6.*

Cullman is perhaps best known for a single attraction, Ave Maria Grotto, which has been called "Jerusalem in Miniature." Off U.S. Highway 278, the four-acre park, filled with 125 small stone and cement structures, is in a sunken garden setting on the grounds of St. Bernard Abbey, the state's only Benedictine monastery. Strolling through the gardens will give you the chance to show your children what ingenuity can produce.

Brother Joseph Zoettl used an assortment of materials—cement, marbles, shells, colored stones, costume jewelry, cold-cream bottles, and chunks of Alabama marble—to build dioramas that illustrate biblical events, complete with miniatures of famous shrines, buildings, and cathedrals. Be sure your family sees Noah's Ark and the Hanging Gardens of Babylon. Brother Joseph, who died in 1961, is buried in the nearby abbey cemetery.

The Fullmans in Cullman

The Fullmans in Cullman We've been many times to Cullman and never grow tired of what's there. With each visit Ave Maria Grotto seems to take on a new look, depending on how the sun is hitting or how the clouds are draped.

We can never resist taking photos there and talking about the precious, bored little monk who crafted those wonders, those "sermons in stones," as they have been called.

If we are there on a weekend, we love nothing better than to take our "mad money" and scour the Cullman Flea Market. Oh, the bargains we've unearthed there—socks and bracelets and such. It's a fun outing for all of us, except maybe Milton, who would rather omit the shopping.

CLARKSON COVERED BRIDGE (all ages)

305 Fourth Avenue NE, Cullman 35055; (256) 734–3369; www.forcullman. com. Open daily from 8:00 A.M. until sunset. Admission is **Free***.*

If your tribe would prefer an outdoor activity, take in Clarkson Covered Bridge and its adjacent pioneer dogtrot-style log cabin and gristmill. The state's largest covered truss bridge sits in a tree-filled park with easy hiking trails and picnic grounds. The 1904 bridge is on the site of the 1863 Battle of Hog Mountain.

It's peaceful here, with the sounds of traffic too distant to penetrate the wooded sanctuary. Walk with your children across the restored bridge and point out the unique lattice-style planks that form a webbing. Explain to them that this truss, an American invention, made the bridge strong enough to withstand excessive weight and to endure the test of time.

Special Events in Cullman

Special Events in Cullman The **Bluegrass Superjam,** held in April and November, features Grand Old Opry–style music and family entertainment.

Held in mid-April, the **Bloomin' Festival at St. Bernard** heralds the arrival of spring with two days of entertainment, crafts exhibits, and demonstrations, and more than one hundred booths. During the festival, admission cost to the grotto is **Free**.

In August the world's largest bass fishing tournament, the **Anderson Fishing Classic,** offers a challenge from Smith Lake to anglers from across the South.

Plan a visit just right and you'll be in town when Cullman, in the first week of October, pays tribute to its heritage with daily German lunches and dinners, Bavarian music, a crafts show, tours, and a ball, all centering around **Oktoberfest.** Don't look for booze, though; this is a dry county.

If your kids are interested in old homes and architecture, visit during December's **Parade of Homes,** when many homes in the historic district are bedecked with garlands and opened to guests.

SPORTSMAN LAKE PARK (all ages)

1523 Sportsman Lake Road (mail: 305 Fourth Avenue NE), Cullman 35055; (256) 734–3052; Fax (256) 736–2898. Open daily from 7:00 A.M. to sunset. Admission is **Free**.

Within the city limits of Cullman, the park overflows with activity on warm days. It is especially popular with locals who convene to fish, picnic, play carpet golf, paddle boats, ride the miniature train, and romp on the playground. If you visit, take peanuts or bread to feed the ducks and geese that come very close for the chance at a snack.

With water on your mind, take your family to Smith Lake, most of which is in Cullman County. The lake's 500 miles of shoreline and

21,000 acres of clear water are a popular place with visitors who like to fish, ski, and boat. Challenge your kids to hold a line steady and see what might bite at this lake, which provided a state-record striped bass that weighed 32.8 pounds. The lake yielded the past five world-record spotted-bass catches, too. In Alabama the lake is billed number one for spotted bass and number three for crappie. So the odds of landing a trophy-size fish are strong.

If you want to up your odds for reeling in bass, plan to visit from February through early April or October and November. Action continues through summer but is best very early or late in the day or at night. Crappie action is best in April and May, with striped-bass fishing good year-round.

 SMITH LAKE PARK (all ages)
416 County Road 385 (mail: 305 Fourth Avenue NE), Cullman 35055; (256) 739–2916. Open daily from 9:00 A.M. until sunset. Tent camping is $10 a night; camper, $13.

The park has a boat ramp, a swimming pool, a water slide, carpet golf, picnic sites, more than 200 campsites (most on the water and all with electricity), and eight shelters.

Where to Shop

Touch of German. *218 First Avenue SE, Cullman 35055; (256) 739–4592.* This quaint shop overflows with cuckoo clocks, antique toy reproductions, and rows of handcrafted nutcrackers and smokers that stare with fixed eyes. This is the place to find traditional German clothing, dolls, and toys. Collectors will also find blue Delft, Russian, and Polish nested dolls, Austrian crystal, music boxes, and steins. Christmas items are sold year-round. When visiting the store, be sure that your children are on their best behavior; the aisles are narrow and the displays are crammed with items, many of which are very expensive.

Cullman Flea Market. *Next to Interstate 65 at U.S. Highway 278; (256) 739–0910. Open Saturday and Sunday from 8:00 A.M. to 5:00 P.M.* If you want some less restrained shopping, and if your youngsters are old enough to appreciate bargain hunting, don't miss this weekend flea market with scores of indoor and outdoor vendors. Count on finding furniture, tools, new (but imperfect) lingerie, ceramics, socks, jewelry, and T-shirts. There are several rest rooms, plenty of bargains, and a few places to get a quick bite to eat.

Where to Eat

All Steak Restaurant. *314 Second Avenue SW, Cullman 35055; (256) 734–4322.* You have to look hard for this popular eatery, because it is on the upper level of a downtown bank building. Enter from the parking deck. Orange rolls are terrific. $

The Creamery. *402 Fifth Street SW, Cullman 35055; (256) 739–3131.* This is a fun place, housed in a building constructed by early German settlers and later used as a dairy for producing cheese for Kraft. Lots of seafood, steaks, and salads. $–$$

Where to Stay

Best Western Fairwinds Inn. *1917 Commerce Avenue, Cullman 35055; (256) 737–5009 or (800) 528–1234.* **Free** continental breakfast and in-room coffee. $

Comfort Inn. *5917 Highway 157 NW (at Interstate 65), Cullman 35057; (256) 734–1240.* **Free** continental breakfast. $

Hampton Inn. *6100 Highway 157 (at Interstate 65), Cullman 35057; (256) 739–4444 or (800) HAMPTON.* **Free** continental breakfast and in-room coffee. $

Holiday Inn Express. *Interstate 65 at exit 304, Cullman 35057; (256) 734–2691 or (800) HOLIDAY.* The 60-unit inn offers **Free** continental breakfast, in-room coffee, and **Free** newspaper. $

For More Information

Cullman Area Chamber of Commerce. *211 Second Avenue NE, Cullman 35055; (mail: Box 1104, 35056-1104);* *(256) 734–0454; Fax (256) 737–7443; Web site www.cullmanchamber.org.*

Warrior

RICKWOOD CAVERNS STATE PARK (all ages)

370 Rickwood Park Road, Warrior 35180; (205) 647–9692 or (800) ALA–PARK; www.bham.net/rickwood/index.html. The park, its nature trails, picnic areas, and playground are open daily from 9:00 A.M. until sundown. Attractions are open daily from Memorial Day through Labor Day from 10:00 A.M. to 5:00 P.M. Park admission is $1.00 per person. Cave tours are $7.50 for adults, $3.50 for children 6 to 11, and **Free** *for younger children. Cave is closed November through February. Swimming pool is $2.50 per person.*

The adventure lover in your family will relish a trip to Rickwood Caverns State Park, off Interstate 65 north of Warrior. The only operational caving park in the state's park system, it has an underground "Miracle Mile," which is a web of passages and lighted rooms accented with thousands of sparkling white limestone formations that are 260 million years old.

When you go into the cave, look for the blind cave fish and underground pools. Remind your children not to disturb the bats, because they do swoop down when annoyed. Noise doesn't bother them, but physical contact will bring them to life. Cavern tours are completely guided, go 175 feet underground, and cover about 1 mile.

If anyone in your group might have trouble with the walk, ask the guide if rests will be permitted along the way. (When a group is small enough, this request usually can be granted.) You can, of course, visit without going into the cave, but who'd want to? When you exit the underground attraction, look around at all the other possibilities: camping, game machines, hiking trails, picnic tables, an Olympic-size swimming pool, a playground, and a miniature train. There's also a snack bar if anyone in your crowd grows hungry while romping.

Oneonta

Oneonta sits in Blount County, a region known as the "Covered Bridge Capital of Alabama." Three of the state's remaining dozen covered bridges are within a few miles of Oneonta. (The other covered bridges are in Sumter, Calhoun, Cullman, Etowah, Talladega, Coosa, and Lee counties.) Set aside a half day to easily see all three.

Of the three Oneonta-area bridges, the most intriguing is Horton Mill Covered Bridge, 5 miles north of town on State Route 75. The latticed bridge stretches some 70 feet above the Warrior River and is said to be higher above water than any other covered bridge in the nation.

Annual Event Each October Oneonta hosts a **Covered Bridge Festival** with bridge tours, arts and craft exhibits, and other fun. You can sign up for a bus trip during the festival or strike out on your own, which may give you more flexibility in scheduling your adventure.

Northwest of Cleveland and a mile off State Route 79, Swann Bridge stretches 324 feet over the Locust Fork of the Black Warrior River. Ten miles from Oneonta, the bridge, built in 1933, is the state's longest. Easley Bridge, 3 miles northwest of Oneonta, is 95 feet across. Built in 1927, it is one of the state's oldest covered bridges.

If water activities draw your brood, you can get wet near Oneonta, where, minutes away off U.S. Highway 231, is 500-acre Highland Lake. It offers public boat ramps, boating, and swimming facilities. Or you can canoe and kayak on the Locust and Mulberry forks of the Black Warrior River, which wind through the county offering lazy drifts and white-water action.

PALISADES PARK (all ages)

U.S. Highway 231, atop Ebell Mountain; (205) 274–0017. Park hours are 9:00 A.M. to 9:00 P.M. during Daylight Savings Time. The park closes at 5:00 P.M. during the rest of the year. Admission is **Free***.*

Once your family has seen the bridges, it may be time for a rest—and Palisades Park is the place, with plenty of places to romp, picnic, and explore. Nationally acclaimed for its design, the park is a fun stop, especially if your family enjoys easy hiking trails, historic log cabins, and picnic areas. There are some rocky gorges here, so don't let little ones too far out of sight. Do, however, keep an eye out for rappelling rockclimbers, who often practice on these ledges and make some impromptu entertainment.

The ninety-acre park offers a spectacular view of the countryside and the foothills of the Appalachians. Pioneer buildings moved to the site include a couple of log cabins, a barn, a corncrib, a meditation chapel, a one-room schoolhouse, and a small museum filled with farm items. At a lodge where quilters sometimes work, you are welcome to look on.

BLOUNT COUNTY MEMORIAL MUSEUM (ages 8 to 12)

201 Second Street North (Box 45), Oneonta 35121; (205) 625–6905. Open Monday through Wednesday from noon to 4:00 P.M. and Saturday from 9:00 A.M. to 1:00 P.M. Admission is **Free***.*

Dedicated to the memory of Blount Countians who served in the nation's wars, the museum has artifacts from the area's early years. It's a nice, **Free** stop while you're in the area.

Where to Eat

Cafe Dupont. *619 Main Street, Oneonta 35146; (205) 467–3339.* Old building once part of a Methodist church compound with foods created by Chef Chris Dupont. Everything is prepared from scratch or by hand. Reservations recommended for weekend nights. $–$$

The Landmark. *601 Second Avenue East, Oneonta 35121; (205) 274–2821.* Some people have described this as "a little bit of France in the middle of nowhere." Seafood buffet on Thursday nights. Reservations suggested. $–$$

Where to Stay

Capps Cove. *4126 County Highway 27, Oneonta 35121; (205) 625–3030 or (800) 583–4750.* Cason and Sybil Capps retired to this acreage, built their own two-story house that has two guest rooms and built two log cabins, complete with microwaves, full baths, front porches with rockers, and rear decks. A real treat to stay here. Children over 12 only. Elaborate breakfast is served in the Cappses' dining room. $$

Windwood Inn. *120 High School Street, Oneonta 35121; (205) 625–3961 or (800) 233–0841.* Fresh, clean, and nice with **Free** continental breakfast. $

For More Information

Blount County–Oneonta Chamber of Commerce. *227 Second Avenue East., (Box 1487), Oneonta 35121; (205) 274–2153; Fax (205) 274–2099; E-mail blount@cheney.net.*

Boaz

Boaz, a shopper's paradise because of its abundance of outlet stores, is fun for youngsters old enough to appreciate bargain hunting. With more than one hundred stores, including Tommy Hilfiger, Osh Kosh, Liz Claiborne, Black&Decker, Polo/Ralph Lauren, and Fieldcrest/Cannon, this is one of the South's largest outlet centers. Outlet store hours typically are Monday through Saturday from 9:00 A.M. to either 6:00 or 9:00 P.M. and Sunday from noon to 6:00 P.M.

Annual Event On the second weekend of every October, Boaz hosts a **Harvest Festival,** which includes an antique car show, cloggers, bluegrass music, and a few hundred booths occupied by craftspeople. As you might guess, there's plenty of food: everything from barbecue to apple fritters and fried pigskins.

For More Information

Boaz Chamber of Commerce. *306 West Mann Avenue (Box 563), Boaz 35957; (256) 593–8154 or (800) 746–7262; Web site www. boazalabama.com.*

Marshall County Convention and Visitors Bureau. *200 Gunter Avenue (Box 711), Guntersville 35976; (256) 582–7015 or (800) 582–6282; E-mail mccvb@mindspring.com.*

Gadsden

The Appalachian foothills are dotted with lakes and threaded with streams and rivers that provide the backdrop to Gadsden, a town with several sites worth visiting.

While in Gadsden, you won't want to miss the approach to the Broad Street Bridge, where you can tell your children a bit of Civil War history. Here a life-size, Italian-marble statue of Emma Sansom honors the sixteen-year-old girl who led Confederate General Nathan Bedford Forrest and his men across a swollen creek. When Forrest stopped at the Sansom house to ask directions, the teen volunteered to show the troops where the family cows crossed the creek. Riding on the general's horse, the young girl dodged bullets. When her skirt was struck, she waved her bonnet and shouted, "They have only wounded my dress." Seeing the young girl, Union troops ceased firing, allowing Forrest and his men to cross the creek. The next day the Rebels captured many of the Union soldiers. Facing downtown Gadsden, the monument, erected in 1907, is in the center of Broad Street at the corner of First Street near the Coosa River.

NOCCALULA FALLS PARK (all ages)
1500 Noccalula Road (Box 267), Gadsden 35999; (256) 549–4663 or (256) 543–7412 (campground). The park is open daily from 9:00 A.M. to sundown. There is no admission to the park, falls, and playground. Admission to the Pioneer Homestead and Botanical Gardens is $2.00 for adults and $1.00 for children under age 12 and seniors 60+. Minitrain rides are $1.50 for adults and $1.00 for

children and seniors 60+. Carpet golf is $2.00 for adults and $1.00 for children and seniors.

A bronze statue of a young Indian princess stands poised to jump into the ravine below. As one old-timer once said, "Every community that owns a waterfall also owns a legend." Gadsden is no different.

The legend is that the young Indian Noccalula jumped to her death at the waterfall when her father forbade her to marry the warrior she loved. Whether or not the tale is true is lost in the fun that families find in this attraction, which has picnic areas, miniature golf, botanical gardens (which are especially breathtaking in spring), and a minitrain. The open-air train, which offers short rides looping through the pioneer homestead, is a good way to get an overview of the complex, which has a blacksmith shop, a gristmill, a barn, and cabins. The rides are narrated, so listen closely even though voices sometimes get muffled.

While your family is at the park, don't miss the War Memorial, dedicated in 1988 to pay tribute to Etowah County's men who died in war.

CENTER FOR CULTURAL ARTS AND IMAGINATION PLACE CHILDREN'S MUSEUM (all ages)

501 Broad Street, Gadsden 35901; (256) 543–2787; Fax (256) 546–7435; www.culturalarts.com. Open weekdays from 9:00 A.M. to 6:00 P.M. (Tuesday's closing is at 9:00 P.M.). Saturday hours are from 10:00 A.M. to 6:00 P.M.; Sunday, from 1:00 to 5:00 P.M. Admission to the center, which includes entrance into the Imagination Place, is $3.00 for adults and $2.00 for children 15 and under. Admission is Free *on Tuesday afternoons.*

The triangular-shaped Cultural Arts Center has three galleries with a wide range of changing exhibits and a permanent 72-foot-long model of Gadsden in the 1940s, with working railroads. Connected via a courtyard is Imagination Place where kids may touch, run and learn. Exhibits include a kids-size city complete with a grocery store, bank, construction site, grandma's house and a health clinic exhibit.

What a Sale! No matter what treasures your family seeks on a shopping expedition, you'll likely find something you like when, in mid-August, the Lookout Mountain Parkway becomes part of "the world's longest yard sale," a 450-mile stretch from Gadsden to Ohio. Look for antiques, collectibles, furniture, housewares, dishes, garden produce, homemade jams and jellies, and loads more. Thousands of vendors take part in the sale.

MOUNTAINTOP FLEA MARKET (all ages)
11301 U.S. Highway 278 West, Attalla, 35954; (800) 535–2286. *Opens every Sunday at 5:00 A.M. and closes at varying times. Admission is* **Free**.

With more than 1,000 dealers displaying their wares on more than ninety-seven acres, you'll find just about anything, new and used, that you can imagine. Among the offerings are jewelry, tools, pets, records and tapes, furniture, fresh fruits and vegetables, crafts, leather goods, clothing, and shoes. There also are spaces (without water or electricity) for campers and motor homes, as well as a snack bar.

Where to Eat

The Olde Warehouse. *315 South Second Street, Gadsden 35901; (256) 547–5548.* Cotton once was stored here; these days it's good food and home-cooked vegetables that draw folks. Lunchtime can get crowded. $–$$

City Grill. *5th and Broad Street, Gadsden 35902; (256) 546–8555.* Inside Gadsden's Center for Cultural Arts, the restaurant offers cloth-covered tables, abundant art, an upscale menu, and the feel of a cafe. From April through October, there is food service, and sometimes live music, in the Center's courtyard. Closed Monday. Reservations accepted. $–$$$

Where to Stay

Days Inn. *1612 West Grand Avenue, Gadsden 35901; (256) 442–7913.* Save at the 55-unit inn with **Free**, continental breakfast. $–$$$

Gadsden Inn & Suites. *200 Albert Rains Boulevard, Gadsden 35901; (256) 543–7240 or (800) 637–5678.* Pets are allowed, and some rooms have kitchenettes. $

Hampton Inn. *129 River Road, Gadsden 35902; (256) 546–2337 or (800) 426–7866.* Sleepy heads will like the in-room coffee; others will love the **Free** continental breakfast. $

For More Information

Gadsden–Etowah Tourism Board. *90 Walnut Street (Box 8267), Gadsden 35902; (256) 549–0351; Fax (256) 549–1854; E-mail getb@cybrtyme.com.*

Author's Top Picks

- Ave Maria Grotto, Cullman (256–734–4110)

- Shady Grove Dude Ranch, Mentone (256–634–4344)

- DeSoto State Park, Fort Payne (256–845–5380)

- EarlyWorks, Huntsville (256–564–8125)

- Noccalula Falls Park, Gadsden (256–549–4663)

- Old MacDonald's Petting Zoo, Woodville (256–776–4332)

- Rickwood Caverns State Park, Warrior (205–647–9692)

- Sequoyah Caverns, Valley Head (256–635–0024 or 800–843–5098)

- Southern Adventures Family Entertainment Center, Huntsville (256–880–6599 or 256–382–PARK)

- U.S. Space and Rocket Center, Huntsville. (256–837–3400 or 800–63–SPACE)

Central Alabama

Alabama's midsection is easy to explore, especially if you anchor your travels in Birmingham, the state's largest city and one filled with a host of offerings, from baseball to ballet.

Mountains, ridges, valleys, and waterways mark this region, where you can visit for a day or stay for a lifetime. Remember to come prepared to romp and play, because the state's central region brims with a wonderland of attractions.

Anniston

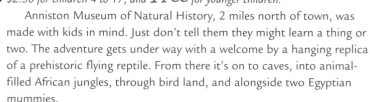

ANNISTON MUSEUM OF NATURAL HISTORY (all ages)
800 Museum Drive, Anniston 36202; (256) 237–6766; Fax (256) 237–6776; www.annistonmuseum.org. Open Tuesday through Saturday from 10:00 A.M. to 5:00 P.M. and Sunday from 1:00 to 5:00 P.M. In summer months the museum is open on Mondays from 10:00 A.M. to 5:00 P.M. Admission is $3.50 for adults, $2.50 for children 4 to 17, and **Free** *for younger children.*

Anniston Museum of Natural History, 2 miles north of town, was made with kids in mind. Just don't tell them they might learn a thing or two. The adventure gets under way with a welcome by a hanging replica of a prehistoric flying reptile. From there it's on to caves, into animal-filled African jungles, through bird land, and alongside two Egyptian mummies.

What began in 1929 as one man's gift to the city of Anniston has become an outstanding natural history museum and popular attraction. Your kids will be intrigued by the museum's various exhibits: "Designs for Living" includes a neat bird collection; and "Adaptations to the Environment" features a mammal collection with African exhibits.

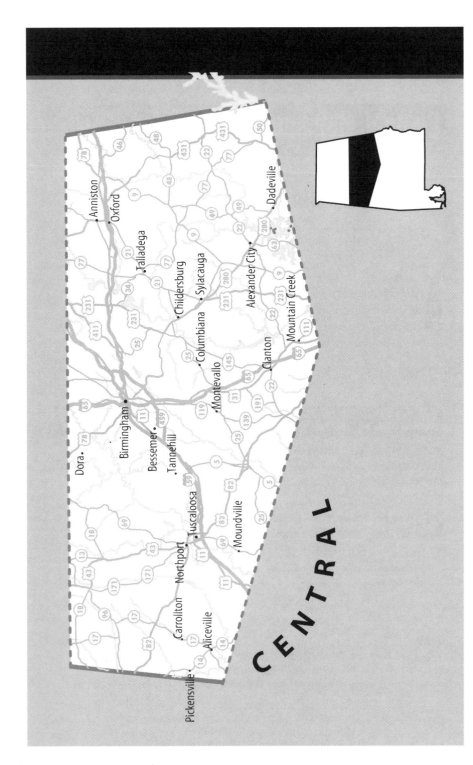

CENTRAL

"Underground Worlds" showcases a realistic Alabama cave environment, and "Attack and Defense" features North American wildlife, live snakes, and an observation beehive. The beehive always is a hit with children, who want to linger to watch the busy bees at work. Your kids surely will be intrigued with "The Mysteries of the Mummies" exhibit, which offers Egyptian mummies whose x-rays, displayed nearby, hint that multiple broken bones must have been the cause of death.

"Dynamic Earth" explores the complex processes and products of the planet Earth. Educational and gift items fill the gift shop, the final leg of a tour before you spill outside to nature trails. Don't miss the west lawn, where you can enjoy a demonstration wildlife garden as well as a wildflower meadow, a birds-of-prey trail, and a live-animal building. There's no tough walking here and not much distance to cover, so take the whole crew with you on this leg of your visit. Not far away there are picnic tables for you to use.

BERMAN MUSEUM (ages 6 to 12)

840 Museum Drive, Anniston 36202; (256) 237–6261; Fax (256) 238–9055. Open Monday through Saturday from 10:00 A.M. to 5:00 P.M. and Sunday from 1:00 to 5:00 P.M. Admission is $3.50 for adults, $3.00 for seniors, $2.50 for children 4 to 12, and **Free** *for children under age 3.*

Depending on the ages of your children, you may want to slip down the street to the Berman Museum, which opened in 1996. It is filled with one man's donated collection of some 6,000 pieces and is worth $100 million. Included in the collection are personal items that once belonged to Hitler, suits of armor, beheading swords, a chastity belt, and tiny guns that look like cigarette lighters. One of the most valuable pieces, worth some $10 million, is a sparkling Persian scimitar (a saber with a curved blade), which dates from the sixteenth century. The handle is embedded with 1,295 diamonds, sixty carats of rubies, and a single, forty-carat emerald set into three pounds of gold.

CHURCH OF ST. MICHAEL AND ALL ANGELS (ages 6 to 12)

1000 West Eighteenth Street, Anniston 36202; (256) 237–4011; Fax (256) 237–4014; www.brasenhill.com/stmikesaa. Open daily from 9:00 A.M. to 4:00 P.M. Admission is **Free**.

You might not think of a church as a place to tour, but it's time to change your mind, especially if your family has never visited any of the world's majestic cathedrals. While you're in Anniston, you should spin by the Church of St. Michael and All Angels. The church's simple exterior is in contrast to its elaborate interior, which contains a 12-foot altar of marble shipped from Italy, archangels alongside Michael behind the altar, a pipe organ installed in the late 1880s, and more than a dozen stained-glass windows of Jesus and the holy family.

On occasion the sexton will remain after Sunday services to give tours. Even though there isn't always someone on hand to give a tour, you can pick up a brochure that is full of information. Although admission is not charged, a donation box accepts contributions for the facility's preservation.

CHEAHA STATE PARK (all ages)

19644 Highway 281, Delta 36258; (256) 488–5111 or (800) 846–2654. Open daylight hours. Park admission is $1.00 per person, all ages.

South of Interstate 20 off U.S. Highway 431, Cheaha State Park is on the state's highest point. Sprawling over some 2,500 acres, the park is a fun place for your family's outdoor adventures. At the foot of Cheaha Mountain, you can swim in a lake served by a bathhouse built by the Civilian Conservation Corps in the 1930s. If you're feeling ambitious, head to the hiking trails and tackle either the half-mile Bald Rock Trail or the Pulpit Rock Trail. The truly brave tackle the steep, mile-long Lake Trail. More than 1,000 acres rise more than 2,000 feet, providing panoramic views of east-central Alabama. These views are especially memorable in fall, when Mother Nature seems to spill her entire collection of colors across the mountaintop.

Overnight facilities allow you to spend the night in this spot. A restaurant serves three meals daily, and a store sells all kinds of souvenirs, including, of course, the obligatory T-shirt. This is one of the state's better spots for viewing fall foliage.

Where to Eat

Betty's Bar-B-Q. *401 South Quintard, Anniston 36201; (256) 237–1411.* Barbecue is king, but try their corn bread and butter beans for a real taste of down-home cooking. Children's menu. $

Top O' the River. *3220 McClellan Boulevard, Anniston 36201; (256) 238–0097.* Every meal starts with a tiny, cast-iron skillet of corn bread served with a measuring cup filled with coleslaw. Great fried catfish fillets. Historic photos on walls. $–$$

Where to Stay

Cheaha State Park. *19644 Highway 281, Delta 36258; (256) 488–5111 or (800) 846–2654.* Very nice motel rooms, cabins, and chalets. $

Hampton Inn. *1600 Highway 21 South, Oxford 36203; (256) 835–1492 or (800) HAMPTON.* Convenient to area museums; kids under 18 stay **Free**. $

Holiday Inn Anniston/Oxford. *Interstate 20 at U.S. Highway 78, Oxford 36203; (256) 831–3410.* In-room coffee, swimming pool, and convenience to interstate. $

The Victoria: A Country Inn. *1604 Quintard Avenue, Anniston 36201; (256) 236–0503 or (800) 260–8781.* A restored Queen Anne-style mansion fronts a modern motel facility that has a swimming pool. The main house is often used for weddings and receptions, so you might get to look on. $$$–$$$$

Wingate Inn. *143 Colonial Drive, Oxford 36203; (256) 831–1921; Fax (256) 831–1952.* **Free**, expanded continental breakfast, **Free** business center with Internet access, fitness center, swimming pool, and whirlpool. $–$$

For More Information

Calhoun County Chamber of Commerce. *1330 Quintard Avenue (Box 1087), Anniston 36202; (256) 237–3536 or (800) 489–1087; Fax (256) 237–4338; Web site www.calhounchamber.org*

Talladega

Some of Talladega's early residents earned their fortunes in textiles and other products. These days, the wealth comes to those persons who take the checkered flag at the world's fastest NASCAR track at Talladega Superspeedway. If your family arrives in Talladega with no idea where to head first, look for the restored railroad depot at 210 East Street South. The depot houses the Talladega Chamber of Commerce, where helpful folks have plenty of information and gobs of good brochures to head you on your way.

Downtown Talladega has some interesting stores, especially antiques shops, which lure collectors from far and wide. Even if your children aren't into shopping, you're bound to pique their interest when you step inside Cowboy Hubbard's Trading Post. Chances are they've not visited stores that sell horse harnesses and cowbells.

TALLADEGA-TEXACO WALK OF FAME/DAVEY ALLISON MEMORIAL (all ages)

Coffee and Court Streets (mail: Box 1179, Talladega 35161); (800) 711–7991. Open twenty-four hours. No admission.

From the chamber office you can walk to the Talladega-Texaco Walk of Fame/Davey Allison Memorial, a combined site that honors racing greats and Davey Allison, who died young, at the track, in a helicopter crash.

TALLADEGA SUPERSPEEDWAY (ages 8 to 12)

3366 Speedway Boulevard (mail: Box 777, Talladega 35161), Talladega 35160; (256) 362–2261. Open daily from 9:00 A.M. to 4:30 P.M. Track van tour is $4.00 for adults, $3.00 for children 7 to 17, and Free *to children under 6. Track tour with museum admission is $10.00 for adults and $8.00 for students. Ask about 50 percent discount for seniors 55+.*

If there are stock-car racing fans in your midst, they probably know about Talladega Superspeedway. Just off Interstate 20 at exit 168, it's the world's fastest speedway and home to the National Association for Stock Car Auto Racing (NASCAR). The speedway, in fact, put this town on the map and made it a household word among racing fans.

Annual Events Two acclaimed events happen each year at the speedway: **Winston Select 500,** which is run on the last Sunday in April; and the **DieHard 500,** which is run in October.

INTERNATIONAL MOTOR SPORTS HALL OF FAME (ages 8 to 12)

3198 Speedway Boulevard, Talladega 35160; (256) 362–5002; www.motorsportshalloffame.com. Open daily from 8:30 A.M. to 5:00 P.M. Admission is $8.00 for adults, $7.00 for children ages 7 to 17, and Free *for younger children. Save by buying a supersaver ticket, which includes a bus tour of the track and museum admission.*

This several-building complex is filled with dozens of famous racing cars and memorabilia. The collection's Daytona Room is muscle-car heaven, with seven muscle cars and a Corvette. You'll also see Richard Petty's red-and-blue STP Dodge Charger that won thirty-one races and took sixteen pole positions before it was retired.

The UNOCAL 76 building has more cars, along with a Richard Petty single-seat-car simulator that kids may operate. A couple of the cars on display gained notoriety, not for wins but for their near tragedies. One ended its career during the 1983 Winston 500 when Phil Parsons wrecked with Darrell Waltrip, causing an eleven-car pileup that sent Parsons' No. 66 bolting through the air. Parsons was the only driver who suffered injuries, and those were minor, especially compared with the tangle of metal left in his wake. Parsons' wrecked car is on display, a reminder of how harrowing those races can become.

Other cars include Bill Elliott's 1985 Ford Thunderbird, which won the 1985 Winston 500 with an average speed of 186.288 miles per hour.

 SILK STOCKING HISTORIC DISTRICT (ages 8 to 12)
Mail: Talladega Chamber of Commerce, Drawer A, Talladega 35161; (256) 362–9075. Open twenty-four hours. Admission is **Free**.

Don't miss driving through the town's Silk Stocking Historic District, south of the town square. Homes in the district were erected from 1835 to 1910 by the town's wealthy residents, whose wives could afford the luxury of wearing expensive silk stockings. On the second weekend in April, several of the district's historic homes shine their silver and open their doors for an annual pilgrimage, which includes tours of churches and antebellum and Victorian homes. It's a great chance to look behind the massive front doors at some incredible craftsmanship.

ALABAMA INSTITUTE FOR THE DEAF AND BLIND (all ages)
205 East South Street, Talladega 35161; (205) 761–3206 or 761–3470. Open Monday through Friday from 8:00 A.M. to 5:00 P.M. Admission is **Free.**

While driving through town, check out the Alabama Institute for the Deaf and Blind, the country's most comprehensive education and rehabilitation program for deaf and blind children and adults. Among the most notably restored buildings are Manning Hall (1850), Jemison House (1898), and Grace Hall (1878). Three murals here detail when Joseph Cinque led a revolt aboard a Cuban schooner to set free fellow Africans in 1839.

 TALLADEGA NATIONAL FOREST (all ages)
Mail: Ranger, Talladega District, 1001 North Street, Talladega 35160; (256) 362–2909; Fax (256) 362–0823. Open daily. Admission is **Free**.

If your family likes hiking, don't miss this place, the southernmost extension of the Appalachian Mountains.

With some 210,000 acres of hardwood trees, lakes, scenic over-looks, waterfalls, and mountain streams, Talladega National Forest is crisscrossed with what many Alabama hikers consider to be the state's best hiking experience. Trails in this forest offer diverse topography, scenic beauty, and varying lengths to meet the needs of both novice and experienced hikers. Elevations range from 800 feet above sea level along the bottom of the eastern slopes of the forest to 2,342 feet above sea level at Odum's Point on Cheaha Mountain.

Where to Eat

Cafe Royale. *110 Court Square East, Talladega 35161; (256) 362–3186.* Situated on the downtown square, the Royale serves lunch Monday through Saturday with choices such as chicken salad, Reuben sandwiches, and pastas. $

Cheaha State Park Restaurant. *19644 Highway 281, Delta 36258; (256) 488–5111 or (800) 846–2654.* Wide range of choices and incredible views. $

Fincher's Real Delight. *521 East Street North, Talladega 35160; (256) 362–2174.* You'll have to look quick or you'll miss this eatery that locals adore and few

out-of-towners spot. Some might call it a hole in the wall, but don't jump to conclusions without trying the fried dill pickles, stuffed peppers, and other house specialties. Kids will like the ice creams. $

Old Mill Restaurant. *Highway 77 at Waldo; (206) 761–0043.* This restaurant is really an old mill, which makes it lots of fun to visit, and, better yet, the food is grand. Known for pond-raised cat-fish but also serves steaks, seafood, oysters, and chicken. Open Friday for dinner and all day on Saturday and Sunday. $–$$$

Where to Stay

Cedars Plantation Bed and Break-fast. *590 Cheaha Road, Munford 36268; (256) 761–9090.* Lots of charm plus a fish pond, screened gazebo, tennis court, and large swimming pool. Two-bedroom apartment allows children age 8 and older. Rooms in the main house allow children age 12 and older. $–$$

Days Inn. *945 Speedway-Industrial Drive, Lincoln 35095; (205) 763–8080.* **Free** continental breakfast and swimming pool. $

Holiday Inn Express. *850 Speedway-Industrial Drive, Lincoln 35095; (205) 763–9777.* **Free** continental break-fast, swimming pool. Kids under age 18 stay **Free**. $

Orangevale Plantation Bed and Breakfast. *1400 Whiting Road, Talladega 35160; (256) 761–1827.* Your family will enjoy the country setting, hiking trails, and personable farm animals. $$

For More Information

**Greater Talladega Area Chamber
of Commerce.** *210 East Street South
(mail: Drawer A, Talladega 35161);*

*(256) 362–9075; Fax (256) 362–9093;
Web site www.talladega.com.*

Alexander City

The fun of Alexander City is its diversity. Here your family can watch the creation process of ornamental ironworks, play in a sprawling artificial lake, and explore a battlefield.

If you are traveling on sunny days, you'll want to spend some time at Lake Martin, which became the world's largest artificial body of water when Martin Dam went up in the 1920s. The distinction has since been relinquished, but the water continues to be a major draw.

Your kids probably won't care, but if you have parents who are looking for a retirement spot, look closely and gather information while you're in town. The area has been noted as one of the nation's top retirement places, because the climate is pleasant year-round, the pace is slow, and the abundance of water creates a playground for fishing, boating, camping, and golf.

ROBINSON IRON (ages 8 to 12)

1856 Robinson Road, Alexander City 35010; (256) 329–8486. Tours are Monday through Friday from 8:00 A.M. to 4:00 P.M. Tours, which are informal, are ${F}$ree.

At Robinson Iron prearranged tours give families traveling with older children a glimpse of the machine shop where fountains, statues, and furniture are made. The showroom offers a few items for sale and spotlights some of the company's handiwork, including the refurbished facade of Raffles Hotel in Singapore, and subway entrances in New York City.

WIND CREEK STATE PARK (all ages)

 4325 Alabama Highway 128, Alexander City 5010; (256) 329–0845; Fax (256) 234–4870.

If you plan to stick around for some lake fun, check out Wind Creek State Park, 7 miles southeast of Alexander City. Alive year-round with activity, the park has a campground, a marina, hiking trails, and picnic pavilions. Situated on the shores of Lake Martin, this 1,445-acre facility is considered one of the South's best places to camp. Many of the campsites are situated so that you can fish from your picnic area or pull your boat right up to your site.

HORSESHOE BEND NATIONAL MILITARY PARK (all ages)

11288 Horseshoe Bend Road, Daviston 36256; (256) 234–7111; Fax (256) 329–9905; www.nps.gov/hobe. Park is open daily from 8:00 A.M. until dark. Museum is open daily from 8:00 A.M. to 4:30 P.M. Admission is Free.

If you've been driving around Alabama while your children's energy levels soared, you might need a stop that's not going to require any prim and proper behavior. In fact you just might be their hero if you'll take them to a wide-open place where feet can run and voices can bellow.

Twenty-three miles from Alexander City, your children will find plenty of places to expend their energy at Horseshoe Bend National Military Park, the site of the bloodiest battle of the Creek War. Here, on March 27, 1814, Andrew Jackson, leading the Tennessee Army, took his first step to national fame when he defeated the Red Stick Creeks and forever broke the power of their nation.

The site includes an exhibit-filled museum. A slide presentation and an electric map make a good starting point for your family's visit.

Living-history programs are presented on the last Saturday of the month. Annually, the battle is celebrated on the last weekend in March.

In the bend of the Tallapoosa River, the site includes a tour road, 2.8 miles of nature trails with markers, and picnic areas. The open field is a good place for running, but before turning your children loose, tell them that they are not allowed to relic hunt.

Where to Shop

Queen's Attic Antiques. *110 Calhoun Street, Alexander City 35010; (256) 329–0653. Open daily (except Wednesday and Sunday) from 10:00 A.M. to 4:00 P.M.* Shoppers will enjoy the store known for its collection of English and American antiques, including armoires, dressers, twin beds, china, silver, mirrors, and needlework.

Russell Retail Store. *3562 Highway 280, Alexander City 35010; (256) 329–4464. Open Monday through Saturday from* *8:00 A.M. to 6:00 P.M. and Sunday from 1:00 to 6:00 P.M.* If you have young athletes or bargain hunters in your clan, don't leave "Alex City" without stopping at the Russell Retail Store, where you can find athletic wear at about one-third the retail price. Look for Russell Athletic, Jerzees, Cross Country shirts, Player Club socks, and university T-shirts and caps. The seasoned bargain hunter won't be able to resist browsing the back room, which is filled with seconds.

Where to Eat

Cecil's Public House. *243 Green Street, Alexander City 35010; (256) 329–0732.* Fun atmosphere in a converted home. $

J.R.'s Wings & Things. *3916 U.S. Highway 280, Alexander City 35010; (256) 234–0770.* Lots of video games to keep kids busy when they aren't downing the popular wings and cheese sticks. $

Kowaliga. *275 Kowaliga Marina Road, Alexander City 35010; (334) 857–2161.* On Lake Martin and known for catfish and seafood but with plenty of things that kids prefer—an Ernie burger, Shirley Temples, chicken fingers, and hot dogs. Your kids will love the wooden Indian statue, made famous by country singer Hank Williams's song, which he wrote while staying nearby. $

Where to Stay

Holiday Inn Express. *2945 U.S. Highway 280, Alexander City 35010; (256) 234–5900 or (800) HOLIDAY.* **Free** continental breakfast. Some rooms have jetted tubs. $-$$$

Jameson Inn. *4335 U.S. Highway 280, Alexander City 35010; (256) 234–9807 or (800) 541–3268.* Nice and new and with a **Free** continental breakfast and a swimming pool. $

Still Waters Resort. *1618 Stillwater Drive, Dadeville 36853; (256) 825–7021 or (888) 797–3767.* A fun place with three swimming pools, two on-site golf courses, marina, activity center, and beach cabana with volleyball court. Baby beds available. $$$-$$$$

Super 8 Motel. *4000 Highway 280, Alexander City 35010; (256) 329–8858 or (800) 800–8000.* Very nice; seniors get a discount. $

Wind Creek State Park Campgrounds. *4325 Alabama Highway 128, Alexander City 35010; (256) 329–0845.* With 642 modern campsites, this is the largest state-operated campground in the United States. You'll find a country store, comfort stations, and a play area. $

For More Information

Alexander City–Lake Martin Area Chamber of Commerce. *120 Tallapoosa Street (Box 926) 35011–0926; (256) 234–3461; Fax (256) 234–0094.*

Dadeville Area Chamber of Commerce. *185 South Tallassee Street, Suite 103, Dadeville 36853; (256) 825–4019. E-mail chamber@lakemartin.net; Web site www.dadeville.com.*

Sylacauga

Sylacauga got is nickname "Marble City" because the town sits on a bed of marble more than 24 miles long and more than 1 mile wide. Marble from here has gone places, including into the construction of the U.S. Supreme Court Building in Washington, D.C. Although no quarry tours are available, you can drive by the marble quarries and see the deep pits.

ISABEL ANDERSON COMER MUSEUM & ARTS CENTER (all ages)

711 North Broadway Avenue (Box 245), Sylacauga 35150; (256) 245–4016. Open Tuesday through Friday from 10:00 A.M. to 5:00 P.M. Admission is Free.

If you need an excuse to stop, you'll find reason enough at the Isabel Anderson Comer Museum. Situated in a former library, the museum has items relating to area history with spotlights on notables, including Jim "Gomer Pyle" Nabors, who hails from here. Once they know what waits downstairs, some kids are quick to run past old pictures, exhibits, and even the replica of a meteorite that in 1954 tumbled from space onto a Sylacauga woman. (The actual meteorite is in the Alabama State Museum of Natural History in Tuscaloosa.) The kids are eager to get downstairs to the log cabin, where they can go inside the cabin, see how early settlers lived, and learn how a fireplace offered the home's only heat. Surrounding the outside of the cabin are stuffed animals, such as deer and beaver, which give an idea what kind of critters would actually have been near a pioneer home.

Where to Stay

Jameson Inn. *89 Gene Stewart Boulevard, Sylacauga 35151; (256) 245–4141 or (800) 541–3268.* Free *continental breakfast.* $

For More Information

Sylacauga Chamber of Commerce. *17 West Fort Williams (Box 185), Sylacauga 35150; (256) 249–0308. Fax (256) 249–0315; Web site www.mindspring.com/~sylacaug.*

*B*oundaries Alabama is bordered

- on the north by Tennessee,
- on the east by Georgia,
- on the south by Florida,
- on the west by Mississippi.

Childersburg

Spanish explorer Hernando De Soto and his men spent more than a month in this area in 1540. Childersburg, during World War II, was a boomtown because of the area's large powder-making plant. In the twentieth century, the town has evolved into a lumber and farm community. For visitors the big draw is DeSoto Caverns Park.

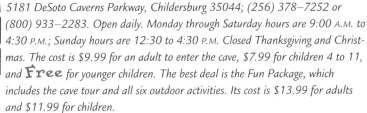

DESOTO CAVERNS PARK (all ages)

5181 DeSoto Caverns Parkway, Childersburg 35044; (256) 378–7252 or (800) 933–2283. Open daily. Monday through Saturday hours are 9:00 A.M. to 4:30 P.M.; Sunday hours are 12:30 to 4:30 P.M. Closed Thanksgiving and Christmas. The cost is $9.99 for an adult to enter the cave, $7.99 for children 4 to 11, and Free *for younger children. The best deal is the Fun Package, which includes the cave tour and all six outdoor activities. Its cost is $13.99 for adults and $11.99 for children.*

Your family can spend a fun-filled day at DeSoto Caverns Park, on Alabama Highway 76 and 5 miles east of Childersburg. You can do everything from touring a cave to tossing water balloons and sharing a picnic. Before arriving you may want to tell your children that the cave is the nation's first recorded cave. It was recorded in 1796 when Benjamin Hawkins, general superintendent of all Indian tribes south of the Ohio River, wrote to President Washington to detail the cavern's beauty.

Visiting is not just fun but is also a study in history as youngsters hear guides tell how the cave's spring-fed well made it a perfect place for Confederate soldiers to mine calcium nitrate, which resulted in the cave's becoming a gunpowder mining and refining center. Visitors still may see a well and leaching trough used by the soldiers.

A laser-light show in the large onyx chamber is a highlight of a visit to the eighty-acre Indian minitheme park, designed with kids in mind.

Tours through the cave take about an hour. You'll enter the cave through the side of a hill, so be sure your family wears functional shoes, preferably with rubber soles. Steps lead into a great cathedral room, which is taller than a twelve-story building and has a ceiling punctuated with thousands of stalactites.

Named for the Spanish explorer Hernando De Soto, who visited the area in 1540, the cave has a year-round indoor temperature of 60 degrees plus an occasional drip of water from above. Anyone who easily gets chilled may want to wear a jacket.

Once your family has been inside the cave, they'll probably want to try the outdoor activities, including a sprawling maze, a place to learn to shoot a bow and arrow, and a spot for "panning" for colored stones. The

Annual Events Every April DeSoto Caverns Park hosts an **Indian Dance and Country Crafts Festival,** and from late November through December it holds a popular Festival of Lights.

energy ant in your crowd will like the balloon battle, which pits players in an Indian teepee against those in a Spanish fort.

Abundant picnic tables are well maintained, so you may want to pack a lunch. If you don't take something with you, you'll find a limited selection of microwavable items available in the gift shop. Or toss nutrition to the wind and settle for the yummy fudge, divinity, or hand-scooped ice cream.

If you're traveling in a recreational vehicle, you can stay overnight in the adjacent campground, which offers full and partial hookups.

KYMULGA GRIST MILL AND COVERED BRIDGE (all ages)

Grist Mill Road (mail: Childersburg Heritage Society, Box 363, Childersburg 35044); (256) 378–7436 or 378–5482. Open daily April through October. Monday through Saturday hours are from 9:00 A.M. to 5:00 P.M., and Sunday hours are from 9:00 A.M. to 5:00 P.M. To enter the grounds is $2.00 per person over age 6.

After leaving DeSoto Caverns head about 7 miles west to Kymulga Grist Mill Park, on County Roads 46 and 36 between Childersburg and Talladega. The still-operating waterpowered mill is a tribute to the skill of the slaves who built it in 1864. Restored in 1984, the mill, on certain days, still grinds corn.

If your children never have seen a mill at work, this is the place to show them how life used to be. Even though some locals bring in their own corn to be ground, you won't have to do so. You'll find bags of cornmeal on sale in a shop adjoining the mill. Outside the mill you'll find tree-studded acres, 2 miles of well-marked hiking trails, and a 105-foot-long covered bridge. There also are picnic tables (some with grills) and a picnic pavilion (you need reservations for the pavilion).The park's entrance fee allows use of trails and picnic areas and includes a mill tour. Even though the mill officially is closed November through March, it is possible you will find someone there who may allow you in, since work and grinding are ongoing.

AFullman Family Adventure Christine and Cameron had a blast when we visited DeSoto Caverns Park. Inside the massive cave they listened closely as a guide told about early inhabitants, about DeSoto's discovery and Native American graves, about moonshiners hiding and bats darting.

When the lights were extinguished for the laser–light show, they could not see their hands in front of their faces. Like others surrounding us, their eyes widened as the show began and lights of all colors began dancing around the cave. Later, when we walked past a bat that clung to a wall, they passed quickly, hoping not to disturb his sleep.

Where to Eat

Dawn's Restaurant. *Highway 280, 35044; (256) 378–7637.* You'll find three meals daily except Sunday evening when closing is at 5:00 P.M. A full breakfast with grits costs less that $3.00. $

Where to Stay

Days Inn. *33669 Highway 280, 35044; (256) 378–6007.* Your kids will like the swimming pool at this forty-unit inn, and you'll like the affordable prices. $

For More Information

Greater Talladega Area Chamber of Commerce. *210 East Street South (mail: Drawer A, Talladega 35161); (256) 362–9075; Fax (256) 362–9093; Web site www.talladega.com.*

Childersburg Chamber of Commerce. *Ninth Avenue and Third Street, Childersburg 35044; (256) 378–5482; Fax (256) 378–5811; E-mai wooeagle@aol.com.*

Columbiana

Columbiana, in Shelby County, is a small town with an unexpected treasure.

 SMITH-HARRISON MUSEUM (ages 8 to 12)
50 Lester Street, Columbiana 35051; (205) 669–4545. Open Monday through Friday from 10:00 A.M. to 3:00 P.M. Closed on weekends and major holidays. Admission is **Free***.*

Inside the Mildred B. Harrison Library Building, the Smith-Harrison Museum holds the largest collection of George and Martha Washington memorabilia outside the Washingtons' Mount Vernon, Virginia, home. The one-room museum has a set dining-room table, which makes it seem that the first First Family might be about to drop in for dinner. Don't miss Martha Washington's prayer book and letters written during Revolutionary War times. If there are boys in your family, expect to see them drawn to the old guns. (A bonus at the museum is a display of an original tintype made by Civil War photographer Mathew Brady.)

Some Shelby County Facts Shelby County's:

- first automobile arrived in 1908.

- first paved street was in 1928.

- first speed limit was 8 miles per hour, set in 1914.

- annual production of lime is between one and one-half to two million tons.

For More Information

North Shelby Chamber of Commerce. *Ball Park Road (Box 324, Pelham 35124); (205) 663–4542; Fax (205) 663–4524; Web site www. shelbychamber.org.*

Clanton

Clanton is best known for its peaches, which are sold, in season, at stands convenient to interstate traffic. Even those tourists who don't stay overnight in Clanton usually can't resist stopping long enough to buy a basket of just-picked-from-the-tree peaches.

Annual Events Clanton's biggest event of the year is its Peach Festival, held the third weekend in June, when the peach harvest is at its peak.

Can You Make A Peach Pie? If you buy a basket of
peaches in Clanton, you may want to bake a peach pie once you're
home. Here's a quick recipe:

1 stick oleo
¾ cup self-rising flour
1 cup sugar
1½ cups sweet milk
3 cups peaches

Melt oleo in pan. Mix together flour, sugar, and milk and stir well. Pour
batter over melted oleo. Spoon peaches over batter. Do not stir. Bake at
350 degrees for one hour.

PEACH PARK (all ages)

*U.S. Highway 31 South and Interstate 65 (mail: Box 48, Clanton 35045); (205)
755–2065. Open April 1 through November 26. Admission is* Free.

In season (mid-May through September) Peach Park, at the junction
of U.S. Highway 31 South and Interstate 65 in Clanton, serves peaches
about every way you can imagine, including those you can buy to carry
home. Prices are reasonable, and there sometimes is special entertainment, such as singing groups from local churches. Adjacent to the park
are gardens, where you are welcome to stroll or sit a spell. Be sure you
and your kids try the peach pie, peach salads, peach cake, and peach ice
cream. This is not a rustic lean-to, but an air-conditioned facility that is
a major stop during peach season, when hundreds of people stop to
taste and buy.

CONFEDERATE MEMORIAL PARK (all ages)

437 County Road 63, Marbury 36051; (205) 755–1990. *The park is open
year-round from dawn to dusk. It is closed major holidays. Museum hours are daily
from 9:00 A.M. to 5:00 P.M. Admission is* Free.

Southeast of Clanton, Confederate Memorial Park at one time was
home for Confederate veterans. A museum includes uniforms, utensils,
artillery, and Confederate money. Two cemeteries contain the graves of
some 300 Confederate soldiers and their widows. There's also the sym-
bolic grave of an unknown soldier.

Hiking trails and picnic pavilions make this an interesting family
stop and a place to ponder the price of war. Be sure your family notices
the cedar trees near the picnic pavilion. The trees are a memorial to a

Confederate veteran who moved to Rio de Janeiro with his wife. The cedars were planted in the early 1900s after the officer's widow wrote from Brazil asking that a tree be planted in her native state to honor her husband's memory.

Where to Eat

Heaton Pecan Farm. *309 Sunrise Boulevard (at exit 208 off I–65),Clanton 35045; (205) 755–8654.* The folks here grow and process their own pecans, which end up in waffles, chicken salad, and nine flavors of ice cream. The eatery, which also serves sandwiches, is in a white, barn-like structure. Save time to browse the arts-and-crafts loft. $

Helen's Place. *407 Second Avenue South, Clanton 35045; (205) 755–9130.* In a house in the heart of a residential area, Helen's serves country cooking. Hours are limited. Best suited to older children because space is small and the menu is limited. $

T & L Restaurant. *215 Sixth Street North, Clanton 35045; (205) 755–5114.* In the heart of downtown Clanton, this landmark is known for affordable meats and veggies. $

Where to Stay

Days Inn. *I–65 and Highway 31 South (mail: Box 2010),Clanton 35046; (205) 755–0510.* A former Holiday Inn, the 100-room property has a swimming pool and restaurant. Pets are allowed. $

Jemison Inn Bed and Breakfast. *212 Highway 191, Jemison 35085; (205) 688–2055.* With arches and a wrap-around porch filled with ferns and antique wicker, the redbrick 1930s house has three guest rooms, a swimming pool, common areas, and a video library. Children are welcome by prior arrangement. $–$$$

Key West Inn. *I–65 and U.S. Highway 31 South, Clanton 35045; (205) 755–8500 or (800) 833–0555.* Pets are welcome. $

Shoney's Inn. *950 Lake Mitchell Road, Clanton 35045; (205) 280–0306 or (800) 222–2222.* More than half of the inn's seventy-three rooms are nonsmoking. Pets are welcome. $

For More Information

Chilton County Chamber of Commerce. *500 Fifth Avenue North, Clanton 35046; (265) 755–2400 or (800) 553–0493.*

State Motto Alabama's motto is *"Audemus Jura Nostra Defendere."* It means: "We Dare Defend Our Rights."

Montevallo Area

Montevallo is a quiet town that bustles with life breathed by university students. A favorite retreat for many of those students is Orr Park, which has wildflowers, walking paths, a creek, waterfalls, a children's play area, and a gazebo where weddings often take place. When you're there, look around at the intriguing cedar carvings created by artist Tim Tingle. Tingle, who's actually a local coal miner, asked permission to transform the storm-damaged trunks. You can make a game of going through the woods and looking for his random, almost-hidden carvings that include a squirrel, a horse's head, a snake, an owl, and a full-length Indian.

UNIVERSITY OF MONTEVALLO (all ages)

Reynolds Circle (mail: Public Relations Department, Station 6230, Reynolds Hall, Montevallo 35115); (205) 665–6230.

The University of Montevallo is the crown jewel of the town of Montevallo, which is in the exact center of the state about halfway between Birmingham and Clanton. Your children will enjoy a ride or stroll through the historic campus. Famous for its red-brick streets and paths, the 160-acre main campus has more than forty buildings surrounded by lawns, groves, and flower beds. The central portion of the campus is a National Historic District with two antebellum structures, including the 1823 King House. A couple of ghosts are said to reside in campus buildings, so stop and ask some residents if they've heard anything unexplainable lately.

Kiss My Grits Actress Polly Holliday, "Flo," whose favorite expression was "kiss my grits," is a graduate of the University of Montevallo.

Ghostly Things

Ghostly Things Reynolds Hall, one of the oldest buildings on the University of Montevallo campus, may be haunted.

Here's the tale: The school closed during the Civil War, and young men traded books for weapons. During the brother-against-brother war, Reynolds Hall was used as an infirmary for wounded and dying soldiers.

Some ghost believers have said that at one point during the war, there was a skirmish with Wilson's Raiders. Reynolds left to fight, and Wilson and his men stormed the infirmary and killed the patients.

Legend has it that the ghost that haunts Reynolds Hall is the spirit of one of the patients slaughtered by Wilson's Raiders.

Historians say the facts are not accurate, but people who like to think about ghosts find it a fun story.

BRIERFIELD IRONWORKS HISTORICAL STATE PARK (all ages)

Route 1 (Box 147), Brierfield 35035; (205) 665–1856. Open daily from daylight to dark. Admission is $1.00 for adults, 50 cents for children 6 to 11 and seniors 62+, and **Free** *to children under 6.*

If your children have energy to burn, take them 8 miles southwest of Montevallo to Brierfield Ironworks Historical State Park. There they can see ruins of the two brick Bibb Furnaces that were destroyed by Union troops on March 31, 1865.

Annual Events

Annual Events Each spring at Brierfield a **Civil War Reenactment** restages the 1865 destruction that took place here. A **Bluegrass Festival** in May is followed in September with a rodeo. October brings **Heritage Days,** which is primarily geared to area fourth graders, but families are welcome to tag along. Of interest to children in December is **The Nights Before Christmas,** when the park is aglow with holiday lights and there are special events, including storytelling.

The furnaces were then rebuilt the following year. When the furnaces were unable to keep pace with advancing technology, their fires were blown out December 24, 1894. In 1906 Henry Weller of Weller Iron Company bought the idle furnaces, salvaged iron, pipes, and equipment, and then dynamited the remains. The ruins are now fenced off and provide the backdrop for a primitive park where your family may camp, swim, and picnic.

BULLDOG BEND (all ages)

Bibb County Road 65, Route 1 (Box 207), Brierfield 35035; (205) 926–7382. Open daily from dawn to dark. Final canoe runs depart at 2:00 P.M. Canoes rent for $30.

If you want to go canoeing while you're near the park, drive a few miles up the road to an outfitter that rents canoes. At Bulldog Bend canoe runs range from a 4.1-mile trip up to an 8.6-mile trip. (Trips take from two to six hours.) The outfitter puts the canoe—and you—into the river and sets a downstream pickup time. The self-guided float is leisurely, allowing time to stop along the way to picnic or to explore river banks.

Star Gazing At the University of Montevallo, a gold star in the front of Main Hall, a girls' dormitory, marks the exact geographic center of Alabama.

Where to Shop

House of Serendipity. *Main Street, Montevallo 35115; no phone.* In a rambling, wood-floored building on a downtown corner, you'll find all kinds of neat things, including children's books, antique glassware, china, art supplies, and gift items. College students like the selection of items with fraternity and sorority lettering.

Where to Eat

Firehouse BBQ. *140 Geronimo, Montevallo 35115; (205) 665–7972.* Owned by a former firefighter, this spot is far from fancy but makes a mean barbecue sandwich. $

Montevallo Grille. *627 Main Street, Montevallo 35115; (205) 665–5111.* A blend of Mediterranean and Middle Eastern foods with some items strictly Southern. $–$$$

Where to Stay

Ramsay Conference Center and Lodge. *Station 6280, University of Montevallo 35115; (205) 665–6280.* Thirty-nine units on the college campus and very affordable. Use of two campus playgrounds. $

For More Information

Montevallo Chamber of Commerce.
966 Main Street, Montevallo 35115; (205)
665–1519.

North Shelby Chamber of Commerce. Ball Park Road, (Box 324,
Pelham 35124); (205) 663–4542;
Fax (205) 663–4524; Web site www.
shelbychamber.org.

Birmingham

Not founded until after the Civil War, Birmingham does not have the abundance of historic sites found elsewhere in the state. What it lacks in roots, however, it makes up for in other attractions that could keep you here for days. Several of the city's sites are especially intriguing to children. Be certain to note the days that the attractions are open, because many city-owned facilities are closed on Monday.

A Few Details

- Alabama is in the Central Time Zone.

- The state's postal abbreviation is AL.

MCWANE CENTER (all ages)

200 Nineteenth Street North, Birmingham 35203; (205) 714–8300; Fax
(205) 714–8400; www.mcwane.org. Open Monday through Friday from 9:00
A.M. to 5:00 P.M., Saturday from 9:00 A.M. to 6:00 P.M., and Sunday from noon
to 5:00 P.M. For adults ages 13 to 59 museum admission is $7.50 and IMAX
admission is $7.50, or buy both tickets for $11.00. For children 6 to 12 and
adults 60+ museum admission is $6.50 and IMAX admission is $6.50, or buy
admission to both for $10.00. For children 3 to 5, museum admission is $5.50
and IMAX admission is $5.50, or buy admission to both for $9.50. Children
under 3 are Free.

Located in a restored department store in downtown Birmingham,
McWane Center offers a hands-on journey into science and technology.
Learning is an adventure in places such as Just Mice Size and Science-
Quest. An IMAX domed theater offers mind-boggling cinematic action
on a giant screen. Chances are your children will want to stay here for
hours.

ALABAMA JAZZ HALL OF FAME (all ages)

1631 Fourth Avenue North (Box 12232), Birmingham 35203; (205) 254–2731; Fax (205) 254–2785; www.jazzhall.com/jazz/. Open Tuesday through Saturday from 10:00 A.M. to 5:00 P.M. and Sunday from 1:00 to 5:00 P.M. Admission is **Free**.

Do you have a music lover in your family? Then don't miss the Alabama Jazz Hall of Fame, which spotlights jazz greats with Alabama ties. Among those featured is Birmingham native Erskine Hawkins, who wrote the now-famous "Tuxedo Junction" about a streetcar crossing west of the city. Heralding the museum is the art deco design of the Carver Theatre. The theater has been a landmark on the western edge of downtown Birmingham since 1935. Youngsters especially like the interactive computer system that lets them touch a screen to hear music, see pictures, and read about Alabama jazz greats who have been inducted into the hall of fame.

ALABAMA MUSEUM OF HEALTH SCIENCES (ages 8 to 12)

1700 University Boulevard, Birmingham 35294–0013; (205) 934–4475. Open Monday through Friday from 8:00 A.M. to 5:00 P.M. Admission is **Free**.

If one of your children shows an interest in medicine—or if you just wish one would—make your way to the Alabama Museum of Health Sciences. On the campus of the University of Alabama at Birmingham, the collection documents various facets of the growth of the medical profession in Birmingham and the development of the state's health sciences. This is not the place to take young children, because most of the displays just aren't geared to their age group. If you have an older child, though, be sure to make time for the museum, where you'll see medical instruments, old photographs, ivory

For More Details The state's Web site address is www.touralabama.org.

anatomical mannequins, and a physician's office. There is a good bit of security, so don't be put off by having to sound a buzzer for admission.

Did You Know?

- Entertainers Kate Jackson, Fannie Flagg, Emmylou Harris, Lionel Hampton, Nell Carter, and Louise Fletcher are from Birmingham.

- The highly acclaimed magazine *Southern Living*, which focuses on the South, is based in Birmingham.

- Birmingham is nicknamed the "Magic City" because of the magical population growth in the city's early years.

- Birmingham is Alabama's largest city and home to the state's largest newspaper, *The Birmingham News*.

 ALABAMA SPORTS HALL OF FAME MUSEUM (all ages)

2150 Civic Center Boulevard, Birmingham 35203; (205) 323–6665; www.angelfire.com/al/SportHall. Open Monday through Saturday from 9:00 A.M. to 5:00 P.M. and Sunday from 1:00 to 5:00 P.M. Admission is $5.00 for adults, $4.00 for seniors, $3.00 for students, and Free *for children under 6.*

You don't have to be a jock to love the Alabama Sports Hall of Fame Museum. Shoot—no pun intended—you don't even have to be able to walk and chew gum at the same time to love this place, where the state's sports legends are remembered. Housed near the Birmingham–Jefferson Convention Complex, the museum is the place to see the University of Alabama's late football coach Paul "Bear" Bryant's game ball from his 315th win, Auburn University quarterback Pat Sullivan's Heisman Trophy, and video clips from memorable moments in sports. Also on display are several major league baseball uniforms from the 1920s and 1930s. These were worn by sports legends who have been inducted into the Alabama Sports Hall of Fame.

If you're like most families, you'll be drawn to the interactive videos and a broadcasting booth, where you can test your announcing skills by describing historical moments in sports. A large diorama displays figures of Hank Aaron, Jesse Owens, Coach Bryant, Bart Starr, Joe Lewis, and announcer Mel Allen.

By the Numbers

- Alabama's Population: 4,319,000

- Area: 51,705 square miles (133,915 square kilometers)

ARLINGTON ANTEBELLUM HOME AND GARDENS (all ages)
331 Cotton Avenue SW, Birmingham 35211; (205) 780–5656. Open Tuesday through Saturday from 10:00 A.M. to 4:00 P.M. and Sunday from 1:00 to 4:00 P.M. Closed Monday and major holidays. Admission is $3.00 for adults, $2.00 for teens, $2.50 for seniors, $1.50 for children 7 to 12, and Free *for children under 6.*

This two-story Greek Revival mansion survived the Civil War because it was used as headquarters for Union officers. The home, restored and refurnished with period furniture, was built in 1842. It is the setting for two popular annual events: the Arlington Country Fair, held the third or fourth Saturday in September, and Christmas at Arlington, when the house is bedecked for the season. During summer, by reservation, lunch with a set menu is served on Thursday in a building behind the main house. This would be a meal probably best appreciated by older children.

 BARBER VINTAGE MOTORSPORTS MUSEUM (all ages)
2721 Fifth Avenue South (mail: 512 Twenty-eighth Street South, Birmingham 35233); (205) 252–8377. Open Wednesday through Friday from 9:00 A.M. to 3:00 P.M. Admission is $5.00 for adults, $2.00 for children 6 to 12, and Free *for younger children.*

Barber Vintage Motorsports Museum claims to be the country's largest motorcycle museum. According to the collection's owner, it is the only museum in the United States to give an accurate account of motorcycles from the turn of the century to the present from an international perspective. Motorcycles are displayed in controlled chaos, motivating you to see a variety of exhibits in a single cluster. Look around at the limited-edition and one-of-a-kind sports and racing bicycles, and expect your children to be drawn to the colorful motorcycles.

 BIRMINGHAM CIVIL RIGHTS INSTITUTE (all ages)
520 Sixteenth Street North, Birmingham 35203; (205) 328–9696. Open Tuesday through Saturday from 10:00 A.M. to 5:00 P.M. and Sunday from 1:00 to 5:00 P.M. Admission is $5.00 for adults, $2.00 for seniors 65+, $1.00 for college students with ID, and Free *to children under age 18.*

The institute is one of the city's most visited attractions. It is the centerpiece of the city's historic Civil Rights District. The district includes the Alabama Jazz Hall of Fame, Kelly Ingram Park (dotted with sculptures commemorating the struggle for equality), and Sixteenth Street Baptist Church. The church has a memorial nook with photographs from the past and a tribute to four girls killed in a 1963 bombing that brought national attention to Birmingham and the civil rights struggle here.

The district and institute are a logical springboard for explaining civil rights and the conflicts of the 1960s to your children. Exhibits are captivating, including a bombed-out bus and a replica of the jail cell where Dr. Martin Luther King, Jr., was held while in Birmingham. This isn't a stuffy place; you and your children can touch things and come away with the feeling of what the struggles must have been.

After leaving be sure that you walk across the street to Kelly Ingram Park, where protesters used to gather for marches and rallies. There are several poignant statues here, most remembering the fire-hoses-and-dog confrontations that most people associate with Birmingham in the 1960s. Outside the institute there are a few pieces of playground equipment where your children can burn off extra energy.

BIRMINGHAM MUSEUM OF ART (ages 8 to 12)

2000 Eighth Avenue North, Birmingham 35203; (205) 254–2565; Fax (205) 254–2714; www.artsbma.org. Open Tuesday through Saturday from 10:00 A.M. to 5:00 P.M. and Sunday from noon to 5:00 P.M. It is closed on Monday and some major holidays. Admission is Free, *except to some special exhibits.*

You might not expect an art museum to top a kid's list of favorite places, but don't underestimate the Birmingham Museum of Art in downtown Birmingham. The Southeast's largest municipally owned art museum, it includes a huge collection of Wedgwood and lots of American, Renaissance, Oriental, and African art.

At the rear of the museum is an outdoor, multilevel sculpture garden. Adjacent parking is Free.

BIRMINGHAM ZOO (all ages)

2630 Cahaba Road, Birmingham 35233; (205) 879–0409; Fax (205) 879–9426; www.birminghamzoo.com. Open daily at 9:00 A.M. with closing at 5:00 P.M. September through early May and at 7:00 P.M. in other months. Closed on a few major holidays. (Closing times indicate when tickets are no longer sold, but if you're already inside the zoo, you may stay until dark.) Admission is $5.00 for adults, $2.00 for seniors and children 2 to 12, and Free *for children under 2.*

The Southeast's largest zoo is one of the state's most visited attractions. A favorite with families, the zoo has a minitrain that winds through the acreage where some 900 rare and exotic animals—including elephants, rhinos, tigers, and cobras—make their homes. There are also picnic tables, a snack bar, and a gift shop. You can spend the whole day here and not spend a bundle.

BIRMINGHAM BOTANICAL GARDENS (all ages)

2612 Lane Park Road, Birmingham 35223; (205) 879–1227; www.bbgardens.org. Open daily from sunrise to sundown. Admission is Free.

Your kids may not be into gardens, but it would be only fair to let them know that near the zoo are the Birmingham Botanical Gardens. Ask if they'd like to stop by and see things that are grown all over the world. Your children will see plants such as rhododendrons, camellias, wildflowers, ferns, delicate bonsai plants, roses, desert flowers, and a Japanese garden complete with a teahouse.

ROBERT R. MEYER PLANETARIUM (ages 8 to 12)

900 Arkadelphia Road, Birmingham-Southern College, Birmingham 35254; (205) 226–4770 or 226–4771 (recorded information). Public presentations are on the first and third weekends each month. Admission is $2.00 for adults and $1.00 for "youth through high school" and seniors.

You and your kids can gaze at the stars and enjoy other special shows at the Meyer Planetarium, on the campus of Birmingham-Southern College. Visiting here also gives you the chance to tour the picturesque campus, not far from exit 123 off Interstate 20/59. A recorded message may answer most of your questions about shows. Just don't be late, because you won't be allowed to enter once a show has begun. To avoid disappointment make reservations. Ask about children's shows.

 OAK MOUNTAIN STATE PARK (all ages)

 200 Terrace Drive, Pelham 35124; (205) 620–2524 or (800) 252–7275. The park is open daylight hours. Admission is $2.00 for adults and $1.00 for children 6 to 12.

Oak Mountain State Park, 10 miles south of Birmingham off exit 246 off Interstate 65, is the largest park in the state's park system. With some 10,000 acres it is in the southernmost part of the Appalachian chain. A drive to the top of Oak Mountain provides spectacular views. Cabins, campsites that face a forty-five-acre lake, a seventy-five-acre lake with a sandy beach, tennis courts, and a BMX track are all here. Your family can also enjoy the park's picnic areas, nature trails, horse trails, eighteen–hole golf course with driving range and putting green, and marina offering canoes and pedal and flat-bottom boats. Your children might especially like the park's demonstration farm. With a variety of animals for viewing and petting, it is the only one of its kind in the state.

RUFFNER MOUNTAIN NATURE CENTER (all ages)

1214 Eighty-first Street South, Birmingham 35206; (205) 833–8112; Fax (205) 836–3960; www.bham.net/ruffner. Trails are open Tuesday through Saturday from 9:00 A.M. to 5:00 P.M. and Sunday from 1:00 to 5:00 P.M. Admission is Free.

Ruffner Mountain Nature Center, 8 miles from downtown Birmingham, is an urban nature center and a great place for families to escape the bustle of city life. The wilderness—with several hundred unspoiled acres—is laced with nature trails and filled with native plants, animals, unusual geological formations, free–flowing springs, and wonderful views. Exhibits detail the mountain's natural and iron-ore histories.

SLOSS FURNACES NATIONAL HISTORIC LANDMARK (all ages)

20 Thirty-second Street North, Birmingham 35203; (205) 324–1911. Open Tuesday through Saturday from 10:00 A.M. to 4:00 P.M. and Sunday from noon to 4:00 P.M. The site is closed on many major holidays. Free *admission.*

The gigantic blast furnaces at the Sloss Furnaces National Historic Landmark on the edge of downtown Birmingham, are idle now, but they are reminders of the industry that gave birth to Birmingham. Shut down in the 1970s, the furnaces have become an industrial museum and a community gathering place for everything from musical festivals to artistic metalworking. Some people say there's even the ghost of Theopholus Jowers, a man who swore that as long as Jefferson County had a furnace, he would be there. This is history that children can touch and feel: the web of pipes, the massive furnace, and the tall, blackened smokestacks. Self–guided tours are available during regular hours. During some special events, though, former workers give tours and explain how the furnaces worked.

SOUTHERN MUSEUM OF FLIGHT (all ages)

4343 Seventy-third Street North, Birmingham 35206; (205) 833–8226; Fax (205) 836–2439. Open Tuesday through Saturday from 9:30 A.M. to 4:30 P.M. and Sunday from 1:00 to 4:30 P.M. Closed on some holidays. Admission is $3.00 for adults, $2.00 for seniors and students, and Free *for preschoolers.*

The future pilot in your family will revel in a tour of the Southern Museum of Flight, near the Birmingham airport. The museum showcases aircraft, models, photographs, and other items related to flight. One intriguing item is the lightbulb that lit the Wright Brothers' first night flight. Also on display are a 1925 crop duster, a 1910 Curtis Pusher, and an F–4 Phantom jet. A variety of short aviation video clips are shown in the museum's small theater, and kids don't seem to mind sitting still long enough to watch.

TEMPLE SIBYL (all ages)

Atop Shades Mountain, where U.S. Highway 31 enters Vestavia Hills. Admission is **Free**.

Although there's nothing in particular to do here, the surrounding grounds are a haven for resting, spreading a picnic, and catching your breath before heading to another Birmingham attraction. The relocated temple stood on the grounds of former Birmingham Mayor George Ward's Greek-style home, which was torn down in the 1970s. It was the temple of Vesta that became the namesake for the community, Vestavia. The estate, with the Vesta Temple as its heart, included extensive grounds with gardens, fountains, statues, and pools. A statue in the garden was the *Temple of Cybele,* now called *Sibyl,* which Ward intended as his tomb. When he died, health officials would not allow his burial there. The temple overlooks Shades Valley and the Samford University campus. Be sure to approach the temple heading up the mountain, because there is no access heading north.

My Man Vulcan
So you think you know some big men. Bet no one you know is as huge as Birmingham's massive statue of Vulcan, god of the forge.

Here are a few facts about Birmingham's main man:

Total height	56 feet
Height to top of head	51 feet
Length of face	7 feet 6 inches
Length of foot	6 feet
Length of arm	10 feet
Distance across shoulders	10 feet
Circumference of chest	22 feet 9 inches
Circumference of waist	18 feet 3 inches
Circumference of neck	11 feet 6 inches
Total weight of figure	100,000 pounds
Weight of anvil block	6,000 pounds
Weight of spear head	350 pounds
Weight of hammer	300 pounds

The College Life Colleges are abundant in Birmingham and will give your children a chance to see what college life is all about. The urban University of Alabama at Birmingham (205-934-4011) sprawls over some 75 city blocks south of downtown. The pulse here is University Hospital, ranked as the nation's third-best center for medical care. UAB is a comprehensive, urban university and medical center with a student enrollment of some 16,000.

Several miles south of UAB, Samford University (205-870-2011 or 800-888-7218) is nestled between Shades Mountain and Red Mountain and offers a different kind of feel with its well–planned campus of Georgian colonial–style buildings. One of the state's largest private universities, Samford in 1999 enrolled more than 4,500 men and women from more than forty states and thirty nations.

West of downtown is Birmingham-Southern College (205-226-4600), which repeatedly has been lauded by national college-guide publications as one of the country's best values in higher education.

VULCAN STATUE AND PARK (all ages)

Atop Red Mountain with entrance to the park at the corner of Twentieth Street South and Valley Avenue; (205) 328–6198. The park currently is closed.

Vulcan, the mythical god of the forge, stands atop Red Mountain and overlooks Birmingham in the valley below. The city's most recognizable site, the towering statue was created as the city's exhibit in the 1904 St. Louis World's Fair. The world's largest iron statue and the second-largest U.S. statue (only the Statue of Liberty is taller), *Vulcan* is cast from 100 percent Birmingham iron ore. The light in Vulcan's uplifted hand is red if there has been a traffic fatality in Metro Birmingham within the previous twenty-four hours and green, if none.

Because of the ravages of time and concern that pieces of the statue might fall off, the park currently is closed as the community raises money for restoration of its most visible landmark. Even though you currently may not enter the park, hike to Vulcan's top, or enjoy surrounding picnic tables, you can spot the statue from afar.

BIRMINGHAM BARONS (all ages)

100 Ben Chapman Drive, Hoover (mail: Box 360007, Birmingham 35236); (205) 988–3200. Season runs April through September. Office open all year.

The Birmingham Barons, Double-A affiliate of the Chicago White Sox, play their home games at the Hoover Metropolitan Stadium south of Birmingham, just off Interstate 459 near the Riverchase Galleria. Over the years baseball fans have watched many future greats pass through the ranks on Birmingham turf. The park was also the home field for Michael Jordan's 1994 rookie season in professional baseball. Promoters with the Barons work diligently to make the ballgame not just a game but an extravaganza that often includes contests, jugglers, a cavorting mascot, fireworks, and music. For about $25 a family of four can attend a game and savor a hot-dog dinner.

BIRMINGHAM BULLS (all ages)

Box 1506, Birmingham 35201; (205) 458–8833; www.birminghambulls.com. Ticket prices range from $8.00 to $12.00 for adults and are $2.00 less for children. Children under age 2 are admitted Free.

From October through April the Birmingham Bulls hockey team plays its regular season games at the Birmingham-Jefferson Convention Complex. It's big-time play, which thrills fans both young and old. Most of the games are played Friday and Saturday nights.

Where to Shop

Riverchase Galleria. *3000 Riverchase Galleria, Suite 905, Birmingham, 35244; (205) 985–3020. Open Monday through Saturday from 10:00 A.M. to 9:00 P.M. and Sunday from 1:00 to 6:00 P.M.* South of Birmingham, the Riverchase Galleria is a shopping mecca with a half dozen anchor stores—JC Penney, Macy's, McRae's, Parisian, Rich's, Sears—and some 200 specialty shops. The complex is among the Southeast's largest malls and boasts the longest skylight in the Western Hemisphere. The food court guarantees a wide range of choices, so there won't be any squabbling at mealtime. Each Christmas the Galleria hosts a spectacular holiday lighting. The centerpiece of the Christmas event is the unveiling of a carousel that is centered in the food court.

Although the Riverchase Galleria garners most of the shopping headlines in Birmingham, there are several malls that many shoppers prefer because they are not as crowded but offer many of the same stores, attentive service, and fewer parking hassles, especially during peak shopping times. The malls are Brookwood Village, The Summit, Century Plaza, Eastwood Mall, and Western Hills Mall.

Where to Eat

Ali Baba Persian Restaurant. *110 Centre at Riverchase, Birmingham 35216; (205) 823–2222.* If your family has never tried Persian foods, this is the place, especially since there is a midday buffet offering lots of things to sample. Extensive menu. Adjacent market. $–$$$

Cobb Lane Restaurant. *One Cobb Lane, Birmingham 35205; (205) 933–0462.* A Birmingham landmark housed in the basement of an old home, the eatery faces an alley, has al fresco dining (that's heated), and cozy inside rooms. She-crab soup and chocolate roulade are signature items. $$–$$$

Klingler's European Bakery & Deli. *621 Montgomery Highway, Vestavia Hills 35216; (205) 823–4560.* A tiny place with noted German foods and display cases laden with sweets. $

La Paz. *99 Euclid Avenue, Mountain Brook 34213; (205) 879–2225.* A popular spot with locals that's known for its Mexican food and seafood dishes. $–$$

Mr. Wang's Chinese Restaurant. *217 Lakeshore Parkway, Birmingham 35209; (205) 945–9000.* A daily grand buffet with seafood added to the evening buffet. Kids love the soft-ice-cream machine, and everyone loves the friendly Wang family. $–$$

Nabeel's Cafe. *1706 Oxmoor Road, Homewood 35209; (205) 879–9292.* Your kids will like the high-backed booths and the sprawling mural on the restaurant's exterior wall. You'll like the Mediterranean foods prepared by the Krontiras family. Don't overlook the adjoining gourmet market stocked with most anything you might find in a Mediterranean market. $

The Original Whistle Stop Café–Irondale Cafe. *1906 First Avenue North, Irondale 35210; (205) 956–5258.* Fannie Flagg put this spot on the map with her book *Fried Green Tomatoes* and its fictitious Whistle Stop Cafe. You'll find a cafeteria line of home-cooked meats and veggies and, of course, those famous fried green tomatoes. $

Sun's Chinese Restaurant. *3780 Riverchase Village Shopping Center, Hoover 35244; (205) 987–9261.* At both lunch and dinner, the restaurant offers a huge buffet. The buffet includes your choice of raw ingredients and sauce, cooked to order by a special chef. Your kids will enjoy the big gold-fish tanks. You'll enjoy the attentive service. There's also an extensive menu for both lunch and dinner if anyone prefers that to the buffet. $

Winston's. *1000 Riverchase Galleria, Birmingham 35244; (205) 987–1600.* A steakhouse off the lobby of the Wynfrey Hotel has great steaks, cloth-covered tables, elegant setting, fine china, and a masculine decor. A prim and proper affair. $$$$

Where to Stay

Courtyard by Marriott. *1824 Montgomery Highway South, Birmingham 35244; (205) 988–5000 or (800) 321–2211.* Children under 18 stay **Free**. Convenient to Riverchase Galleria and Hoover Met. $-$$

Hampton Inn/Mountain Brook. *2731 U.S. Highway 280, Birmingham 35233; (205) 870–7822 or (800) HAMPTON.* **Free** continental breakfast; kids under 18 stay **Free**. $-$$

Key West Inn & Suites/Colonnade. *4400 Colonnade Parkway, Birmingham 35243; (205) 968–3700 or (800) 831–8485.* **Free** continental breakfast, swimming pool, and convenient location. $-$$

La Quinta Inn & Suites. *60 State Farm Parkway, Homewood 35209; (205) 290–0150 or (800) NU–ROOMS; www.laquinta.com.* Your kids will like the heated swimming pool and 25-inch televisions with Nintendo game systems. You'll like the in-room coffeemaker, exercise facility, and **Free** "First Light" breakfast. Children under 18 stay **Free** with parents. $

La Quinta Inn & Suites. *120 Riverchase Parkway East, Hoover 35244; (205) 403–0096.* Heated swimming pool and 25-inch televisions with Nintendo game systems, in-room coffeemaker, exercise facility, and **Free** "First Light" breakfast. Children under 18 stay **Free** with parents. $

Mountain Brook Inn. *2800 U.S. Highway 280, Birmingham 35233; (205) 523–7771.* In-room coffee, swimming pool, and great lunch buffet in their Cafe Savannah. $$

Studio Plus at Wildwood. *40 State Farm Parkway, Birmingham 35209; (205) 290–0102 or (800) 646–8000.* Spacious, nice, and convenient to lots of restaurants. $

Twin Pines Resort. *1200 Twin Pines Road, Sterrett 35147; (205) 672–7575.* A whole world to play in and not too far from Birmingham. Lake, paddleboats, hiking trails, volleyball, and lots more. $$-$$$

Wynfrey Hotel. *1000 Riverchase Galleria, Birmingham 35244; (205) 987–1600 or (800) 476–7006.* The state's only four-star, four-diamond preferred hotel is a good place to stay if you're planning a shopping excursion. When making reservations, ask about shoppers' specials, which include reduced overnight rates and discount coupons to Galleria stores. $$-$$$

For More Information

Greater Birmingham Convention and Visitors Bureau. *2200 Ninth Avenue North, Birmingham 35203; (205) 458–8000 or (800) 458–8085;* Fax *(205) 458–8086;* E-mail *info@birminghamal.org;* Web site *www.bcvb.org.*

Dora

ALABAMA MINING MUSEUM (all ages)
120 East Street, Dora 35062; (205) 648–2442. Open Monday through Friday from 8:30 A.M. to 3:00 P.M. and Saturday from 10:00 A.M. to 3:00 P.M. Admission is Free.

One of the state's best-kept secrets is the Alabama Mining Museum, north of Birmingham in Dora. The museum preserves the state's mining heritage with Alabama's largest collection of mining artifacts. Exhibits that give an idea of what life was like for early miners include a reproduction of a camp commissary store, a fully detailed shotgun house, items coal miners used at work, and tools and machinery used to scratch coal from below the earth's surface.

Children especially like the company store, which has authentic items such as a hoop cheese cutter, old bottles, and bolts of fabric. Signs explain that company stores were centers of activity for miners and their families. Here men would sit on nail kegs, play checkers, and swap stories while women bought food and supplies.

Your youngsters are going to like the children's area, where they can draw water from a "well," play in a post office, and learn old-fashioned games such as spin the top, clicking wheel, or marbles.

Outside the museum there are several structures that have been moved to the site to help visitors better understand a miner's times. You'll find a one-room school, an old post office, a depot, a locomotive, and a caboose. These are open usually by appointment and most often for school groups, but you may be able to persuade the museum keeper to allow you to go inside.

A Fullman Family Adventure A coal mining museum might not seem a glamorous destination, but Christine and Cameron discovered that it can be when your great-grandfather had spent his entire worklife in the mines. They had heard him talk of those days, and they had heard mention of a work-related condition called black lung. But not until they saw the exhibits and photographs at the Mining Museum did they really understand life under the earth. Exhibits of a coal miner's family life also struck home with them as Milton remembered lunchboxes and utensils that he, as a youngster, had seen in his grandparents' home.

Before you leave the museum, be sure your children get one of the tiny chunks of Alabama coal. It will be a reminder of the booty that day after dreary day sent miners trudging into the earth.

Bessemer

About 12 miles west of Birmingham, Bessemer grew up around manufacturing. These days, it's an amusement park that's drawing folks west of Birmingham.

VISIONLAND THEME PARK (all ages)

5051 Prince Street, Bessemer 35022; (205) 481–4750; Fax (205) 481–4758; www.visionlandpark.com. Open daily from 10:00 A.M. to 10:00 P.M. from Memorial Day through Labor Day and on weekends only April, May, September and October. Call for waterpark hours. General admission is $22. For children 3+ but less than 48 inches tall, admission is $18. Admission for seniors is $15. Admission is **Free** *for children under age 3. Season passes are available.*

Man with a Vision Larry Langford, who led the way in construction of VisionLand, once had to take a young relative out of state to an amusement park. As Langford made his trek to Six Flags in Atlanta, it struck him that Birmingham needed its own attraction. That way, he reasoned, people could stay right at home and have fun—plus those driving through would find an added reason to stop.

For more than a decade, Langford worked to make his vision a reality. His vision opened in 1998.

Just west of Birmingham, the theme park, which opened in the summer of 1998, has something for all ages. There are four themed areas: Main Street, with brick streets and shops; Marvel City, with kids' rides; Celebration City, with games and thrill rides; and Steel Waters, a seven-acre waterpark with an enclosed tube ride and a 1,100-foot long meandering river inner-tube ride with a water tower and a cave with misters that give riders a cool shower of fine water.

A river-rapids ride has special effects and the thrill of riding white-water rapids. Three dozen species of animated dinosaurs occupy Dino Domain, an outdoor walk-through facility with life-size animals with moving eyes, heads, legs, or tails.

The park's main attraction is Rampage, a wooden roller coaster with the largest drop of any wooden roller coaster in the Southeast. Rampage's most dramatic drop is 120 feet at a 52-degree slope. With eighteen crossovers and a dozen turns, the coaster reaches a top speed of 56 miles per hour.

BESSEMER HALL OF HISTORY (all ages)

1905 Alabama Avenue, Bessemer 35020; (205) 426–1633. Open Tuesday through Saturday from 9:00 A.M. to noon and 1:00 to 4:00 P.M. Admission is **Free**.

Perhaps the quickest history lesson in the area is at the Bessemer Hall of History, housed in a renovated Southern Railway Depot. The museum's exhibits include old photographs, Civil War items, Indian artifacts, 1800s furnishings and farm implements, antique telephones, and a typewriter once used by Adolf Hitler.

BESSEMER PIONEER HOMES (ages 8 to 12)

Eastern Valley Road (mail: 1859 Edgehill Road, Hueytown 35023); (205) 491–5543. Open first Sunday in December and other times by appointment. Admission to all three houses is $5.00 for adults and **Free** *for children; however, no tours are given for less than a total payment of $20.00.*

On the outskirts of Bessemer are several plantation homes, each within a few miles of one another. The homes, formerly owned by members of the same family, include the 1840s McAdory Plantation Home, which was the center of a plantation covering more than 2,000 acres; the Owen Plantation Home, built in the mid–1830s; and the 1838 Sadler Plantation Home, considered one of the state's finest examples of plantation architecture. Most children nose around and ask where the water came from, how the house was heated, and how the families once living there refrigerated their foods. Many children seem genuinely surprised to hear that those residents put their butter and milk in buckets and stored them in a spring and heated their homes only with fireplaces. The homes were deeded to the city's historical society in the early 1970s, making it possible for volunteers to teach a new generation about early life here.

Although tours are by appointment with two days' notice, you can drive by and peek through windows anytime. If you choose to see all three houses, plan to spend a couple of hours.

TANNEHILL IRONWORKS HISTORICAL STATE PARK (all ages)

12632 Confederate Parkway, McCalla 35111; (205) 477–5711. Open daily from 7:00 A.M. to sunset. Admission is $2.00 for adults, $1.00 for children 6 to 11, and Free *for younger children. Train rides cost $2.00 per person.*

Tannehill Ironworks Historical State Park, 20 miles southwest of Birmingham, is the birthplace of the Birmingham iron industry. The park is built around reconstructed furnaces that in the past produced iron for Confederate forces.

Things bustle here all year, but never as much as on Tannehill Trade Day, usually the third weekend of the month, March through November. This event is the chance to haggle, bargain, and look for treasures, which include everything from painted-on T-shirts to old tools, knives, and collectibles.

Your children will enjoy the miniature train that circles the park and gives an overview of the land, which is tied snugly to the area's history.

While you're in the park, you'll want to see the Alabama Iron and Steel Museum with its large collection of ironwork artifacts that show the evolution of the steel industry responsible for Birmingham's growth.

If you want to stay longer, reserve one of the park's cabins. And don't forget to ask about horseback riding.

Fullman's Pullman Fact Bessemer was the longtime home of Pullman-Standard, manufacturer of famous railroad cars.

Where to Eat

Bob Sykes Bar-B-Que. *1724 Ninth Avenue, Bessemer 35020; (205) 426–1400.* Great barbecue and homemade pies. $

Bright Star. *304 Ninth Avenue, Bessemer 35020; (205) 424–9444.* In business since 1907 and known for home cooking, generous portions, and lunch specials. $–$$

Where to Stay

Days Inn. *1121 Ninth Avenue SW, Bessemer 35022; (205) 424–6078.* Restaurant, room service, and swimming pool. $–$$

For More Information

Bessemer Area Chamber of Commerce. *321 North Eighteenth Street, Bessemer 35020 (mail: Box 648, Bessemer 35021); (205) 425–3253 or (888) 4–BESSEMER; Fax (205) 425–4979.*

Tuscaloosa

Tuscaloosa is the place where youngsters can absorb prep spirit and college-football fever. Even if the city had nothing more to offer than a look at the University of Alabama, college life alone would be enough reason to take children to this town, where the university offers a wide variety of sports events, music, dance, theater, and movies year-round. There is, however, much more than a college in "T-Town."

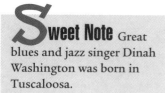

Sweet Note Great blues and jazz singer Dinah Washington was born in Tuscaloosa.

MERCEDES-BENZ VISITOR CENTER (all ages)

11 Mercedes Drive, Vance 35490 (mail: Box 100, Tuscaloosa 35403); (205) 507–2252 or (888) 286–8762. Open Monday through Friday from 9:00 A.M. to 5:00 P.M. and Saturday from 10:00 A.M. to 5:00 P.M. Closed Sunday and major holidays. Admission is $4.00 for ages 12 and older, $3.00 for seniors 55+ and children 6 to 11, and Free *to children under age 6.*

In the only Mercedes-Benz museum outside of Europe, your kids will have a blast seeing cars of all sorts. The German automaker has a great story to tell, and the center is an ideal showcase for sharing it.

The museum features historic Mercedes vehicles and takes you down a multimedia path through the past, present, and future of automotive technology.

Here, your children can explore the pioneering spirit of the people who developed the first automobile in 1836—and can witness some of the greatest racing triumphs in history. Also showcased are technological innovations that have catapulted Mercedes-Benz to its status as one of the world's safest automobiles.

The 24,000-square-foot center holds displays with historical and current photography, video, artifacts, interactive modules, and actual vehicles. Together, the exhibits tell the company's story, including the decision to locate its first North American passenger vehicle plant in Alabama.

Exhibits, which trace the company from 1886 to the present, help you understand why Mercedes-Benz is considered a leader in automotive performance, engineering, safety, and quality. The highlight is seeing an M-Class All-Activity Vehicle, which is manufactured in the adjacent plant. Several vintage Mercedes vehicles also are on display. Among the exhibits are photos of famous people—Gary Cooper, Errol Flynn, Yul Brenner, Elvis Presley, and Bing Crosby, among them—alongside their own Mercedes.

The Visitor Center is both a training center and destination for those who choose to pick up their new vehicles at the factory, a practice more common in Europe than in the United Sates.

Your family will really like the gift shop, with the Mercedes symbol applied to all kinds of things—from key tags and money clips to bicycles, windbreakers, sweaters, T-shirts, calculators, leather carry-on bags, golf balls, and puzzles.

Factory tours, by advance reservation and for children at least age 12 only, are included with museum admission price. (There are no factory tours on Saturday.) Remember, too, that open-toed shoes and short skirts are not appropriate attire for touring the plant.

 ### JEMISON–VAN DE GRAAFF MANSION (ages 8 to 12)

1305 Greensboro Avenue, Tuscaloosa 35401; (205) 391–9200 or (800) 538–8696. Open Monday through Friday from 8:00 A.M. to 5:00 P.M. Admission is Free.

The best beginning for a Tuscaloosa visit is the Jemison–Van de Graaff House. The restored antebellum, Italianate-style home includes offices of the town's tourism folks, who are eager to help. They have lots of brochures and information that will help you decide what you want to do while you're in T-Town. Be sure to pick up a self-guided brochure for Capitol Park.

 ### PAUL W. BRYANT MUSEUM/UNIVERSITY OF ALABAMA MUSEUMS (all ages)

300 Bryant Drive (Box 870385, Tuscaloosa 35487–0385); (205) 348–4668; www.au.edu/bryant/htm. Open daily from 9:00 A.M. to 4:00 P.M. Closed major holidays. Admission is $2.00 for adults, $1.00 for seniors 55+ and children 6 to 17, and Free *for younger children.*

The people working here are quick to tell you that one of the town's most popular attractions is the Paul Bryant Museum, named for the Alabama Crimson Tide's legendary coach, Paul W. "Bear" Bryant. (He received the nickname because as a youngster he tried wrestling a bear.)

Begin your museum visit by watching *The Bryant Legacy,* a short film outlining Bryant's life, career, and philosophy. Next, you need to see what's a favorite with children: a reproduction of Coach Bryant's office. Don't miss his houndstooth hat and field jacket.

Bryant was not just a local favorite. He won national acclaim as a three-time winner of National Coach of the Year, an eight-time winner of Southeastern Conference Coach of the Year, and the first coach since the formation of the NCAA to win one hundred games in a decade.

Museum exhibits include photographs, uniforms, programs, videos, and sports memorabilia dating from 1892. There are films, documents, memorabilia, and publications pertaining to Southeastern Conference sports. One exhibit extols the game's fans, cheerleaders, and staff, a reminder to children that teamwork is essential both in the spotlight and behind the scenes.

GORGAS HOUSE (ages 8 to 12)

Ninth Avenue and Capstone Drive (Box 870266, Tuscaloosa 35487–0266); (205) 348–5906; www.ua.edu/gorgas.htm. Open Tuesday, Wednesday, and Friday from 10:00 A.M. to 4:00 P.M., Saturday from 10:00 A.M. to 3:00 P.M., and Sunday from 2:00 to 4:00 P.M. Closed on major holidays and university holidays and during special events. Admission is $1.00 per person.

If early history intrigues your children, don't miss another campus site, the Gorgas House. Built in 1829, it was once used as a campus dining hall. The house's fame, however, is linked to its most famous residents, the Gorgas family, whose son, William Crawford Gorgas, gained an international reputation for helping to eliminate yellow fever epidemics. His work made it possible for construction of the Panama Canal to be completed. Built in 1829 as a dining room and steward's residence, the Gorgas House was an original building of the University of Alabama. It was the campus's only original building not burned by Union soldiers. When Josiah B. Gorgas retired in 1879 as the university's seventh president, he became university librarian and was allowed to move with his family into the structure. Working from home, his wife, Amelia Gayle Gorgas, served the university as matron of the infirmary and postmistress. Following her husband's death in 1883, Mrs. Gorgas remained in the house until her death in 1913. After the last Gorgas daughter died in 1953, the state set aside the structure as a memorial to the Gorgases' son, Brigadier General William Crawford Gorgas, who never lived with his family in the house.

The house today is filled with a wealth of nineteenth-century furniture and silver.

 ### ALABAMA STATE MUSEUM OF NATURAL HISTORY (all ages)

Sixth Avenue (mail: Smith Hall, Box 870340, Tuscaloosa 35487); (205) 348–9742; www.au.edu/history.htm. Open weekdays from 8:00 A.M. to 4:30 P.M. and Saturday from 1:00 to 4:30 P.M. Admission is $2.00 for adults and $1.00 for children.

Another on-campus must-see is the Alabama State Museum of Natural History, in Smith Hall off University Boulevard, where exhibits focus on portions of state geologic formations and fossils are displayed in re-created natural habitats. What most intrigues kids is the only meteorite said to have struck a person. This particular meteorite fell through the roof of a Sylacauga house in November 1954, bounced off a radio cabinet, and brushed the leg of a woman who later donated the meteorite to the museum.

Some people say the museum is haunted, but few are willing to stick around after hours to verify whether tales of late-night ghostly visits are true.

Annual Events Tuscaloosa hosts several annual events that should interest your family.

- Each March the **Sakura Festival** celebrates the city's friendly ties with Japan and its sister city, Narashino City.

- Another springtime event is an annual **pilgrimage of homes,** when the city pays tribute to its Southern roots.

- In mid-October, downtown Tuscaloosa hosts **CityFest.** Stages on city streets are filled with name entertainment presenting sounds from zydeco to jazz. Costume contests, arts and crafts, a children's parade, and plenty of regional foods are part of the fun.

- In mid-December Tuscaloosa hosts **Christmas Afloat,** when local boat owners plow their decorated boats down the Black Warrior River.

CHILDREN'S HANDS-ON MUSEUM (all ages)

2213 University Boulevard, Tuscaloosa 35403; (205) 349–4235. Open Tuesday through Friday from 9:00 A.M. to 5:00 P.M. and Saturday from 1:00 to 5:00 P.M. Admission is $5.00 for ages 2 and older and **Free** *to children under 2.*

Your kids will want you to put the Children's Hands-On Museum at the top of your must-see list. Housed in a former department store, CHOM is the place where kids can be kids or play act at being someone else. They can pretend to be a doctor or nurse or bank clerk, try on clothes in Grandma's attic, run a store, and experience a planetarium. An Indian village teaches how Native Americans ground corn and made pottery.

THE OLD TAVERN MUSEUM (all ages)

500 Twenty-eighth Avenue (mail: Tuscaloosa County Preservation Society, Box 1665, Tuscaloosa 35403); (205) 758–2238. Open Monday through Friday from 8:00 A.M. to 4:00 P.M., Saturday from 10:00 A.M. to noon and from 1:00 to 4:00 P.M., and Sunday from 1:00 to 4:00 P.M. Admission is **Free***.*

Your children won't be as free to touch things here as they were at the Children's Hands-on Museum, but they should have fun inside what has been a stagecoach stop, a residence, and an inn. These days, the attraction lets you see how things used to be. Built in 1827, the building stands near the ruins of the 1826 state capitol when Tuscaloosa was the seat of state government. Filled with period furnishings and items from the city's capital period, the tavern in those days was frequented by legislators.

When you stopped first at the Jemison–Van de Graaff House, you should have picked up a self-guided brochure for Capitol Park, next to Old Tavern. Newly excavated grounds here have revealed original pillars and part of the rotunda. Kids can actually climb on these old stones and use their imaginations about how the old capitol building must have looked.

MILDRED WARNER HOUSE (ages 8 to 12)

1925 Eighth Street, Tuscaloosa 35401; (205) 553–6200. Open Saturday and Sunday from 1:00 to 5:00 P.M. Admission is **Free***.*

If your kids are older and appreciate fine things, swing by the Mildred Warner House, which holds an impressive collection, including authentic furnishings dating from 1730 to 1860. The house, which began as a two-room cabin, also has a noted art collection. A warning, however: Only go here if your kids know how to behave and keep their hands to themselves. If they're too young for that, skip this and plan to return when they're older.

GULF STATE PAPER CORPORATION (ages 8 to 12)

1400 River Road NE, Tuscaloosa 35404; (205) 553–6200. Guided tours are given weekdays at 5:30 and 6:30 P.M. On Saturday tours are on the hour from 10:00 A.M. to 4:00 P.M. and Sunday from 1:00 to 4:00 P.M. Admission is Free.

The nerve center for a national company is home to one of the country's finest art collections, offering historic Americana, classical and modern paintings, as well as African and Southern Pacific primitive sculptures.

MURPHY AFRICAN-AMERICAN MUSEUM (ages 8 to 12)

2601 Bryant Drive at the corner of Lurleen Wallace Boulevard South, Tuscaloosa 35401; (205) 758–2861 or 758–2238. Hours are irregular, so call first. Admission is $3.00 for adults, $2.00 for seniors 62+ and students ages 6 to 18, and Free *to younger children.*

The museum is housed in what was the home of the city's first black mortician, who later became one of the city's outstanding black leaders and businessmen. The 1920s cottage is filled with many original furnishings that stand alongside African-American exhibits, all designed to showcase achievements and contributions of black people. When you visit, ask about the house's two beams taken from the Alabama capitol building in Tuscaloosa. Don't miss the chance to discuss with your children this nation's ever-changing economy: Murphy built his two-story bungalow with materials that cost him $900.

DENNY CHIMES (all ages)

University of Alabama campus.

While you're in town, listen for the Denny Chimes, erected in 1929 and named for the then-president of the university. The chimes, at the center of the campus in the quadrangle, ring every quarter hour and play a late-afternoon concert.

PICKENS COUNTY COURTHOUSE/FACE IN THE WINDOW (all ages)

Court House (mail: Box 270, Carrollton 35447); (205) 367–8149. Available anytime. Looking is **Free**.

If you find yourself in Carrollton, don't miss seeing the face imprinted on a windowpane at the Pickens County Courthouse. The legend of the mysterious face involves a young black man accused of burning the courthouse in 1876. As he looked through the window at an angry mob below, an electrical storm passed over, and a sudden bolt of lightning etched his terrified likeness onto the window. The pane has survived more electrical storms and even hailstorms, yet the face remains. Look for the face under the eaves of the north side of the courthouse. So many tourists have stopped by to see the famous site that the locals added an arrow on the window to help lookers spot the image. If you're still having trouble, ask anybody walking by; the people here are friendly and accustomed to lookers outside their courthouse.

Where to Eat

DePalmas Italian Restaurant. *2300 University Boulevard, Tuscaloosa 35401; (205) 759–1879.* A favorite with locals who savor the fine Italian cuisine. $–$$

The Mezzanine. *508 Greensboro Avenue, Tuscaloosa 35403; (205) 752–0020.* French-made chairs and large urns with floral arrangements help to create a European setting in a one-time mercantile store. France meets the South on their menu, which includes some popular lunch choices. An elegant restaurant with reasonable prices. $–$$$$

Old Venice Pizza Company. *2321 University Boulevard, Tuscaloosa 35401; (205) 366–1209.* Great pizza in a kid-friendly environment. $–$$

Wings Sports Grill. *500 Harper Lee Drive, Tuscaloosa 35404; (205) 556–5658.* Very family-friendly. Kids under age 10 eat **Free** on Tuesday night. $

Where to Stay

Best Western Park Plaza Motor Inn. *3801 McFarland Boulevard East, Tuscaloosa 35405; (205) 556–9690 or (800) 235–7282.* Great choice with **Free** continental breakfast, restaurant, in-room coffee, **Free** newspaper, and **Free** local calls. $

Courtyard by Marriott. *4115 Courtney Drive, Tuscaloosa 35405; (205) 750–8384 or (800) 228–5150.* Swimming pool and kitchenettes. $–$$

Fairfield Inn by Marriott. *4101 Courtney Drive, Tuscaloosa 35405; (205) 366–0967.* **Free** continental breakfast and an exercise room. $

Four Points by Sheraton Capstone Hotel. *320 Paul Bryant Drive, Tuscaloosa 35401; (205) 752–3200.* Next to the Bryant Museum. **Free** cribs. $$$$

Hampton Inn. *6400 Interstate Drive, Tuscaloosa 35453; (205) 562–9000 or (800) HAMPTON.* **Free** continental breakfast and a swimming pool. $

Hampton Inn University. *600 Harper Lee Drive, Tuscaloosa 35404; (205) 553–9800 or (800) HAMPTON.* **Free** continental breakfast and a swimming pool. $

Key West Inn. *4700 Doris Pate Drive, Tuscaloosa 35405; (205) 556–3232 or (800) 833–0555.* **Free** continental breakfast, **Free** local calls, and a restaurant. $

La Quinta Inn. *4122 McFarland Boulevard East, Tuscaloosa 35405–3833; (205) 349–3270 or (800) NU–ROOMS; www.laquinta.com.* Nice amenities, including 25-inch televisions with Nintendo game systems, in-room coffee-maker, **Free** local telephone calls, and **Free** breakfast. Children under 18 stay **Free** with parents. $

Sleep Inn. *4300 Skyland Boulevard East, Tuscaloosa 35405; (205) 556–5696.* In-room minirefrigerators, oversized showers, and **Free** continental breakfast, which means savings for traveling families. $

For More Information

Tuscaloosa Convention and Visitors Bureau. *1305 Greensboro Avenue, Tuscaloosa 35401; (205) 391–9200 or (800) 538–8696. Fax (205) 391–2125; Web site www.tcvb.org.*

Northport

If one of your children has a hankering for art, don't miss Northport. Although it's small, Northport has impressive exhibits of contemporary and traditional American crafts and fine art. Better yet, this is the place to discover the state's rich folk-art tradition and to see artists at work. Northport's downtown area continues a metamorphosis with the addition of shops and restaurants. Brick-lined sidewalks and streetlights help to perpetuate a small-town charm.

 GALLERY AT KENTUCK (all ages)
503 Main Avenue, Northport 35476; (205) 758–1257. Open Monday through Friday from 9:00 A.M. to 5:00 P.M. and Saturday from 10:00 A.M. to 4:30 P.M. Admission is **Free**.

At the four-building artists' colony, your children can watch woodworkers, a harpsichord maker, a blacksmith, a bookbinder, a photographer, and a painter at work. The gallery's gift shop

Annual Event **Kentuck Festival of Arts, held the third weekend in October, is one of the region's best crafts events.**

is filled with treasures that would make good souvenirs of Alabama. Artists set their own hours, so nothing here is written in stone, but there's usually someone at work during regular weekday business hours.

Where to Eat

The Globe. *430 Main Avenue, Northport 35476; (205) 391–0949.* Housed in a former drugstore with lots of atmosphere and incredible food. $-$$$

Henson's Cypress Inn. *501 Rice Mine Road North, Northport 35476; (205) 345–6963.* Even though evening meals are served on tables draped in white cloths, this place is not hoity-toity, just elegantly casual. Don't miss the homemade yeast rolls and raisin-bran muffins. If it's warm enough, ask to sit on the deck so you can watch for passing boats. If you're good at golf, try hitting a ball across the river. Beside the restaurant are two tee markers, one measuring 250 yards and another 261 yards from the target, which is the opposite bank of the river. Clear the river from the back tee and you win a **Free** dinner; make it from the front tee and you get a drink on the house. The few people who have been successful are named on a bronze plaque near the tees.

Where to Stay

Econo Lodge & Suites. *1930 McFarland Boulevard, Northport 35476; (205) 330–0345 or (800) –ECONO.* **Free** continental breakfast and swimming pool. $-$$

For More Information

Tuscaloosa Convention and Visitors Bureau. *1305 Greensboro Avenue, Tuscaloosa 35401; (205) 391–9200 or* *(800) 538–8696. Fax (205) 391–2125; Web site www.tcvb.org.*

Pickensville

TOM BEVILL VISITOR CENTER (all ages)

(mail: Route 2, Box 352-X, Carrollton 35447); (205) 373–8705. The center is open daily. Summer hours are from 9:00 A.M. to 5:00 P.M.; winter hours are from 8:00 A.M. to 4:00 P.M. Admission is Free.

Tom Bevill Visitor Center, just south of the junction of State Routes 14 and 86 in Pickensville, is 10 miles outside Aliceville. Don't be deceived by the building's elder-statesman air; designers combined architectural features from several of the state's most beautiful mansions, and the house was actually built in the mid-1980s.

Children will love climbing the sweeping stairway to the second floor exhibits, which present the history of the Tennessee-Tombigbee Waterway. The network connects some 16,000 miles of inland waterways and provides a route to the Gulf of Mexico for commerce between the interior of the United States and Mobile and other ports on the Gulf.

Be sure your children look at the 22-foot-wide relief map outlining the waterway's course through locks and dams. Save time to trudge to the roof where, with luck, you'll see a vessel passing through the lock and dam below.

Docked beside the center is an attraction popular with youngsters: the U.S. snag boat, *Montgomery,* a retired steam-powered sternwheeler, which at one time kept Southern rivers navigable by removing debris that threatened river traffic. Visitors are allowed to peer into the crew's tiny sleep quarters, sit in heavy rocking chairs in a screened area, and read through work-related notes left behind by the boat's last crew. For a moment it seems that the men have only stepped away and might, at any time, return to resume plowing Alabama's waterways.

Aliceville

Aliceville is another of Alabama's quiet towns, where Sundays are quiet times, where people rarely lock their cars, and everyone seems to know everywhere else. It was into that bucolic environment that German prisoners of war arrived during World War II. Far from home, the men remained in Aliceville for the war's duration and left an imprint that is remembered today in the city's most popular attraction, the nation's only museum recognizing German prisoners of war.

ALICEVILLE MUSEUM AND CULTURAL ARTS CENTER (all ages)
104 Broad Street, Aliceville 35442; (205) 373–2363 or (888) 751–2340.
Open Monday through Friday from 10:00 A.M. to 4:00 P.M. Admission is $3.00
for adults, $2.00 for seniors and students, and **Free** *for younger children.*

Housed in what formerly was a soft-drink bottling plant, the museum recognizes the World War II prisoners who were detained here until the war ended. The soldiers were German Field Marshal Erwin Rommel's finest, captured during fighting in North Africa. Among the prisoners were artists, engineers, and professors—educated men who produced works of art, wrote and published a camp newspaper, carved chess sets, painted pictures, created drawings, and made furniture. Using a homemade kiln, the Germans made bricks and constructed a small amphitheater where they presented performances, including concerts by the prisoners' orchestra.

Several years ago Aliceville hosted a reunion of former prisoners, and the town realized the need for a museum. Residents donated items, and former prisoners have rallied to contribute. A sixth-generation German toymaker, who had been a prisoner, sent a bundle of small, magnetized blocks that are the biggest hit with visiting children. Another prisoner sent a Bavarian dollhouse outfitted with miniature furniture.

The museum also has a re-creation of a bottling line and displays that explain bottling history.

 BETHANY CEMETERY (all ages)
Alabama Highway 14 East; (no phone).

Five miles south of Aliceville, in Bethany Cemetery, is the grave of James McCrory, who served as George Washington's bodyguard at Valley Forge during the American Revolutionary War. Your family may not think of cemeteries as fun places to visit, but this small one, adjacent to a church, is interesting, especially if you take time to look at the old grave markers. If you have a camera, you probably won't resist the urge to snap a few shots of the towering angels. Just be sure the light hits right or your shots will turn out with featureless faces.

Where to Eat

Broad Street Bistro. *212 Broad Street, Aliceville 35442; (205) 373–6540.* Salad bar, deli sandwiches, plate lunches, and pizzas. Very affordable. Dinner hours are limited, so call first. $

Gates Lodge. *Highway 14 West, Pickensville (mail: Box 163, Aliceville 35442); (205) 367–8700.* In an old hunting lodge with a large, rustic fireplace. Known for steaks, seafood, catfish, and chicken. Salad bar and children's plates. $–$$

The Plantation House Restaurant. *202 Memorial Parkway East, Aliceville 35442; (205) 373–8121.* Meat and veggies in a wonderful old house and within walking distance of museum and bed-and-breakfasts. $

Where to Stay

Myrtlewood Bed and Breakfast, *601 Broad Street, Aliceville 35442; (205) 373–2916 or (800) 367–7891.* This 1909 Victorian-style home, with wide porches, is convenient to downtown sites. No restriction on ages of children. Park is 1 block away. $

WillowBrooke Bed and Breakfast. *501 Broad Street, Aliceville 35442; (205) 373–6133.* Home has wraparound porch and spacious rooms and offers deluxe continental breakfast. Owner has a preschooler, so you'll find indoor and outdoor toys, a VCR, and loads of videos; use of stroller, too. $

For More Information

Aliceville Area Chamber of Commerce. *416 Third Avenue (mail: Drawer A, Aliceville 35442);* *(205) 373–2820; Web site www.pickens.net/~commerce/.*

Moundville

 MOUNDVILLE ARCHAEOLOGICAL PARK (all ages)
1 Mound Parkway, Moundville (mail: Box 66, Moundville 35474); (205) 371– 2572 or 371–2234. The park is open daily from 8:00 A.M. to sunset. Museum is open daily from 9:00 A.M. to 5:00 P.M. Closed some holidays. Admission, which includes entry into the museum, is $4.00 for adults and $2.00 for children.

Moundville Archaeological Park, 17 miles south of Tuscaloosa, is one of the state's best opportunities to learn about the Indians who at one time lived here. The site is nationally recognized as

Annual Event In the first full week of October, the Moundville Archeological Park hosts a **Native American Festival.** Indian artisans showcase crafts, ranging from beadwork to basketweaving.

the most important prehistoric Indian settlement and ceremonial center of the South. The settlement supported more than 3,000 people.

Your family can see and climb the twenty-six mounds built by the Indians, who lugged dirt into huge heaps that overlook the Black Warrior River. Nobody is sure why these Indians built mounds, but everyone seems to agree that they are fun to visit and explore. For children visiting the site, a bonus is a reconstructed Indian village that shows how the early residents lived and worked.

The park and museum are on 320 acres, which include walking trails dotted with wildflowers and small mounds. Nearby are camping facilities with water and electrical hookups, tent pads, and grills. Also offered are primitive camping sites, picnic tables, and grills.

Author's Top Picks

- Anniston Museum of Natural History, Anniston (256–237–6766)

- International Motor Sports Hall of Fame, Talladega (256–362–5002)

- DeSoto Caverns Park, Childersburg (256–378–7252)

- Bulldog Bend, Brierfield (205–926–7382)

- McWane Center, Birmingham (205–714–8300)

- VisionLand Theme Park, Bessemer (205–481–4750)

- Birmingham Zoo, Birmingham (205–879–0409)

- Paul W. Bryant Museum, Tuscaloosa (205–348–4668)

- Children's Hands-On Museum, Tuscaloosa (205–349–4235)

- Moundville Archaeological Park, Moundville (205–371–2572)

Southwest Alabama

Bet your children never thought they'd come face to snout with an alligator, but they can do just that in the state's southwest section. This is the place to sun on sandy beaches, sail gulf waters, tour magnificent gardens, and discover the hometown of a famous author. It is the place for outdoor dramas, Southern mansions, thrill rides, petting zoos, and building sand castles. So pack your sunscreen, your sand pail, and your sense of adventure, because southwest Alabama is unlike any other part of the state.

Marion

One of the state's oldest towns, Marion, began as a cultural center for planter society. The town centers the Black Belt, a region named for its dark and fertile soil.

In Marion your children can learn more about war and its costs at Confederate Rest, where both Yank and Rebel dead are buried. And they can learn about heroes of another kind at Marion Cemetery, where a monument honors "Harry," a servant who died saving students from a fire.

Marion's downtown has a gaggle of antiques shops clustered around the town square.

The town may be best known as home to Marion Military Institute (800-664-1842). With an emphasis on preparation for the nation's service academies, the high school and junior college have turned out some 200 generals and admirals who began their military educations here. Women first were admitted in 1971.

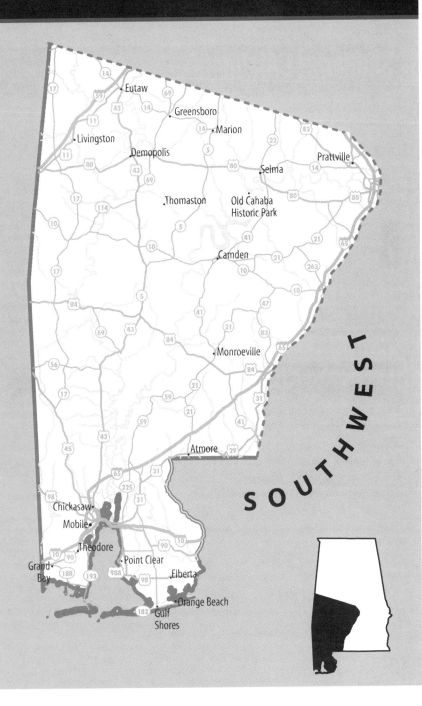

SOUTHWEST

ALABAMA WOMEN'S HALL OF FAME (ages 8 to 12)

Judson College, corner of Bibb Street and East Lafayette (Box 120), Marion 36756; (334) 683–5109. Open Monday through Friday from 8:00 A.M. *to 4:30* P.M. *Admission is* **Free***.*

If there's a girl in your family, be sure your trek into Marion includes a stop at the Alabama Women's Hall of Fame. The tribute to outstanding women is a reminder that ambition and dreams know no bounds.

Begun in 1979 on the campus of Judson College, the hall of fame recognizes outstanding women who have close ties to the state and have made significant contributions on a state, national, or international level.

Hall inductees include Helen Keller, blind and deaf educator and lecturer; Julia Tutwiler, a pioneer in women's education and a prison-reform advocate; actress Tallulah Bankhead; and Margaret Washington, leader, teacher, and wife of black educator Booker T. Washington.

There are dozens of other women also honored, so don't miss this opportunity to let your children learn about these women and their contributions.

JUDSON COLLEGE (ages 8 to 12)

302 Bibb Street, Marion 36756; (334) 683–5100.

While you are in the area, don't leave without a drive through the picturesque campus of Judson College, one of the nation's oldest women's colleges. Begun in 1838 by Baptists, Judson, today with some 450 students, offers a liberal arts curriculum with more than thirty fields of study including literature, computer, Bible, business, music, and psychology.

State Song The state's official song, "Alabama," was written by Julia S. Tutwiler, and its music was composed by Edna Goeckel Gussen.

Here's the first verse of that song:

Alabama, Alabama,
We will aye be true to thee,
From thy Southern shore where groweth,
By the sea thy orange tree.
To thy Northern vale where floweth
Deep and blue thy Tennessee,
Alabama, Alabama,
We will aye be true to thee!

ALABAMA MILITARY HALL OF HONOR (ages 8 to 12)
1101 Washington Street, Marion 36756–9988; (800) 664–1842. Hours are limited. Admission is 𝔉𝔯𝔢𝔢.

Make advance arrangements to stop by the Alabama Military Hall of Honor located in the town's former city hall, which was moved to the Marion military school campus. The hall invites children to learn about heroes and heroism.

When you're visiting the military institute, savor a few minutes in the chapel, which, like many Alabama structures, served as a makeshift hospital for wounded Civil War soldiers. Outside the chapel are hundreds of signatures scrawled on bricks. Sanctioned by the school, the signings have become a cadet tradition. If you're in town on Friday from September through May, you might catch students drilling on one of the school's fields. You are welcome to sit on bleachers to watch these young people perform precise and impressive moves. Call the school to confirm when parades will be held.

Women Remembered Stories of the first twenty-five inductees into the Alabama Women's Hall of Fame are told in *They Also Served: Twenty-five Remarkable Alabama Women* by Mildred Griffin Yelverton. Published by Ampersand Publishing in Dothan, the book is sold in some bookstores and at the hall.

Where to Shop

Angel Wings. *321 Washington Street, Marion 36756; (334) 683–4900.* Consignment dealers are clustered in old buildings with plenty of treasures.

Browse About Antiques. *105 East Jefferson Street, Marion 36756; (334)* 683–9856. The shop is on the square and offers abundant choices.

Old Victoria Antiques. *216 Washington Street, Marion 36756; (334)* 683–2095. On the downtown square, you'll love these antiques.

Rule of Our Roads Alabama law requires all front-seat occupants to buckle up. In front and back seats, children under age six must occupy federally approved safety restraints. Four- and five-year-olds may use safety belts or the child safety seats required for younger children.

Where to Eat

Calico Kitchen. *Alabama Highway 5, Marion 36756; (334) 683–6739.* Family eatery with a lunch buffet. $

Gateway Restaurant. *1615 Alabama Highway 5, Marion 36756; (334) 683–9166.* Walls laden with historic photos and items and plates laden with home cooking (fried okra, lemon pie, biscuits, and yummy desserts). $

Old Victoria Cafe. *216 Washington Street, Marion 36756; (334) 683–2095.* Kids love this quaint shop, housed in Old Victoria Antiques. $

Where to Stay

Gateway Inn. *1615 Alabama Highway 5 South, Marion 36756; (334) 683–9166.* Twenty-three very clean and affordable units. $

Myrtle Hill Bed and Breakfast. *303 West Lafayette Street 36756; (334) 683–9095.* An elegantly restored ante-bellum home, complete with a resident ghost, four-poster beds, and back-porch rocking chairs. $

For More Information

Perry County Chamber of Commerce. *Washington Street (Box 951); Marion 36756; (334) 683–9622.*

Marion City Hall. *123 East Jefferson (Drawer 959), Marion 36756; (334) 683–8969.*

Greensboro

Greensboro is not a hot tourist city, but it's worth a stop if you're in the area. You won't find amusement parks or tourist traps, but you will see architecture and history. Unlike many Alabama towns, Greensboro was spared Civil War devastation, so antebellum homes still exist. The downtown district, with 150 nineteenth-century structures, is listed on the National Register of Historic Places.

 MAGNOLIA GROVE (ages 8 to 12)
1002 Hobson Street, Greensboro 36744; (334) 624–8618. Open Tuesday through Saturday from 10:00 A.M. to 4:00 P.M. and Sunday from 1:00 to 4:00 P.M. Admission is $3.00 for adults and $2.00 for students.

The columned, two-story house was the birthplace and childhood home of Spanish-American War hero Richard Pearson Hobson. As your family walks through the house, observe the furnishings, many of which are original. Then head outside to see an abundance of magnolias, camellias, boxwoods, and other traditional Old South plants on the home's dozen acres.

Annual Event In mid-September Greensboro hosts the **Alabama Catfish Festival,** a salute to tasty freshwater catfish. The fun includes catfish fingerling races, arts and crafts, a children's carnival, a rodeo, and bus tours of catfish farms.

Where to Eat

The Inn Motel's Restaurant. *1302 State Street, Greensboro 36744; (334) 624–3031.* The motel's restaurant has good food at affordable prices. $

Where to Stay

Blue Shadows Bed and Breakfast. *Highway 14 West (Box 11265), Greensboro 36744; (334) 624–3637.* Situated on 320 acres, the overnight accommodations are adjacent to a main house. The above-garage, three-room suite has a living room, kitchenette, and bedroom, plus couch and roll-away bed for extra sleepers. Breakfast foods are furnished in the suite. Access to fishing pond and nature trails. $

For More Information

City of Greensboro. *1101 Main Street (Drawer 77), Greensboro 36744; (334) 624–8119.*

Eutaw

Eutaw, another sleepy little town in the state's Black Belt, is filled with stately homes worth a closer look.

When you're traveling U.S. Highway 43 about 15 miles south of Eutaw, don't miss the whimsical Hay Sculptures erected by Green County farmer Jim

Bird, who has mechanical and marine engineering degrees. His works, which have captured international attention, are made mostly from driftwood and bales of hay, stacked to create all kinds of shapes, which he constantly is changing. Children especially like the creatures: a bull, E.T., a shark, and a snake. Some people even get out of their cars to take photos, and Bird is just as happy as a lark to make their world brighter.

Where to Eat

Main Street Eatery and Deli. *208 Main Street, Eutaw 35462; (205) 372–0209.* You might want to sit outside and eat. Great burgers, sandwiches, and homemade cookies. $

Cotton Patch. *Union Road (Box 270), Eutaw 35462; (205) 372–4235.* Rustic log cabin known for great fried chicken and catfish, pickled watermelon rinds, and hand-dropped biscuits, a favorite with young diners. $

Mama Leone's Pizzaria. *305 Prairie Avenue, Eutaw 35462; (205) 372–0007.* On the town square with the best pizza around and brownies that are to die for. $

Where to Stay

Kirkwood Bed and Breakfast. *State Route 14 and Kirkwood Drive, Eutaw 35462; (205) 372–9009; www. kirkwoodplantation.com.* A restored 1850s, belvedere-topped mansion has eight massive columns, marble mantels, and original furnishings. Beware of stairs with young children. Baby bed available. $$

Western Inn. *Union Road (Route 3, Box 49–B), Eutaw 35462; (205) 372–9363 or (800) 343–3490.* Nice and with a swimming pool. $

For More Information

Eutaw Area Chamber of Commerce. *110 Main Street (Box 31), Eutaw 35462; (205) 372–9002.*

Batter Up

- Alabama-born baseball player Hank Aaron had a lifetime batting average of .305.

- *Sporting News* magazine named Alabama-born Willie Mays Baseball Player of the Decade, 1960 to 1969.

Livingston

Livingston is best known as the home of the University of West Alabama (formerly Livingston State University), but as you pass through, check out several sites. One is the Alamuchee Covered Bridge on the university campus across from the Baptist Student Union. Dating from 1861, it is one of the South's oldest covered bridges. Built of heart pine, the bridge originally spanned a river south of the town before being disassembled and moved to its present site.

Don't speed away without touring the college campus and its two lakes. From the campus drive downtown to see the domed Sumter County Courthouse, which dates back to around 1900.

From here, it's onto Demopolis.

For More Information

City of Livingston. *220 South Washington Street (Drawer W), Livingston 35470; (205) 652–2505.*

Demopolis

Demopolis offers families old homes, water sports, and a slow-paced escape.

Annual Events Several annual events draw people to Demopolis. An evening **fireworks display** held each July 4 is sponsored by the Demopolis Area Chamber of Commerce. The town's most noted celebration is **Christmas on the River,** held annually on the first week in December. The holiday salute includes parades, tours, and special events leading up to the grand finale: a huge arts-and-crafts show and a night parade of floats that drift down the river. Crowds of 70,000 have watched the decorated boats floating down the Tombigbee River.

BLUFF HALL (ages 8 to 12)
405 North Commissioners Avenue, Demopolis 36732; (334) 289–1666. Guided tours Tuesday through Saturday from 10:00 A.M. to 5:00 P.M. and Sunday from 2:00 to 5:00 P.M. Admission is $5.00 for adults and $1.00 for students under 12.

Overlooking the Tombigbee River, Bluff Hall is a majestic showplace of two architectural trends in the antebellum South. Built in 1832 as a father's gift to his daughter, the house later was modified from its original Federal style to Greek Revival. Discussing how a father could afford to build such an elaborate house for his daughter may spark interesting conversation with your children.

GAINESWOOD (ages 8 to 12)

805 Whitfield Street East, Demopolis 36732; (334) 289–4846. Open Monday through Saturday from 9:00 A.M. to 5:00 P.M. and Sunday from 1:00 to 5:00 P.M. Admission is $5.00 for adults, $3.00 for ages 13 to 18, $2.00 for ages 6 to 12, and Free *for younger children.*

Built mostly by slave labor before the outbreak of the Civil War, the home began as a two-room cabin squatting on 1,000 acres of cotton. When you visit, point out to your children the skilled carpentry and plaster work, a testimony to the workers' talents. The house evolved into a Greek Revival–Style mansion, which now is filled with many original furnishings.

FOSCUE CREEK NATIONAL PARK (all ages)

Box 520, Demopolis 36732; (334) 289–3540 or 289–5535.Open daily. Free *admission.*

If your family has an urge for outdoor activities, head to Foscue Creek National Park, where year–round you can fish, camp, picnic, hike, and boat. Operated by the U.S. Corps of Engineers, the park is 2 miles west of downtown Demopolis, off Maria Street on the lock and dam.

Where to Eat

Faunsdale Ca-John's Grill. *Box 218, Faunsdale 36738; (334) 628–3240; www.ca-johns.com.* East of Demopolis at the intersection of Alabama Highway 25 and U.S. Highway 80, the two combined mercantile stores have exposed brick, plaster walls, scarred wood floors, a pot-bellied stove, and eclectic items (from cattle brands to a Rebel flag) covering walls. Crawfish is a specialty. When traveling with children, dine before 8:00 P.M., when the adjoining lounge starts hopping and the band strikes up. $–$$

Annual Event Faunsdale Ca-John's Grill and the surrounding area are the setting for mid-April's **Alabama Crawfish Festival,** with entertainment and, yes, crawfish.

Jolly Roger's. *135 Yacht Basin Drive, Demopolis 36732; (334) 289–8103.* At Riverview Inn and known for ribs, sandwiches, seafood, and steaks. There's a kids' menu. $–$$

Red Barn. *901 Highway 80 East (Box 39), Demopolis 36732; (334) 289–0595.*

Don't let the outside fool you. Inside there's great food, especially seafood. Children's menu. $–$$

Stables Restaurant. *North Walnut Street, Demopolis 36732; (334) 289–2967.* A family place with a lunch buffet and great catfish. $–$$

Where to Stay

Best Western. *1034 Highway 80 East, Demopolis 36732; (334) 289–5772.* Kids under 12 stay **Free**. $

Days Inn. *1005 Highway 80 East, Demopolis 36732; (334) 289–2500.* Kids under 13 stay **Free**. $

Riverview Inn. *Highway 43 (Box 1024), Demopolis 36732; (334) 289–0690.* Stay at a marina and watch as yachts and pleasure boats dock. $

For More Information

Demopolis Area Chamber of Commerce. *102 East Washington Street (Box 667), Demopolis 36732; (334)*

289–0270; Fax (334) 289–1382; Web site www.chamber.demopolis.al.us.

Selma

Once you reach Selma you may want to put down roots for a couple of days and do some serious exploring.

Selma is a town where two Kings have left their mark. In 1820 Selma (which means "throne" in Greek) was incorporated and given its name by William Rufus King, who later became vice president of the United States. Later, it would be here that Dr. Martin Luther King, Jr., confronted the racist voting regulations of the South. During the Selma-to-Montgomery Voting Rights March in the spring of 1965, the national media was on hand to record "Bloody Sunday," an event that shaped Selma's—and the nation's—direction in the civil rights movement.

A Fullman Adventure

A Fullman Adventure I was in high school 250 miles north of Selma in 1965 when the world turned its attention on this sleepy Southern town.

My classmates and I were stunned by the events on the nightly news when protesters, seeking to draw attention to the voting rights issue, marched from Selma to Montgomery. In a first attempt marchers were trompled by horses and beaten with billy clubs as photographers captured the atrocities on film.

The several hundred people on that failed, first march were joined three weeks later by some 20,000 people and civil rights leader Dr. Martin Luther King, Jr., who led a successful, and carefully guarded, march into the capital.

In Selma, where the march began, there are tangible links to events so significant that the National Park Service has named the stretch of Highway 80 between Montgomery and Selma a National Historic Trail. The highway also has been named a National Scenic Byway and an All-American Road.

NATIONAL VOTING RIGHTS MUSEUM (ages 8 to 12)

1020 Water Avenue, Selma 36701; (334) 418–0800. Open Tuesday through Friday from 9:00 A.M. to 5:00 P.M. and Saturday from 10:00 A.M. to 3:00 P.M. Open other times by appointment. Admission is $4.00 for adults, $2.00 for students, and Free *for children under 6.*

The city's role in the civil rights struggle is remembered in a museum that is not far from the Edmund Pettus Bridge, where people protested on that fateful march. Exhibits look at Reconstruction, women's suffrage, and "Bloody Sunday."

Your children most likely are going to be drawn to the cast footprints of many of those who participated in the Bloody Sunday march, and they're going to be impressed with the handwritten notes attached to a mirrored wall on the left of the museum's front room. Called "I Was There," the wall is splattered with tiny notes scrawled by visitors who have helped to chronicle their roles in the march. In their own handwriting they have recorded memories from that day, which changed the course of the nation.

OLD DEPOT MUSEUM (all ages)

4 Martin Luther King Street, Selma 36702; (334) 874–2197. Open Monday through Saturday from 10:00 A.M. to 4:00 P.M. and other times by appointment. Admission is $4.00 for adults, $3.00 for seniors, $1.00 for students, and Free *for younger children.*

If you've found a good parking spot and want a several-block exercise, you can walk from the museum past the Pettus Bridge to the Old Depot Museum, at the corner of Martin Luther King Street and Water Avenue. Your family will discover an interpretive museum that recalls Selma's history, with displays that include everything from a railroad boxcar to old photographs, a wooden bicycle, silverware, china, a spinning wheel, and a bank's Victorian mahogany cages.

STURDIVANT HALL (ages 8 to 12)

713 Mabry Street, Selma 36701; (334) 872–5626. Open Tuesday through Saturday from 9:00 A.M. to 4:00 P.M. Admission is $5.00 for adults, $2.00 for students.

If you want to look inside a columned and stately mansion, don't miss Sturdivant Hall, a ten-room mansion designed by Robert E. Lee's cousin, Thomas Helm Lee. The house—with a spiral staircase, marble mantels, servant pulls, and period furnishings—has a well-stocked gift shop nestled among the home's back gardens in what was formerly a carriage house. Tours are guided.

LIVE OAK CEMETERY (all ages)

110 West Dallas Avenue, Selma 36701; (334) 875–7241 or (800) 457–3562.

If your family can't resist wonderful old cemeteries, you'll kick yourself if you miss Live Oak Cemetery. Filled with moss-draped trees, the cemetery has graves that are marked with beautifully crafted monuments. It might sound morbid, but if you're a camera nut, you can get some neat shots here, especially if the sun's just right when you visit.

Ghost Woman Former newspaperwoman Kathryn Tucker Windham, now in her eighth decade, is perhaps Selma's most noted celebrity. She claims a ghost, which she has nicknamed Jeffrey, lives with her in the home where she raised her three children after her husband's untimely death. When once asked if the ghost in his mother's house were real or not, her son, Ben, himself a newspaperman, replied, "All I know is that he helped to put three kids through college."

Annual Events Selma has several annual events that draw thousands of visitors:

- On the fourth weekend in March, Selma hosts a **pilgrimage** that showcases its collection of nineteenth-century buildings.

- On the fourth weekend in April, Selma is the setting for a **Reenact-ment of the Battle of Selma,** remembering April 2, 1865, when Union General James Wilson attacked the city, which housed the Confederate Naval Ordnance Works. The outnumbered Confederate troops, led by General Nathan Bedford Forrest, were defeated.

   The four-day event, which is a favorite with families, is one of the country's largest reenactments and includes authentic encampments, nighttime artillery-firing exhibits, and a Saturday-night ball held at Sturdivant Hall. Thousands attend the ball, and all must be in period clothes. (Many of Selma's grand homes were destroyed during the war but speculation is that Sturdivant was spared because Abraham Lincoln's wife's half-sister lived next door.) Even spectators attending the "battle" often are in clothes typical of that era. Look around and you'll see children in tiny Confederate uniforms and women and young girls in hooped skirts. Chat with some of the children and you'll quickly be impressed with how much they know about the battle that was fought a week before Lee surrendered to Grant at Appomattox. You'll find several items for sale, including food and period costumes.

- On the second Friday and Saturday in October, Selma is the setting for a **Tale Tellin' Festival** and **Riverfront Market Day.** Chief among the tellers is local resident and regional ghost watcher Kathryn Tucker Windham, a former newspaper woman. (Her books about ghosts include antics about her own ghost, Jeffrey, who lives in her Selma home.) On Saturday during the festival, Riverfront Market Day is held on downtown's historic Water Street, which is filled with more than 500 vendors selling foods and arts and crafts.

Where to Eat

Hancock's Bar-B-Q. *72 County Road 46 (Highway 22 West), Selma 36701; (334) 872–5541.* Interesting stuff such as fish trophies and old license plates decorate the walls. $

Major Grumbles. *1300 Water Avenue, Selma 36701; (334) 872–2006.* In an old cotton warehouse, with a real skeleton at the front door. $$–$$$

Troup Restaurant at St. James Hotel. *1200 Water Avenue, Selma 36701; (334) 872–3243.* Elegant setting and outstanding food. $$–$$$

Where to Stay

Comfort Inn. *1812 Highway 14 East, Selma 36703; (334) 875–5700.* New in 1999. All 50 rooms have microwaves and minirefrigerators. Eight minisuites, swimming pool, exercise room, and **Free** continental breakfast. $

Jameson Inn. *2420 Broad Street, Selma 36701; (334) 874–8600 or (800) 526–* 3766. Exercise room and swimming pool. $

St. James Hotel. *1200 Water Avenue, Selma 36701; (334) 872–3243.* Old hotel restored with modern amenities, overlooking the river; with **Free** continental breakfast. $–$$$

For More Information

Selma–Dallas County Chamber of Commerce. *513 Lauderdale Street (Drawer D), Selma 36702; (334)* *875–7241 or (800) 457–356;. E-mail: selmacofc@zebra.net; Web site www.olcg.com/selma.*

Cahawba

OLD CAHAWBA ARCHAEOLOGICAL PARK (all ages)

9518 Cahawba Road, Orrville 36767 (mail: Box 289, Selma 36702); (334) 872–8058 or (800) 45–SELMA. Open daily from 8:00 A.M. to 5:00 P.M. and closed on Thanksgiving and December 25. Admission is **Free**.

Nine miles southwest of Selma, Old Cahawba Archaeological Park is the site of the state's first permanent capital. The town is gone—abandoned after floods, yellow fever, and the Civil War took their tolls—but among the moss-covered ruins is a welcome center, which has literature and historical displays of the community's glory days.

Your family can spend hours discovering this ghost town and imagining what stood where. Self-guided brochures and interpretive signs help with the challenge of mentally reconstructing the town.

Behind the visitors center is a hands-on history room designed just for kids. A discovery trunk is filled with items such as child-size Confederate uniforms they can try on. Children also are drawn to the miniature cotton gin and the Spanish coat of arms; the latter resembles what early explorers would have worn when traipsing through Alabama. The site has picnic tables with grills plus loads of grassy fields and wide-open spaces where your youngsters can run, romp, yell, and imagine what must once have been here.

A **nnual Event** Try to be at the Old Cahawba Archeological Park on the second Saturday in May for the annual **Old Cahawba Festival.** It offers music and frog-jumping and greased-pole climbing contests that are favorites with kids.

Monroeville and the Surrounding Area

Not too many small towns can lay claim to a famous author. Imagine the joy in Monroeville, which has dibs on two: native Harper Lee and frequent visitor Truman Capote.

Lee's Pulitzer Prize-winning novel *To Kill a Mockingbird,* since its publication in 1960, has helped to define this south Alabama community. It took thirty years for the tale to return to its roots after it gained international fame by focusing on racism and changing relationships in the Deep South.

Before leaving town be sure to see the historical marker on South Alabama Avenue not far from the courthouse. It notes the location of a now-demolished house where the late author Truman Capote regularly visited relatives and lived for several years. Best known for his book *In Cold Blood,* an account of the murder of a Kansas farm family, his time spent in the South is reflected in his writings.

OUTDOOR DRAMA: *TO KILL A MOCKINGBIRD* (ages 8 to 12)

Monroe County Courthouse; (334) 575–7433. Performed annually on two weekends in May. Tickets for the outdoor drama are $20 and go on sale March 1 (but not a minute sooner). You'll need reservations. In 1999 tickets sold out in a single day.

When the outdoor drama of *To Kill a Mockingbird* was presented in November 1991, it was the first time the tale had been produced in Monroeville. Now the town presents the outdoor drama every May and draws visitors to a tale set in 1935 in a small Southern town much like Monroeville.

The two-part drama unfolds first outside the courthouse, using sets that remain in place year-round. Following the outside scene, cast, crew, and audience move indoors, where the reality of injustice and racism is stark.

The court scene, which ends with a falsely accused black man convicted by an all-white jury, is reminiscent of the era when the tale took place. With no air conditioning in the turn-of-the-century building, the courtroom often gets very hot, so warn your kids what to expect. When people begin fanning themselves, though, it seems much like how things would have been during the fictional trial.

MONROE COUNTY HERITAGE MUSEUM (all ages)
Courthouse Square (Box 1637), Monroeville 36461; (334) 575–7433. Open Monday through Friday from 8:00 A.M. to noon and from 1:00 to 4:00 P.M. and on Saturday from 10:00 A.M. to 2:00 P.M. Closed December 25 through January 1. Admission is Free.

Although the drama is a major draw to Monroeville, the town is worth a visit any time of year. A section of the courthouse includes the Heritage Museum, filled with items detailing the area's history, so you may want to give the collection a look. There's a great gift shop in the courthouse, and you can sometimes find a copy of *To Kill a Mockingbird,* signed by its author.

RIKARD'S MILL (all ages)
Alabama Highway 265, Beatrice 36425; (334) 789–2781 or (334) 575–7433. Open Thursday through Sunday from 11:00 A.M. to sundown, April through mid-December. Admission is $3.00 for adults and $2.00 for seniors and children under 12.

Twenty-three miles north of town, the mill, established in 1845, is a living-history park that includes nineteenth-century gristmilling, black-smithing, cane-syrup making, and agriculture of bygone days. The mill, which locals say is the state's only restored gristmill still standing on its original site, has an official reopening the first Saturday of April, with gristmilling and smithing demon-strations and arts and crafts. The park also

Annual Events Rikard's Mill hosts several annual events including a **FolkFest & BBQ** contest (with Alabama restaurants vying for the title of "Alabama's Best Barbeque Restaurant") on the fourth Saturday of September, a **Civil War Living History Weekend** on the last weekend in October, and **Cane Syrup Makin' Days** on the second Saturday of November.

has a covered bridge, gift shop, nature trail, and carriage house.

CLAUDE D. KELLEY STATE PARK (all ages)

580 H. Kyle Road, Atmore 36502; (334) 862–2511; www.vten.com. Open daily from 7:00 A.M. to sunset. Park admission is $1.00 for adults, 50 cents for seniors 62+ and children 6 to 11, and **Free** *to children under 5. Cabin rental is $41.60; paddleboat rental is $4.00 per hour; boat and canoe rental $7.50 for all day or $5.00 for four hours. Overnight campers may rent boats for $5.00 for twenty-four hours.*

Ten miles north of Interstate 65 not far from the Atmore exit, the park has one cabin (with others planned), picnic grounds (first-come-first-serve unless they are reserved for $15.00), primitive camping ($6.24 per night), a refreshment center, rental boats, and a twenty-five-acre lake where your family can fish, swim, and pedal boats. The lake in the summer of 1998 yielded two record 13-pound bass.

Where to Shop

Vanity Fair Outlet. *900 Drewry Road, Monroeville 35460; (334) 575–2330. Open Monday through Saturday from 9:00 A.M. to 6:00 P.M. and Sunday from noon to 5:30 P.M. You'll find Vanity Fair, Healthtex and Lee and pay half of the ticket price.*

Where to Eat

David's Catfish. *Highway 84 East, Monroeville 36460; (334) 575–3460. Great catfish. $$*

Java Hut. *54 East Claiborne, Monroeville 36460; (334) 575–2983. Small but good, with lunch sandwiches and salads plus great pastries. Works by local artists on walls. $*

Mel's Dairy Dream. *263 South Alabama Avenue, Monroeville 36460; (334) 743–2843. On site of Harper Lee's childhood home and known for great ice (no kidding!). $*

Radley's Deli. *1616 South Alabama Avenue, Monroeville 36460; (334) 575–3354. Cozy and popular spot, with sandwiches, soup, burgers, pizza, and dinner menu. Closed Sundays. $-$$*

Sweet Tooth Bakery. *105 West Claiborne, Monroeville 36460; (334) 575–7040. Old South cooking and daily lunch buffet. $*

Alabama's Flag The state flag, adopted in 1895, bears a crimson cross on a white field. The flag's cross is suggestive of the Confederate battle flag.

Where to Stay

Best Western Inn. *4419 South Alabama Avenue, Monroeville 36460; (334) 575–9999 or (800) 528–1234. Swimming pool. $–$$*

Budget Inn. *605 South Alabama Avenue, Monroeville 36460; (334) 575–3101. Very affordable. $*

Days Inn of Monroeville. *4389 South Alabama Avenue, Monroeville 36460; (334) 743–3297 or (800) 329–7466. Nonsmoking rooms. $–$$*

For More Information

Monroeville Area Chamber of Commerce. *Alabama Avenue, Old Courthouse Square (Box 214), Monroeville 36461; (334) 743–2879;*

Fax (334) 575–7934; E-mail monroeco@frontiernet.net; Web site www.frontiernet.net/~monroeco or www.tokillamockingbird.com.

Chickasaw

You're in for a treat in the tiny community of Chickasaw, where boat captain Gene Burrell daily glides through the swamps north of Mobile.

 WILDLAND EXPEDITIONS SWAMP TOURS (all ages)
Chickasaw Creek Marina, Alabama Highway 43, Chickasaw (mail: 7536 Tung Avenue, Theodore 36582); (334) 460–8206. Tours are daily, except Monday, at 8:00 and 10:00 A.M. and 2:00 P.M. Closed December 15 through January 31. Cost is $20 for adults and $12 for children under 13.

Your crew surely will be mesmerized as Captain Gene Burrell stops his boat from time to time to tell about this wild world, which seems to fit him better than a suit and tie fit many men.

As his self-designed boat crawls through the south Alabama swamp, the captain occasionally will silence the engine and challenge you to listen. You might hear birds or crickets and the distant wail of a passing train.

Even if you don't know an iota about nature, Burrell and his insatiable curiosity make it possible for you to explore one of America's most diverse wildlands and the nation's largest inland delta.

Trips typically run two to two and a half hours and cover from 20 to 26 miles. Midway in the tour the boat returns to the marina, so you get a quick break for a cold drink or the rest rooms.

To reach Chickasaw Creek Marina, take exit 13 off Interstate 65 and drive 2 miles east to Highway 43. Go south about one-half mile to the marina.

Mobile

Mobile is different from other Alabama towns. It's moss-draped trees and long history have given rise to many of the area's attractions, which families find enticing.

You will find here something to match the interests of everyone in your clan: a retired battleship, a hands-on science center, restored forts, and antebellum homes. About the only problem your family will have is deciding where to begin.

FORT CONDE MOBILE VISITOR WELCOME CENTER (all ages)

150 South Royal Street, Mobile 36602; (334) 434–7304; Fax (334) 208–7659. Open daily from 8:00 A.M. to 5:00 P.M. Closed Mardi Gras and December 25. Admission is **Free**.

To get an overview you should begin your Mobile trip with a stop at Fort Conde, a restored fort that presently serves as the city's official welcome center. The fort leaves no doubt that Mobile is one of the nation's oldest cities. (Mobile dates back to the early 1700s, when the site's original fort was headquarters for the French Louisiana Territory.) At Fort Conde, with its low-slung doors and thick walls, you'll see replicas of eighteenth-century French cannons and muskets, which are demonstrated by guides dressed like French soldiers of the era. The center has displays of artifacts excavated from the fort, which was occupied during much of the 1700s. Partially reconstructed, the fort now is the place to find brochures, information, and answers. Ask one of the costumed interpreters if he will fire his musket—then hold your ears as you await a deafening boom.

Armed with brochures and advice gathered at the visitors center, begin your Mobile explorations with a trek downtown.

MUSEUM OF THE CITY OF MOBILE (all ages)

355 Government Street, Mobile 36602; (334) 208–7569. Open Tuesday through Saturday from 10:00 A.M. to 5:00 P.M. and Sunday from 1:00 to 5:00 P.M. The museum is closed on major holidays. Admission is **Free**.

A downtown must-see is the Museum of the City of Mobile, where children are drawn to the collection of Mardi Gras costumes. Among the items detailing the city's past are Civil War exhibits and antique carriages, another favorite with youngsters.

PHOENIX FIRE STATION (all ages)

203 South Claiborne Street, Mobile 36602; (334) 208–7554. Open Tuesday through Saturday from 10:00 A.M. to 5:00 P.M. and Sunday from 1:00 to 5:00 P.M. Closed major holidays. Admission is Free.

It's a safe bet your family is going to love the Phoenix Fire Station. With turn-of-the-century steam engines, fire-fighting equipment, tools, and keepsakes of the men who at one time fought the city's fires, the museum is always a hit with kids. Besides, who wouldn't love a bright-red fire truck?

OAKLEIGH PERIOD HOUSE MUSEUM (ages 8 to 12)

350 Oakleigh Place, Mobile 36604; (334) 432–1281. Open Monday through Saturday from 10:00 A.M. to 4:00 P.M., with each day's final tour beginning at 3:30 P.M. Admission is $5.00.

Mobile is blessed with wonderful old homes, many of which your family can tour. If seeing inside appeals to your crew, then you're in for a treat. Five minutes from downtown is Oakleigh Period House Museum, the city's official period house museum that dates back to 1833. Here former President Garfield sipped his first mint julep.

nnual Mobile Events

- If you think Mardi Gras was born in New Orleans, ask around and you'll learn that Mobile has celebrated the occasion longer than any other U.S. city. **Mardi Gras** is a two-week celebration with parades and fun that draw thousands of families to a mid-winter revelry.

- On the second Friday and Saturday in March, Mobile hosts **Home Tours,** which give you a chance to look inside some of the stately historic homes not normally open to the public.

- On the first weekend in December, Mobile's Oakleigh is the setting for a **Candlelight Tour.** Local boys, dressed as the Mobile Rifle Company, pay tribute to the young daughter of the house's former owner.

RICHARDS-DAR HOUSE MUSEUM (ages 8 to 12)

256 Joachim Street, Mobile 36603; (334) 208–7320. Open Tuesday through Saturday from 10:00 A.M. to 4:00 P.M. and Sunday from 1:00 to 4:00 P.M. Admission is $4.00 for adults, $1.00 for children 6 to 12, and **Free** *to younger children.*

Mobile's most significant example of Italianate style may be best remembered by your kids as the one with several portraits of young children and the tea and goodies served in the gift shop.

You also may want to see the Conde-Charlotte House (105 Theatre Street) and the Bragg-Mitchell Mansion (1906 Spring Hill Avenue). You can save on house admission costs by buying combination tickets, available at any of the houses.

GULF COAST EXPLOREUM OF SCIENCE (all ages)

65 Government Street, Mobile 36602; (334) 208–6873 or (877) 625–4386. From June through August, open Sunday through Thursday from 9:00 A.M. to 8:00 P.M. and Friday and Saturday 9:00 A.M. to 9:00 P.M. From September through May, hours are Sunday through Thursday from 9:00 A.M. to 5:00 P.M. and Friday and Saturday from 9:00 A.M. to 9:00 P.M. Admission is $6.50 for adults and $5.50 for children ages 13 through 17 and seniors 60+; $4.00 for children under 13. IMAX tickets are separate. Save with combination tickets.

If your kids tolerated your insatiable desire to look inside old houses, then you owe them time at The Exploreum, across from the Mobile Convention Center. The center is a total sensory immersion, hands-on science museum and the place to touch, smell, magnify, build, and explore. Great movies are shown in the IMAX theater. Don't be surprised if your children don't know where first to head.

USS *ALABAMA* BATTLESHIP MEMORIAL PARK (ages 5 to 12)

2703 Battleship Parkway (off Interstate 10), Mobile 36601; (334) 433–2703 or (800) 426–4929. Open daily from 8:00 A.M. until sunset. Closed December 25. Admission is $8.00 for adults, $2.00 for seniors 55+, $4.00 for children ages 6 to 11, and **Free** *to younger children.*

Have a future sailor with you or maybe a retired one? Then don't miss this one hundred-acre site 1 mile east of Mobile. The decommissioned battleship, which was launched in 1942, may be your children's favorite part of a Mobile visit. Go inside the ship to see boiler rooms, a sickbay, lockers, the kitchen and mess, and bunkrooms. And, yes, you can crawl onto a bunk. (It's actually a pretty neat place to take a picture.) Nothing's really off-limits at the ship, a winding maze of corridors and rooms. This is not the place for the weary. Also, because there is so much to cover, be careful to keep your family together or you may be calling a "man lost on board" alert. Before you descend into the ship, it would be a good idea to designate a rendezvous point should you get separated.

Adjacent to the battleship are military aircraft and equipment, hundreds of varieties of roses, a boardwalk, and a two-story observation deck with a view of the wetlands. It's also not every day you can go through a submarine, so be sure you save time for your family to explore the USS *Drum*. Topside at the submarine, your children can man a gun and imagine for a moment the intensity of fighting at sea.

 ### MOBILE BOTANICAL GARDENS (ages 8 to 12)
Pat Ryan Drive (Mobile Municipal Park, Box 8382, Mobile 36608); (334) 342–0555. Open daily from dawn to dusk. Admission is **Free**.

Nature lovers in your family won't want to miss the sixty-four-acre Mobile Botanical Gardens. Even those not smitten with flowers will enjoy the walking trails. For the physically challenged there is a texture-and-fragrance garden.

 ### FORT MORGAN STATE HISTORIC SITE (all ages)
51 Alabama Highway 180 West, Gulf Shores 36542; (334) 540–7125; Fax (334) 540–7665. Fort opens weekdays at 8:00 A.M. and closes 5:00 P.M. in winter and 6:00 P.M. in spring and summer. Hours on Saturday and Sunday are from 9:00 A.M. to 5:00 P.M. Museum is open daily from 9:00 A.M. to 5:00 P.M. Closed on major holidays. Admission is $3.00 for adults, $1.00 for children 6 to 12, and **Free** *for children under 6.*

This fort's the place to run, romp, and learn about history. Even with your gang's whooping and hollering, it will be far quieter than it was on the morning of August 5, 1864, when Union Admiral David Farragut, stung by the sinking of the *Tecumseh* and undeterred by underwater mines strung across the channel, yelled words still remembered: "Damn the torpedoes; full speed ahead!" He then led his fleet to victory in the Battle of Mobile, eliminating the Confederacy's final gulf stronghold.

Your children will want to spend time atop the ramparts and beneath the archways of Fort Morgan, whose star-shaped structure—built with more than seven million bricks—remains relatively intact. Your kids are going to love exploring the fort's low-ceilinged dank rooms and topside vantage point that still has cannons aimed toward sea and any would-be enemy.

Although most of the fun is outdoors, don't miss the visitors center, with exhibits covering military history from the fort's early years through World War II. Especially poignant are the letters and poems written by soldiers on both sides during the Civil War.

FORT GAINES (all ages)

51 Bienville Boulevard (Box 97), Dauphin Island 36528; (334) 861–6992. Open daily from 9:00 A.M. to 5:00 P.M., with closing at 6:00 P.M. during summer. Admission is $3.00 for adults, $1.00 for children 5 to 12, and Free *for children under 4.*

After seeing Fort Morgan board the Mobile Bay Ferry (334-540-7787). The thirty-minute trip to Fort Gaines will give you a coastal glimpse of the gulf. (Ferry schedules vary by season and prices are subject to change, so call before going.)

As the salt water sprays your face, look ahead to Fort Gaines, a brick fortress standing guard at the western approach to Mobile Bay on Dauphin Island. Here several dozen Confederate soldiers were killed or wounded during the 114-hour barrage by Farragut's forces, who overtook both forts. Take time to roam the grounds and explore vaulted tunnels and bastions where Civil War cannons remain.

Annual Events Throughout the year **Civil War Reenactments** and other tributes are held at the forts. On a July weekend, Fort Gaines is the site of a reenactment of life at the fort in the years before the Union gained control. A Saturday-night tour takes you through a fort lighted only by lanterns and candles. Other reenactments take place in August and October.

ESTUARIUM AT THE DAUPHIN ISLAND SEALAB (all ages)

101 Bienville Boulevard (mail: Box 369–370, Dauphin Island 36528); (334) 861–7500; Fax (334) 861–4646. Open Monday through Saturday from 9:00 A.M. to 5:00 P.M. and Sunday from 1:00 to 5:00 P.M. Admission is $6.00 for adults, $3.00 for children 5 to 18, and $5.00 for seniors. Children under 5, Free. *Take exit 17-A off Interstate 10.*

Local habitats of Mobile's estuary, delta, bay, barrier islands, and Gulf of Mexico are highlighted with visual displays and interactive exhibits. It's a fun place built with kids in mind.

PUNTA CLARA'S CANDY KITCHEN (all ages)

17111 Scenic U.S. Highway 98 (Drawer 49), Point Clear 36564; (334) 928–8477. Open Monday through Saturday from 9:00 A.M. to 5:00 P.M. and Sunday from 12:30 to 5:00 P.M. Admission is **Free***.*

Journey from Mobile to Point Clear for a shopping spree to Punta Clara's Candy Kitchen. Housed in an 1897 Victorian home known as Miss Colleen's house, the business has been family operated for more than thirty-five years. Look for exquisite candies, preserves, and other specialties. You can watch candy being made, browse through the gift shop, or amble down the hallway to see several roped-off rooms furnished in the once-popular cluttered style. (Maybe that's the look your kids have been trying to bring back.) Don't take a calorie counter with you when you visit.

HISTORIC BLAKELEY PARK (all ages)

33707 U.S. Highway 225, Spanish Fort 36527 (Box 7279, Spanish Fort 36577); (334) 580–0005; E-mail blakeley@dibbs.net; Web site www.siteone.com/tourist/blakeley/index.html. Open daily at 9:00 A.M. with closing at dusk. Admission is $2.00 for adults; $1.50 for children 6 to 12, and **Free** *to younger children. Screened shelters rent for $23 nightly.*

While you're in the vicinity, save time for a visit to nearby Spanish Fort, east of Mobile. In the past a thriving riverfront town, Blakeley played a dominant role in early Alabama history. In time, though, yellow-fever epidemics and greed eradicated the once-booming town. The last major battle of the Civil War was fought in Blakeley, ending the same day that General Robert E. Lee surrendered at Appomattox.

Despite its sorrowful early years, the 3,800 acres are the place for families in search of primitive camping, hiking trails, picnic areas, and a fishing wharf.

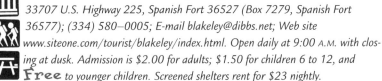

A Fullman Family Adventure On a chilly morning when first we visited Historic Blakeley Park, children raced up and down ripples of earth as their voices of merriment echoed and bounced off towering pine trees. As their parents looked on, the girls scaled what had been Union rifle pits. In that moment it seemed ironic to us that a place where battles had been fought had become a place of tranquility, with walking trails and picnic tables. As gunshots once rang out, who could have imagined that this same land one day would offer a peace not afforded the soldiers who had battled here.

If you don't need a lot of creature comforts, stay overnight in one of the park's two "squirrels' nests," which have two screened sides and a deck, but no plumbing or electricity. Two shelters share an outhouse and are furnished with futons, a bar with stools, and a deck with table and chairs. It's a great way to feel at one with nature.

Where to Eat

Dreamland Bar-B-Que. *3314 Old Shell Road, Mobile 36607; (334) 479–9898.* World-famous ribs begun by "Big Daddy" Bishop. Limited menu but ideal for rib lovers. $

Mayme's. *359 Church Street, Mobile 36602; (334) 438–4701.* In old carriage house connected to Malaga Inn. Brick floors, cloth-covered tables, outstanding seafood. $$–$$$

Roussos. *166 South Royal Street, Mobile 36602; (334) 433–3322.* Nautical treasures and old photos decorate the walls in this family-run business that has been named a Mobile attraction. $–$$$$

Sadie's Buffet. *3787 Airport Boulevard, Mobile 30337; (334) 460–0297 or (800) 345–5134.* Affordable family dining with loads of choices. $

Where to Stay

Adam's Mark. *64 South Water Street, Mobile 36602; (334) 438–4000; Fax (334) 415–3060.* Waterfront high rise connects with Mobile Convention Center. Hot tub, exercise room, swimming pool, convenience to downtown attractions. $–$$$

Hampton Inn. *930 South Beltline Highway, Mobile 36609; (334) 344–4942.* Free continental breakfast and Free use of crib. $

Holiday Inn Express/Historic District. *301 Government Street, Mobile 36602; (334) 694–0100 or (800) 692–6662; Fax (334) 694–0160.* Some rooms with kitchenettes. Convenient to downtown sites. $

La Quinta Inn. *816 South Beltline Highway, Mobile 36609–1302; (334) 343–4051 or (800) NU–ROOMS; www.laquinta.com.* You'll find upscale amenities not typically found at mid-priced hotels. Your kids will like the 25-inch televisions with Nintendo game systems, and you'll like the in-room coffee- maker, Free local telephone calls, and Free "First Light" breakfast. Children under 18 stay Free with parents. $

Malaga Inn. *359 Church Street, Mobile 36602; (334) 438–4701.* Lots of atmosphere in now-connected twin homes dating from 1862. Restaurant, swimming pool, patios/balconies, 39 guest rooms. $–$$

Marriott's Grand Hotel. *Scenic High-way 98, Point Clear 36564; (334) 928–9 201 or (800) 544–9933; Fax (334) 928–1149.* Beneath moss-draped oaks and sprawling magnolias, the site at one time was a gathering place for antebellum Southern society. Mostly rebuilt, the property now offers hiking/jogging trails, a swimming pool, and horseback riding. Children's pro-gram includes croquet, kickball, soft-ball, miniature golf, nature hikes, story times, sand-castle building, beach and other outdoor games, swimming, pool games, volleyball, movies, cartoons, musical chairs, fishing, relays, arts and crafts, scavenger hunts, and duck feed-ing. Campers get snacks and meals. $$–$$$

Radisson Admiral Semmes. *251 Government Street, Mobile 36602; (334) 432–8000 or (800) 333–3333; Fax (334) 405–5942.* Restored landmark. Some rooms have minirefrigerators. Some suites. Convenient to Exploreum. $$–$$$

For More Information

Mobile Convention and Visitors Corporation. *One South Water Street, Mobile 36602; (334) 208–2000 or (800) 566–2453; Fax (334) 208–2060; E-mail info@mobile.org; Web site www. mobile.org.*

Theodore

 BELLINGRATH GARDENS AND HOME (all ages)
12401 Bellingrath Road, Theodore 36582; (334) 973–2217 or (800) 247–8420; Web site www.bellingrath.org; E-mail bellingrath@juno.com. Gardens open daily at 8:00 A.M. and close at dusk. Tickets range from $7.50 to $18.00, depend-ing on a package for home and garden tours and boat rides.

If your family is in search of beautiful gardens and abundant color, head to Bellingrath Gardens, where something always is in bloom. The gardens sprawl across sixty-five landscaped acres nestled in a semitropical forest. Overflowing with flowers, trees, and birds, the gardens have been described by *American Garden Guidebook* as "perhaps the most beautiful garden in the Southeastern United States and one of America's top five."

You should begin your garden tour by looking at exhibits in the wel-come area, then head down a path across a pedestrian bridge overlook-ing a sprawling rose garden. Next you'll see the Oriental area, complete with teahouse, red bridges, and an abundance of resident waterfowl. Outlined by seasonal bloomings, the walkway directs you to Mirror Lake. Be sure to have your camera ready for this segment of the gardens. Don't go dashing too fast or you might miss seeing the sculptures, reflecting pools, waterfowl, winding paths, wrought-iron bridges, waterfalls, lily pads, and singing birds.

In 1918 Walter Bellingrath (who helped introduce Coca-Cola to a thirsty South) and his wife, Bessie, bought this riverfront land to use as a fishing camp. Inspired by travels in Europe, Mrs. Bellingrath busied herself transforming the site. Interest from the public was intense, prompting the couple in 1932 to open their gardens to the public. When they did, response was so heavy that police were needed to control traffic.

Five years after the gardens opened, the couple built a riverbluff home of old brick and trimmed it with antebellum wrought iron. Highlighting the formal gardens, the house, listed on the National Register of Historic Places, was opened to the public after the owners' deaths in the 1950s.

If you go inside the house, look around at the Bellingraths' fine antique furniture, Oriental rugs, silver, china, and what is considered the world's largest public display of Boehm porcelain.

Only recently have visitors had the chance to view the gardens from the *Southern Belle* riverboat (334-973-1244), which offers a narrated forty-five-minute cruise on the Fowl River. The boat leaves from a dock at the house, then glides through an estuary of the river before passing wildlife and vegetation such as delta grasses, cypress, and southern pine. The boat also offers dinner cruises, which are a relaxing way to enjoy the river. Nine years before building his mansion, Bellingrath promised his mother that he intended "to make the world better and brighter by my being here." Ask your children if they think the son honored his promise.

Plan to spend at least ninety minutes touring the gardens. Guided tours of the home take from thirty to forty minutes.

A Fullman Family Adventure I can barely drag Milton away from Bellingrath Gardens. When he's there, his cameras snap frame after frame then almost sing as film is rewound. In these gardens something always is blooming, and no matter what the season, he finds something to shoot. Reds and pinks and greens and yellows seem to burst from the earth—and he loves few things better than capturing the explosions on film. Walter Bellingrath probably would have been pleased to know just how many people feel the same way about this flowering little corner of the world.

Where to Eat

The Magnolia Cafe. *12401 Bellingrath Road, Theodore 36582; (334) 973–2217 or (800) 247–8420.* Adjacent to the gardens' gift shop. The menu offers soup, salad, and sandwiches year-round and adds a hot entree and veggies in the spring. $

Gulf Shores and Orange Beach

Of all the cities in Alabama, the coastal towns of Gulf Shores and Orange Beach have the largest concentration of places that kids can play. Amusement parks, miniature golf, and playgrounds abound. But your first surprise may be that the state has 32 miles of such beautiful beaches.

The state's coastline offers plenty to do besides tan, fish, build sand castles, and swim (although these aren't bad choices). There are places for those who love nature or the outdoors, or for those wanting to ride thrill rides, play miniature golf, sail the high seas, or do nothing at all.

If it's fishing you want, you can wet your line from the shore or take a full- or half-day charter-fishing trip into the deep blue sea. Some of the country's best fishing happens in Gulf Shores and Orange Beach. You can take part even if you're skittish about baiting a line; the crew might actually do it for you aboard a chartered fishing boat. The captains here know where the fish bite and how to show a novice a good time. When you take to the waters, pack some sunscreen and, if it's fall or spring, maybe even a jacket because the winds can turn chilly.

Your family might prefer to stick to shore, work on a tan, or go bicycling or moped riding. Maybe they'd like to take a helicopter ride and get a whole new perspective on the beaches.

In this town where the weather is pleasant almost all year, there are all kinds of neat things that kids love doing.

GULF STATE PARK (all ages)

20115 Alabama Highway 135, Gulf Shores 36542; (334) 948–7275 or (800) ALA–PARK. No general admission. Costs for using picnic and swimming facilities are $1.00 for adults, 50 cents for children 6 to 12, and Free *for younger children. Beach-pavilion access is $2.00 per car. Camping typically costs from $120 to $125. Greens fees, with cart, are $36 Monday through Thursday and $40 on Friday, Saturday, and Sunday. Cabin rentals, depending on the season, range from $55 to $109.*

For three years running the 6,000-plus-acre facility received *Family Circle*'s prestigious Family Resort of the Year Award. You'll find here more than 2 miles of beach and a long pier jutting into the gulf, a great place for fishing. There also are campsites, picnic areas, and boat ramps. Your family could spend your entire vacation here at one of Alabama's most popular state parks.

ZOOLAND ANIMAL PARK (all ages)

1204 Highway 59 South, Gulf Shores 36542; (334) 968–5731. Open daily at 9:00 A.M. Closes 4:00 P.M. except June through August, when closing is at 5:00 P.M. Park admission is $7.00 for adults, $5.00 for seniors 55+, $4.50 for children 3 to 11, and Free *for younger children.*

Your children will want to spend hours playing miniature golf or having an up-close wilderness adventure at Zooland Animal Park. The sixteen-acre park has exotic animals, including alligators and zebras, that you can see in their natural habitats. Don't miss the petting zoo, either. After you've seen animals, which number more than 250, you'll want to play a round or two at the animal-themed miniature golf course. It is a welcome escape from the beating sun, since you can play beneath the cool shade of towering oak trees.

WATERVILLE, USA (all ages)

906 Gulf Shores Parkway (Box 1017, Gulf Shores 36547), Gulf Shores 36542; (334) 948–2106; www.waterville.com. Water park is open Memorial Day through Labor Day. Amusement park is open spring through Thanksgiving. Water-park hours are 10:00 A.M. to 6:00 P.M. Amusement-park hours are from 10:00 A.M. to midnight. Minimum height requirements apply to some rides. Water park admission is $18.00 for anyone over 42 inches tall; $9.00 for those under 42 inches, and Free *to children under 2 years old. No general admission to amusement park. Instead, pay for what you ride, with most rides $3.00 to $6.00. Ejection-seat ride is $25 per person or $40 for two in one seat.*

Here's a guaranteed day of fun with a freshwater wave pool, raft rides, tube rides, and two eighteen-hole golf courses. Your children are going to love zooming in the Nascarts racers, riding the cannonball roller coaster, playing laser-storm tag, and maybe even dropping some coins in what Waterville calls the largest game arcade on the coast. An ejection-seat ride, not for the faint of heart, soars riders 150 feet into the air in 1.5 seconds.

S**hrimp Festival** On the second weekend in October, Gulf Shores hosts the **National Shrimp Festival,** which has been called the biggest beach party of the year. You'll find shrimp served all kinds of ways, plus music, and arts and crafts.

THE TRACK RECREATION CENTER (all ages)

3200 Gulf Shores Parkway, Gulf Shores 36542; (334) 968–8111. Open daily (except December 25) at 10:00 A.M. and closes "when the last person leaves." No general admission. Pay as you ride. Go-carts are $5.00; kiddie rides are $2.50; bungee jump is $15.00; sky coaster is $20.00; miniature golf is $2.50 for ages 4 to 7 and $5.00 for older players. Ask about ride packages to save.

This family fun center has four go-cart tracks, bumper boats, Kids Kountry, a 5,000-square-foot arcade, a skycoaster, thrill rides, bungee jumping, and a miniature golf course.

PIRATE'S ISLAND ADVENTURE GOLF (all ages)

3201 Gulf Shores Parkway, Gulf Shores 36542 (Box 2490, Gulf Shores 36547); (334) 968–GOLF. Summer hours are from 9:00 A.M. to 10:00 P.M. Hours November through February are 10:00 A.M. to 5:00 P.M.; other months, 9:00 A.M. to 8:00 P.M. (It's best to call ahead to confirm hours.) Playing the Lafitte course costs $5.00 for adults, $4.00 for children 4 to 10, and $\mathbf{Free}$ for children under 3 with a paying adult. To play the more challenging Blackbeard Course is $6.00 for adults and $5.00 for children. You can save by playing both courses; the two-course cost is $8.50 for adults and $7.00 for children.

Putt around historical markers of Jean Lafitte and Blackbeard on two eighteen-hole courses, and your family will enjoy the tropical trees and flowers, waterfalls, caves, and pirate ships.

ADVENTURE ISLAND (all ages)

24559 Perdido Beach Boulevard, Orange Beach 36561; (334) 974–1500. Open daily 10:00 A.M. to 10:00 P.M. except in summer, when hours are from 9:00 A.M. until midnight. Pay per ride, mostly $5.00 to $5.50 each.

Adventure Island has a go-cart track, an arcade plus laser tag, paddleboats, miniature golf, children's rides, and double carts so that small children may ride with their parents.

FUN MARINA/ALABAMA PARASAIL (all ages)

Highway 182 East, Orange Beach 36561; (334) 980–5122 or (334) 981–8877. Open daily from 10:00 A.M. to 5:00 P.M., with closing at 6:00 P.M. in summer months. Parasailing, which begins daily at 10:00 A.M., costs $45 to go 400 feet high (about ten minutes) to $70 to go 1,200 feet high (about twelve minutes). Pontoon boats rent for $95 for two hours or $150 for four hours. Runabouts rent for $85 for two hours or $140 for four hours.

If your family is looking for more to do, this is the place to rent personal water craft, pontoons, and runabouts. Or launch from the back of a boat and try parasailing.

BON SECOUR NATIONAL WILDLIFE REFUGE (all ages)

12295 Alabama Highway 180, Gulf Shores 36542; (334) 540–7720. Trails are open daily during daylights hours. Museum open Monday through Friday from 8:00 A.M. to 4:00 P.M. **Free** *admission.*

If your family wants to find Mother Nature, visit Bon Secour National Wildlife Refuge, which has more than 2 miles of beachfront accessible by nature trails. Six miles west of Gulf Shores, this wildlife oasis is where you can freshwater and saltwater fish and hike trails. You can see pelicans, bobcats, and alligators year-round at the park. And in mid-April you can see the arrival of migratory songbirds.

*B*irds, Lots Of Birds Dauphin Island is one of the major paths traveled each spring and fall by thousands of neotropical migratory birds.

Where to Shop

Riviera Centre. *2601 U.S. Highway 59, Foley 36535; (334) 943–8888 or (888) SHOP333 (for brochure). Open Monday through Friday from 10:00 A.M. to 9:00 P.M. and Sunday from 11:00 A.M. to 6:00 P.M.*

For shoppers, this place is paradise, with more than 120 outlet stores selling brand names such as Nike, Mikasa, Coach, and Polo/Ralph Lauren.

Alvin's Island. *24949 Perdido Beach Boulevard, Orange Beach 36561; (334) 974–1123 and 100 West Beach Boulevard, Gulf Shores 36542; (334) 948–3121.* You'll find two locations and could probably shop until you drop as you rifle through choices you likely won't spot at home.

Souvenir City. *Gulf Shores Parkway, Gulf Shores 36542; (334) 948–7280.* Have your picture made in the shark's mouth; then shop for everything from T-shirts to hermit crabs.

Teeing Off

Teeing Off If you want to play grown-up golf, the only problem is deciding where to tee off. There are more than a dozen courses within a forty-five-minute drive of the coast. One of the most noted is Craft Farms (334-968-7500 or 800-327-2657), 3840 Cotton Creek Drive, where golf great Arnold Palmer has said, "Any player, no matter what their handicap is, will have fun on this course."

Where to Eat

Bayside Grill. *Canal Road, Orange Beach 36561; (334) 981–4899.* Adjacent to beautiful Sportsman Marina. Award-winning Creole and Caribbean food. Great menu for children. Dine inside or out. Enjoy the boats. $$

Calypso Fish Grille & Market. *At Orange Beach Marina, Marina Road, Orange Beach 36561; (334) 981–1415.* Very casual with Caribbean cuisine. Kids eat 𝐅𝐫𝐞𝐞 on Tuesday night. Fun place with five TVs and exciting Hermit Crab Races. $$

Fish Camp Restaurant. *4297 County Road 6, Gulf Shores 36547; (334) 968–2267.* Fresh local seafood, catfish, po' boys, bottomless salad. Casual dining on the water. Kids' menu. $$

Hazel's Family Restaurant. *Highway 182, Orange Beach 36561; (334) 981–4628.* Family restaurant with rea-sonable prices and traditional home-cooked food. Kids buffet for breakfast, lunch, dinner. Kids 3 and under eat 𝐅𝐫𝐞𝐞. $

King Neptune's. *1137 Gulf Shores Parkway, Gulf Shores 36452; (334) 968–5464.* More than twenty seafood meals for less than $10. Specializing in delicious Gulf Coast seafood. Kids' menu. $

Original Oyster House. *Bayou Village Shopping Center, Gulf Shores Parkway, Gulf Shores 36542; (334) 948–2445.* Dine on the bayou and look for alligators. Great seafood. Kids' menu. Their motto is "We love kids." Shop after you dine. $$

Sea-n-Suds. *405 East Beach Boulevard, Gulf Shores 36542; (334) 948–7894.* Overlooks the gulf. Family dining specializing in seafood. Hot dogs, hamburgers, and grilled cheese, too. Watch the dolphins play. $

Where to Stay

(Note: Along the coast rates vary greatly by seasons, with the best prices during winter. Rates are moderate in fall and spring and peak, often doubling, from Memorial Day to Labor Day.)

Gulf State Park Resort Hotel. *20115 Alabama Highway 135 (Box 437), Gulf Shores 36547; (334) 948–4853 or (800) ALA–PARK.* Basic rooms have two double beds and are on the beach. Ask about vacation packages, typically available all months except summer. $-$$

Gulf Shores Plantation. *Highway 180 West (Fort Morgan Road), Gulf Shores 36542; (800) 554–0344.* Wide, secluded beach. Six gulf-side pools, heated indoor pool, lighted tennis courts, beach-volleyball courts, and game rooms. Jet-ski, catamaran, and aqua-cycle rentals available. $$-$$$

Hilton Garden Inn. *23092 Perdido Beach Boulevard, Orange Beach 36561; (334) 974–1600 or (888) 644–5866.* In-room coffeemakers, microwaves, and minirefrigerators. On the beach. Swimming pool. $-$$$

Holiday Inn Express. *24700 Perdido Beach Boulevard, Orange Beach 36561; (334) 974–1634.* In-room coffee makers and microwaves. On the beach, with swimming pool and great off-season rates. $-$$$

The Island House Hotel. *26650 Perdido Beach Boulevard, Orange Beach 36561; (800) 264–2642.* Rooms face the gulf. Outdoor pool with adjacent kiddie pool. On-site laundry facilities, beach volleyball, game room, boogie-board rentals, and poolside cookouts on the weekend. Kid-friendly. $$-$$$

A Fullman Family Adventure One of the tree-shaded trails at Bon Secour leads to Gator Lake, where a tiny, two-person boat is tied to a tree and available to anyone who wants to forge into the water. When we were there, I thought it would be fun to venture into alligator land, and Milton went along with my idea.

As we glided in the tiny boat, I realized for the first time that Milton never had canoed. Frustrated by going in circles, I urged him to take pictures and to leave the paddling to me. With camera in hand he spotted an alligator yards and yards away and requested that I paddle him there for a great shot. (I don't think he realized I cannot produce the same power as an outboard motor.) Once we laughed so hard at ourselves that we thought the boat would tip over. As several 'gators slid past, it was not a good thought. I don't know about Milton, but I was sure happy to get back and tie that boat back up.

The Lighthouse Resort. *462 East Beach Boulevard, Gulf Shores 36542; (334) 948–6188.* Apartments with fully equipped kitchens, three swimming pools, one of which is indoor and heated. Private beach. $–$$$

Microtel. *Highway 59, Gulf Shores 36542; (334) 967–3000 or (800) 771–7171.* Trade beach view for very affordable rates. Only 2 miles from the beach and very nice, with an outdoor pool and putting green. $

Phoenix Condominiums I–IV. *24132 Perdido Beach Boulevard, Orange Beach 36561; (800) 221–0258.* Equipped kitchens, washer/dryer, indoor and outdoor pools, hot tubs, tennis and racquetball courts, video-game rooms, and fitness rooms. On the beach. $$–$$$

Windemere Condominiums. *23010 Perdido Beach Boulevard, Orange Beach 36561; (888) 974–1120.* On the gulf, with one- and two-bedroom condos, each with washer, dryer, kitchen, and bunk beds for the kids. Heated pool. Tiki Hut offers hot dogs, hamburgers, sno-cones. $$–$$$

For More Information

Alabama Gulf Coast Convention and Visitors Bureau. *3150 Gulf Shores Parkway (Drawer 457), Gulf Shores 36547; (334) 968–7511 or (800) 745–7263*

(SAND); Web site www.gulfshores.com and www.orangebeach.com; E-mail info@gulfshores.com.

Elberta

BALDWIN COUNTY HERITAGE MUSEUM (all ages)

25521 U.S. Highway 98 East (mail: Box 356, Elberta 36530); (334) 986–8375. Open Friday and Saturday from 10:00 A.M. to 5:00 P.M. and Sunday from 1:00 to 5:00 P.M. Admission is $4.00 for adults, $2.00 for children ages 13 to 18, $1.00 for children 6 to 12, and **Free** *to children under 6.*

If you're in the area, check out the county's rural heritage that is preserved in a rambling old building. Displays include everything from old farm equipment and cooking utensils to an Edison phonograph. Kids especially like the carriage that at one time carried visitors from the ferry to a grand hotel at nearby Point Clear. On occasion there are live demonstrations—such as a blacksmith at work or someone extracting turpentine from a tree—that kids especially like.

Surrounding the museum in a wooded setting is a nature trail that is a favorite with children who need to stretch their legs.

Author's Top Picks

- National Voting Rights Museum, Selma (334-418-0800)

- Old Cahawba Archaeological Park, Orrville (334-872-8058 or 800-45-SELMA)

- Outdoor Drama: *To Kill a Mockingbird*, Monroeville (334-575-7433)

- Wildland Expeditions Swamp Tours, Chickasaw (334-460-8206)

- Gulf Coast Exploreum of Science, Mobile (334-208-6873 or 887-254-4386)

- USS *Alabama* Battleship Memorial Park, Mobile (334-433-2703 or 800-426-4929)

- Fort Gaines, Dauphin Island (334-861-6992)

- Estuarium, Dauphin Island (334-861-7500)

- Zooland Animal Park, Gulf Shores (334-968-5731)

- The Track Recreation Center, Gulf Shores (334-968-8111)

Atmore

Atmore was founded in 1866 as a supply stop along the Mobile and Great Northern railroads and early on was named Williams Station. In 1897 the sawmill town was renamed Atmore to honor Charles Pawson Atmore, the general ticket agent for the Louisville-Nashville railroad. The city retains a small-town, rural style of living.

Annually on the fourth Saturday of October, the community celebrates its railroad and sawmill heritage with a regional festival, Williams Station Day.

The Poarch Creek Indian Reservation, 8 miles north of town, has members who are active in the community and well known for their Bingo Palace that is near Interstate 65.

During a Thanksgiving Day Poarch Creek Indian Pow Wow, members return to visit friends and family on land that formerly belonged to the Creeks. If you want to interest your children in Indian lore and heritage, this is the perfect occasion. It offers dancers in colorful regalia and demonstrations of

Native American culture, herbal medicine, and food drying. Your youngsters may sample Indian foods such as hominy and fry bread, and they may watch as baskets, beadwork, and quilts are made. At day's end they should leave with a new understanding of our nation's early inhabitants.

A museum (334-368-9136) is filled with tribal artifacts and is open weekdays from 8:00 A.M. to 5:00 P.M. Admission is Free.

For More Information

Atmore Area Chamber of Commerce. *501 South Pensacola Avenue, Atmore 36502; (334) 368–3305; Fax (334) 368–0800; Web site www. frontiernet.net/~commerce.*

Southeast Alabama

Southeast Alabama is where Civil War and civil rights histories were written. It is historic land, some rural, some very modern. Life is unhurried in south Alabama. This is the place to find moss-draped trees, the state capital, farmers who labor to produce cotton, and Southern hospitality. Listen closely and you're likely to hear often, "Ya'll come back now, you hear?" And, when you hear the invitation, you can be assured that these people mean just that.

Brewton

Brewton is not a major Alabama destination, but it has one museum and a fun annual event. You may want to combine a visit to include both.

THOMAS E. MCMILLAN MUSEUM (ages 8 to 12)

220 Alco Drive, Brewton 36426; (334) 867–4832. Open Monday through Thursday from 8:00 A.M. to 2:00 P.M. and Friday from 8:00 A.M. to 1:00 P.M. Closed major holidays, the first weeks of June and September, and again in the second half of December. Admission is **Free**.

The Thomas E. McMillan Museum, which is in the fine arts center of Jefferson Davis Community College, has exhibits that relate to Native Americans, several of the nation's wars, and archaeology; displays include old carpenters' tools, medical instruments, and a stuffed black bear, coyote, and turkey. Your children are probably most going to like the prehistoric fossils and Indian items. Together the collection gives some understanding of the area's heritage. If you read the signs explaining exhibits, you'll probably need about an hour here. Bypass the signs and you could breeze through in half that time.

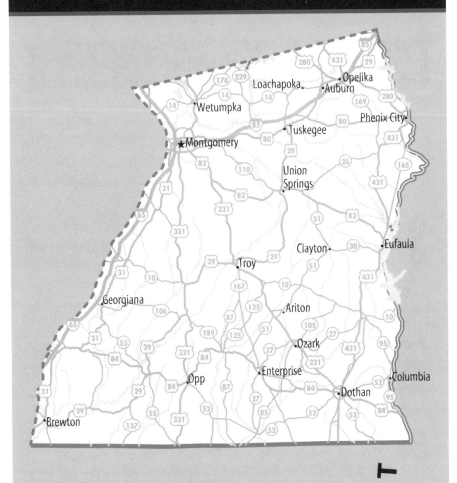

SOUTHEAST

*B*erry Madness On the third Saturday in June, the campus of Jefferson Davis Community College is the setting for a **Blueberry Festival** that draws thousands of visitors. Expect to find blueberries served in every way you can imagine, plus arts and crafts and live music.

About 10 miles north of Brewton, Castleberry hosts a **Strawberry Festival** on an April Saturday. It's held downtown in this tiny town, midway between Evergreen and Brewton. As one local explains, "Look for more than three cars parked together and you'll find the festival."

Where to Eat

Green House Restaurant. *1115 Douglas Avenue, Brewton 36426; (334) 867–9999.* In Brewton Motor Inn, it offers a buffet and weekend specials. $

Jalisco Mexican Restaurant. *1614 Douglas Avenue, Brewton 36426; (334) 809–0244.* A hot spot with locals, especially on Friday and Saturday nights when there's often live music. Real Mexican food prepared by real Mexicans. $

Ole Willie's Place. *204 Belleville, Brewton 36426; (334) 867–3341.* Favorites are burgers and seafood. $–$$

Where to Stay

Brewton Motor Inn. *1115 Douglas Avenue, Brewton 36426; (334) 867–5741.* Swimming pool and very affordable rates. $

Days Inn. *611 South Boulevard, Brewton 36426; (334) 867–9999.* **Free** continental breakfast; kitchenettes. $

For More Information

Brewton Chamber of Commerce. *1012 Douglas Avenue, Douglas 36426; (334) 867–3224.*

Georgiana

Georgiana is a small Alabama town that nurtured a future star. The late country music great, Hank Williams, grew up in this town not far from Interstate 65.

Annual Event In early June Georgiana hosts a **Salute to Hank Williams Day** with a barbecue, a jam fest, a street dance, arts and crafts, and "old-fashioned fun."

HANK WILLIAMS, SR., BOYHOOD HOME AND MUSEUM (ages 8 to 12)

127 Rose Street (Box 310), Georgiana 36033; (334) 376–2555; www.georgiana@alaweb.com. Open Monday through Saturday from 10:00 A.M. to 5:00 P.M. and Sunday from 1:00 to 5:00 P.M. Admission is $3.00 for adults and $2.00 for students.

The house is the only remaining home Williams lived in before becoming a Nashville celebrity. After buying the 1850 house, the city reopened it as a museum and filled it with the singer's memorabilia, artifacts, pictures, and personal belongings. Poke around inside and consider with your children what thrust a man from this tiny town into stardom.

For More Information

City of Georgiana. *400 East Railroad Avenue, Georgiana 36033; (334) 376–2396; Fax (334) 376–9850; E-mail georgian@alaweb.com.*

Opp

Opp is void of tourist attractions, but it has a humdinger of an annual event.

Annual Event Drawing thousands of people from all over, the **Rattlesnake Rodeo** is held on the first weekend in March. Although the fun centers on snakes and even includes snake races, there are other happenings—arts and crafts, dancing contests, and programs on rattlesnake education. Your family can learn snake history, how to milk a snake for its venom, and what to do if you're bitten by a snake. The rodeo is held at the town's stadium.

Where to Stay

Holiday Inn Express. *812 Florala (Highway 3315), Opp 36467; (334) 493–6399 or (800) HOLIDAY.* You'll enjoy the swimming pool at this 43-unit property. $

For More Information

Opp and Covington County Area. *Box 148, Opp 36467; (334) 493–3070 or (800) 239–8054; Fax: (334) 493–6666.*

Enterprise

Your first stop in Enterprise should be at the Welcome Center (334–393–3977), on U.S. Highway 84 bypass east of the city, to gather brochures and maps detailing things to do in the region. Guides here are full of information about their area. The center, which is a replica of an early nineteenth-century log home, is open Monday through Friday from 10:00 A.M. to noon and from 1:00 to 3:00 P.M. Admission is **Free**.

LITTLE RED SCHOOLHOUSE (all ages)

U.S. Highway 84 bypass (mail: Pea River Historical Society, Box 310628), Enterprise 36331–0628; (334) 393–3977. Open Monday through Friday from 10:00 A.M. to noon and from 1:00 to 3:00 P.M. Admission is **Free**.

Adjacent to the Welcome Center, a schoolhouse replica is filled with desks, schoolbooks, a pot-bellied stove, and other nostalgic reminders of rural American schools.

BOLL WEEVIL MONUMENT (all ages)

553 Glover Avenue, Enterprise 36330; (334) 347–0581 or (800) 235–4730. The monument is accessible anytime. Viewing is **Free**.

Your family has probably never seen a statue to an insect. That's because there is only one in the world and that one stands on Main Street in downtown Enterprise. If you have time for only one stop while here, this should be it.

You might think that an insect that devoured the bulk of local farmers' cotton crops would not be cherished. Hindsight, however, showed the farmers that the cotton-eating rampage nudged them into diversifying their crops and thus surviving and prospering when the introduction of peanuts resulted in a new primary crop.

The Boll Weevil Monument depicts a woman standing on a pedestal and holding an oversized, but still tiny, boll weevil in her uplifted hand.

DEPOT MUSEUM (ages 8 to 12)

106 Railroad Street (mail: Pea River Historical Society, Box 310628) Enterprise 36331–0628; (334) 393–2901. Open Monday through Friday from 10:00 A.M. to 4:00 P.M. (occasionally open on Saturday). Admission is **Free**.

Near the center of town, the museum has a collection of items relating to the area. Kids especially like the Indian relics, old medical equipment, and military uniforms.

Where to Eat

Cutts. *417 East Lee Street, Enterprise 36330; (334) 347–1110.* Down home cooking in a family restaurant with a buffet and child's plates. $

Gazebo Restaurant. *630 Glover Avenue, Enterprise 36330; (334) 347–0783.* Fine dining inside the Ramada Inn. $–$$$

The Lobby Restaurant. *116 South Main Street, Enterprise 36330; (334) 393–1360.* In the old Rains Building with lots of ambience. $

Where to Stay

Comfort Inn. *615 Boll Weevil Circle, Enterprise 36330; (334) 347–2271.* In-room coffee for all your sleepyheads. $

Days Inn. *714 Boll Weevil Circle, Enterprise 36330; (334) 393–3297 or (800) DAYS–INN.* You'll enjoy the swimming pool after a long day traveling. $

Ramada Inn. *630 Glover Avenue, Enterprise 36330; (334) 347–6262 or (800) 272–6232.* Restaurant, room service, and **Free** newspaper. $

For More Information

Enterprise Chamber of Commerce. *553 Glover (mail: Box 310577), Enterprise 36331; (334) 347–0581 or (800) 235–4730; Web site www. entercomp.com/users/chamber/.*

Dothan

Your family will have a ball in Dothan, where the locals are friendly and the attractions diverse. Should you arrive with no information in hand, head first to the Dothan Area Convention and Visitors Bureau on Ross Clark Circle where it meets Choctaw Street. Gather all the information you need, but don't leave too quickly. In the parking lot take time to snap your crew's photo next to the gold statue of a peanut, the farm product most associated with this town.

Downtown would be a good starting point for your Dothan explorations. You'd have to have your eyes closed tighter than a stored strand of Christmas lights to miss seeing the giant murals covering the walls of several buildings. Painted by world-renowned artists, the paintings, known as the Wiregrass Festival of Murals (334–793–0450), tell the region's history and make it clear that local roots run deeply into agriculture.

Annual Event Known as "The Peanut Capital of America," Dothan annually hosts the **National Peanut Festival,** a two-week affair with national celebrities, a carnival, fair, parade, beauty pageant, and peanut recipe contest. The festivities begin on the first Friday in November.

WIREGRASS MUSEUM OF ART (all ages)

126 Museum Avenue (Box 1624), Dothan 36302; (334) 794–3871; Fax (334) 671–0380. Open Tuesday through Saturday from 10:00 A.M. to 5:00 P.M. and Sunday from 1:00 to 5:00 P.M. Admission is **Free**.

After checking out the murals, head next to the Wiregrass Museum of Art. If you're thinking, "Yeah, sure, as if my children want to see that," think again. Among the changing exhibits of nineteenth- and twentieth-century art is a second-floor room where exhibits can be touched and imaginations unleashed. Be sure your children go into the shadow box and crawl through the tunnel filled with their own reflections, making it complex to choose a path.

You need to see two more downtown spots before leaving the city's heart. Not far from the art museum, look for the Mule Marker in Poplar Head Park (corner of East Main and College Streets). The landscaped and bricked park pays tribute to the mule, which was instrumental in the region's development.

PORTER HARDWARE (all ages)

136 East Main Street, Dothan 36301; (334) 792–3158. Open Monday through Friday from 7:00 A.M. to 5:00 P.M. and Saturday from 7:00 A.M. to 1:00 P.M. Admission is **Free***.*

From the Mule Marker, walk up the street to discover a store that time seems to have forgotten. Porter Hardware, downtown at 136 East Main Street, is like taking a step back in time. While locals do their shopping here, visitors come mostly to look. Your children will enjoy seeing the rolling ladders, the scarred, wooden floors, and the team of old-timers who still work in this place. The men sit, when not needed, in straight-back chairs just inside the front door, where they watch the world pass by.

WATER WORLD (all ages)

401 Recreation Road, Dothan 36302; (334) 793–0297. Open daily from Memorial Day through Labor Day weekends. Open only on weekends in early May and in late summer after school starts. Closed after Labor Day. Hours Monday, Wednesday, and Friday are from 10:00 A.M. to 6:00 P.M., Tuesday and Thursday from 10:00 A.M. to 9:00 P.M., Saturday from 10:00 A.M. to 7:00 P.M., and Sunday from noon to 7:00 P.M. Admission is $7.00 for adults, $5.00 for children 3 to 12, and **Free** *for children under 3 and adults over 60.*

If you visit Dothan on a hot Alabama day, your youngsters will welcome the relief available at Water World.

At the area's only wave pool, your children can ride ocean-size waves in the giant pool, speed down the twisting 400-foot water slides (there are three), and ride the crazy-water bumper boats. When they need a break, they can cavort with the lovable mascot, Aquaduck, who's always strutting around and making people laugh. You'll like the picnic pavilion, barbecue grills, and kiddie play area, and your children will probably take all your loose change to the arcade.

ADVENTURELAND THEME PARK (all ages)

3738 West Main Street, Dothan 36301; (334) 793–9100. Summer hours are Monday through Saturday from 10:00 A.M. to midnight. Winter hours are Monday through Thursday from 2:00 to 10:00 P.M., Friday from 2:00 P.M. to midnight, Saturday from 10:00 A.M. to midnight, and Sunday from noon to 10:00 P.M. **Free** *general admission. Cost is per activity.*

If Water World doesn't sap the final drop of your children's energy, take them next to Adventureland, a mini-theme park that's family-oriented and includes two eighteen-hole miniature golf courses, a figure-eight go-cart track, bumper boats, an arcade, video and novelty games, and a snack bar.

LANDMARK PARK (all ages)

Highway 431 (Box 6362), Dothan 36302; (334) 794–3452. Open Monday through Saturday from 9:00 A.M. to 5:00 P.M. and Sunday from noon to 6:00 P.M. Closed some major holidays. Except during special events admission is $2.00 for adults, $1.00 for children 3 to 16, and Free *for children under 3.*

You should set aside a full day to visit Landmark Park, a living-history farm 3 miles north of Dothan on Highway 431. You'll find sheep, goats, a rooster, a smokehouse, a cane-mill syrup shed, a blacksmith shop, a log cabin, and outbuildings typical of an 1890s farm. This is a great place for children to romp and run and to see what life was like in another century.

In addition to the farm, the sixty-acre park has a turn-of-the-century church, a gazebo, a one-room schoolhouse, a country store, a planetarium, wildlife exhibits, and an 1,800-foot-long boardwalk. When you walk the boarded trail, look for beaver, opossum, fox, and turtles. If anyone in your family tires easily, they can take advantage of the several benches and pavilions along the path.

Annual Events To add to the experience, schedule your trip to Landmark Park to coincide with one of the multitude of special events held here annually, including **Pioneer Peanut Days**, highlighting old-fashioned harvesting methods, and a **Fall Folklife Festival**, with demonstrations in how to make soap, grind cane, dip candles, and sew quilts.

Pack a lunch and use the picnic area adjacent to the visitors center. Just remember that picnickers are asked to carry their trash away with them.

FARLEY NUCLEAR VISITORS CENTER (ages 6 to 12)

7388 North State Highway 95 (Box 470, Ashford 36312), Columbia 36319; (334) 899–5108 or (800) 344–8295. Open Monday through Friday from 9:00 A.M. to 4:00 P.M. Admission is Free.

Located south of Columbia, Farley Nuclear Visitors Center is a hands-on interpretive center where kids have a ball with activities such as playing computer games and using muscle power to generate energy on a treadmill. The museum has duplicated the control room of a nuclear power plant. Films trace the story of energy, but the big hit with youngsters is meeting Wattsworth, a robot that's an energy expert. Even though he appears only for groups, you might be lucky and visit when a scheduled group is meeting this charming fellow. Kids also like the neutron gun that aims a beam of light at a board, causing a chain reaction that's fun to watch. (To get there go east on U.S. Highway 84 and turn left on County Road 95.)

Where to Eat

Garland House. *200 North Bell Street, Dothan 36301; (334) 793–2043.* In an early 1900s house, lunch is served on weekdays only. Lots of charm but not for rambunctious children or picky eaters. $–$$

The Mexican Connection. *4185 Montgomery Highway, Dothan 36303; (334) 793–2496.* Offers a children's menu, crayons, and color sheets. On Monday

night two kids, age 12 and younger, eat **Free** with purchase of one adult entree priced at $7.50 or more. $

Mrs. Boomer's. *256 North Foster Street, Dothan 36301; (334) 793–7810.* Home of the famous "Boomer Burger." Children's menu, crayons, and coloring/ activity sheet, balloons, **Free** ice cream for kids who finish their meal. Great atmosphere. $

Where to Stay

Comfort Inn. *3593 Ross Clark Circle, Dothan 36303; (334) 793–9090.* Award-winning property with cheerful staff, exercise room, swimming pool, convenient location, and **Free** continental breakfast. Kids under 18 stay **Free** with adults. $–$$

Courtyard by Marriott. *3040 Ross Clark Circle, Dothan 36301; (334) 671–*

3000 or (800) 321–2211. Indoor pool means your kids can swim no matter what the temperature is outside. $–$$

Shoney's Inn. *1075 Ross Clark Circle, Dothan 36303; (334) 793–2525 or (800) 222–2222.* **Free** breakfast, in-room coffee, and great rates. $

For More Information

Dothan Area Convention and Visitors Bureau. *3311 Ross Clark Circle NW (Box 8765), Dothan 36304; (334)*

794–6622 or (888) 449–0212; E-mail dothancvb@mail.ala.net.; Web site www.dothanalcvb.com.

Ozark

Ozark is best known as the home of Fort Rucker, but you'll also find here a quaint downtown shopping area and Dale County Lake, which has been called the state's No. 1 lake for bass fishing. The county park also has walking trails, picnic areas, and a huge playground, called Kid Zone, that overflows with neat tunnels and wood structures waiting to be climbed.

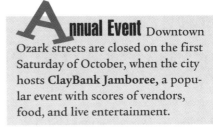

Annual Event Downtown Ozark streets are closed on the first Saturday of October, when the city hosts **ClayBank Jamboree**, a popular event with scores of vendors, food, and live entertainment.

 UNITED STATES ARMY AVIATION MUSEUM (ages 8 to 12)
Building 6000, corner of Andrews and Novusel Streets (mail: P.O. Box 620610, Fort Rucker 36362–0610); (334) 598–2508; E-mail avnmuseum@ala.net; Web site www.aviationmuseum.org. Open Monday through Saturday from 9:00 A.M. to 4:00 P.M. and Sunday from noon to 4:00 P.M. Closed some holidays. Admission is Free.

Just outside of Ozark your kids will fly high after a visit to Fort Rucker. Home of the Apache helicopters, the site is the training base for military helicopter pilots and home to a museum that captivates children interested in powerful machines. The museum details the history of U.S. Army aviation with one of the world's largest collections of helicopters.

Begin your explorations by watching a brief film; then plunge into the exhibits that include the R-4, the Army's first helicopter; Army One, the helicopter used by President Dwight Eisenhower; General Douglas MacArthur's Bataan helicopter; and the AH-74 Apache, the hero of Desert Storm. Exhibits include life-size dioramas, films, and interpretive material.

If your kids want a memento of their visit, don't miss the gift shop, which has a wide selection of aviation-related items.

Where to Eat

Deloney's. *U.S. Highway 231 North, Ozark 36360; (334) 774–5901.* Home cooking and low-priced buffet. $

Kelly's Bar-B-Q. *U.S. Highway 231 North, Ozark 36360; (334) 445–9676.* Heaping helpings at good prices. $

Vic's Restaurant. *U.S. Highway 231 North and Deese Road, Ozark 36360; (334) 445–2707.* Oyster bar and great seafood. $

Where to Stay

Best Western. *U.S. Highway 231 South (Box 1396, Ozark 36361); (334) 774–5166.* Always clean; **Free** continental breakfast. $

Holiday Inn Ozark/Fort Rucker. *151 U.S. Highway 231 South, Ozark 36360; (334) 774–7300 or (800) HOLIDAY.* You can't go wrong here—and there's a swimming pool. $

Jameson Inn. *Highway 120 at U.S. Highway 231 South, Ozark 36361; (334) 774–0233 or (800) 526–3766.* Breakfast room and some suites. $

For More Information

Ozark Area Chamber of Commerce. *308 Painter Avenue, Ozark 36360; (334) 774–9321 or (800) 582–8497; Fax (334) 774–8736; E-mail ozarkcc@snowhill.com; Web site www.snowhill.com/ozarkcc.*

Christmas Lights If you visit this region during the Christmas holidays, swing by Ariton, north of Ozark. The tiny town at year's end becomes a winter wonderland, thanks to one man who started the outdoor displays to amuse his grandchildren. More than three million lights and dozens of animated displays are strung along a 2½-mile driving tour, and folks turn out by the thousands to see the displays. For one cover charge ($4.00 per person over age three), visitors get two and a half hours of entertainment, including a drama called *City of Bethlehem*. There are eighteen shops and an area called "chatter box," with eighty rocking chairs, so sit a spell if you find a vacancy.

Christmas City USA takes place from Thanksgiving night through December. Call (334) 762–2227 for information.

Troy

This commercial city is the seat of Pike County and perhaps best known as the home of Troy State University (334-670-3000). Don't pass through without a glimpse of the campus and a visit to Pike Pioneer Museum.

 PIKE PIONEER MUSEUM (ages 6 to 12)

248 U.S. Highway 231 North (Box 486), Troy 36081; (334) 566–3597. Open Monday through Saturday from 9:00 A.M. to 5:00 P.M. and Sunday from 1:00 to 5:00 P.M. Admission is $3.00 for adults, $2.00 for seniors 60 or older, $1.00 for students, and **Free** *for younger children.*

The museum actually is a several-building complex created when structures were moved here from other parts of the county. On display are old farming equipment, period merchandise from an old general store, and artifacts displayed in a split-log house and tenant house. When groups tour, the museum schedules demonstrations of arts, such as weaving and spinning. If you happen to be there during a group tour, you are welcome to watch.

Where to Eat

Mossy Grove Schoolhouse. *1902 Elba Highway, Troy 36079; (334) 566–4921.* In an old school dating from 1856, a former schoolteacher prepares Southern foods, catfish, pork chops, steaks, shrimp, fried mushrooms, clam strips, and chicken, all fried, grilled, or charbroiled. Children may draw on a wall chalkboard. $–$$

Where to Stay

Days Inn and Suites. *1260 U.S. Highway 231 (Box 761), Troy 36081; (334) 566–7007 or (800) DAYS–INN.* Swimming pool plus **Free** continental breakfast. $–$$

Holiday Inn Express. *U.S. Highway 231 at U.S. Highway 29, Troy 36081; (334) 670–0012.* **Free** continental breakfast and **Free** newspaper. $

For More Information

Pike County Chamber of Commerce. *246 Highway 231 North, Troy 36081; (334) 566–2294;* *Fax (334) 566–2298; E-mail pikecoc@trojan.troyst.edu; Web site www.pikecounty.com.*

Clayton

Clayton has a couple of sites worth seeing if you're passing through the area. You'll find an amusing site at Clayton Baptist Church Cemetery, on North Midway Street. A tombstone that draws attention is one shaped like a whiskey bottle. It marks the grave of W. T. Mullen, who died in 1863. The story is told that Mullen's wife promised to erect the unusual tombstone if he really managed to drink himself to death. He did, so she did.

OCTAGON HOUSE (ages 8 to 12)

103 North Midway Street (mail: Thelma Teal, Box 454, Clayton 36016); (334) 775–3546. Tours by appointment only. Admission is $5.00 for adults, $2.50 for children.

Perhaps the town's most impressive site is the Octagon House. Children who see the unusual eight-sided structure begin to realize the endless possibilities in the minds of those who design and build. The house is the state's only remaining antebellum, octagon-shaped house. Even if you haven't arranged a tour, which is the only way to see inside the house, you still can drive by and observe the unusual shape and the four chimneys that jut above the cupola.

For More Information

Historic Chattahoochee Commission. *211 North Eufaula Avenue, Eufaula 36027; (334) 687–9755;* Fax *(334) 687–6631; Web site www.hcc-al-ga.org.*

Eufaula

If your family wants to see an abundance of columned antebellum homes set against moss-draped trees, Eufaula is the place to go.

Seth Lore and Irwinton Historic District is filled with hundreds of historic and architecturally significant structures. The district is said to have the state's most complete collection of intact mid- to late-nineteenth-century small-town commercial buildings.

Begin your tour by visiting the offices of the Historic Chattahoochee Commission, which is open regular weekday business hours and is the place to get details on all the sites and attractions in the eighteen-county Chattahoochee Trace. The two-state region, which straddles the Chattahoochee River along the Alabama-Georgia border, is filled with antebellum homes, lakes, and scenic wonders.

SHORTER MANSION (ages 8 to 12)

340 North Eufaula Avenue, Eufaula 36027; (334) 687–3793. Open Monday through Saturday from 9:00 A.M. to 4:00 P.M. and Sunday from 1:00 to 4:00 P.M. Closed major holidays. Admission is $4.00 for adults, $1.00 for children under age 12, and **Free** *for children under 6.*

Most of Eufaula's homes and buildings are privately occupied and not routinely open, but that's not the case at Shorter Mansion, a neoclassical-style columned home dating from 1884. It houses the offices of the Eufaula Historical Museum and Eufaula Heritage Association. Parking is available behind the building. At the mansion you will find brochures relating to other area sites.

HART HOUSE (ages 8 to 12)

211 North Eufaula Avenue, Eufaula 36027; (334) 687–9755; Fax (334) 687–6631; www.hcc-al-ga.org. Open Monday through Friday from 8:00 A.M. to 5:00 P.M. Admission is **Free***.*

The restored Greek Revival house has not changed much since it was built in 1851. Its porch is noted for its six fluted Doric columns.

LAKEPOINT RESORT STATE PARK (all ages)

104 Lakepoint Drive (Highway 431 North), Eufaula 36027; (334) 687–8011 or 687–6676. Open daily sunrise to sunset. Park admission is **Free***. Picnic area admission is 50 cents per person.*

Five miles north of Eufaula, Lakepoint Resort State Park is an ideal setting for your family's vacation. The park's focal point is sprawling Lake Eufaula, often referred to as "the large-mouth bass capital of the world." Although fishing is ideal here, there are other recreational opportunities, too, including hiking, tennis, swimming, and picnicking.

Give your kids a choice: Would they prefer to stay in a heated and air-conditioned cabin or would they like a room in the lodge? If they can't quite decide, you may sway their thinking by telling them that some of the cabins have fireplaces that are ideal in colder months. The lodge, however, has more convenient access to the park's restaurant. Decisions, decisions.

Families who prefer camping will be pleased with the 244-site campground, which has water and electric hookups, a community center, beach, boat ramp, bath house, laundry, and camp store.

While you're visiting, be sure your children get to see one of the fish weigh-ins following a fishing tournament at the marina. Or, if they'd rather fish than watch, you can rent both boats and guides and wet your own lines.

EUFAULA NATIONAL WILDLIFE REFUGE (all ages)

509 Old Highway 165, Eufaula 36027; (334) 687–4065; Fax (334) 687–5906; www.fws.gov. Open daily from sunup to sundown. Admission is **Free**.

Now here's a place for those little legs to run and for wide eyes to spot wildlife. Eufaula National Wildlife Refuge is a federal preserve that protects waterfowl and wild game. Humans enjoy the land, too; boating, hiking and wildlife observation are permitted in designated areas. You may want to drive through the park, get your bearings, then decide which activity to pursue.

The refuge is 7 miles north of U.S. Highway 431.

TOM MANN'S FISH WORLD AQUARIUMS (all ages)

1951 North Eufaula Avenue, Eufaula 36027; (334) 687–3655. Open daily from 8:00 A.M. to 5:00 P.M. Admission is $2.50 for adults, $1.00 for seniors 55+, $1.50 for children in first through twelfth grades, and **Free** *to younger children.*

Tom Mann's Fish World is a noted aquarium complex where your youngsters can watch large-mouth bass and other fish species, and they can see Mann's collection of Indian artifacts. Mann, who runs a pro shop here, keeps fishermen updated on local lake conditions.

Your children will be intrigued by the tale of—and monument to—Leroy Brown. His marker reads, "Most bass are just fish, but Leroy Brown was something special." Several hundred people attended the fish's funeral, paying their final respects to a bass who had eaten from Mann's hand and jumped through hoops. Leroy endeared himself to Mann by "testing" the lure designer's latest inventions. If Leroy bypassed a lure, Mann went back to the drawing board but if the bass nibbled, Mann proceeded with production. Leroy, after being hooked by Mann, lived seven years in the aquarium before he died in 1981. (The governor declared a day of mourning.) Pallbearers were tuxedo-clad professional bass fishermen.

Special Events If you can't decide when to visit Eufaula, you might consider going during one or both of two popular events. The first is a three-day **Spring Pilgrimage**, when residents shine their silver and fling wide their doors to give you a look inside. The pilgrimage takes place the first weekend in April. (If Easter falls on that Sunday, the pilgrimage is held the following weekend.)

Each fall the town hosts an **Indian Summer Arts and Crafts Festival** that commemorates the city's Indian heritage and the area's moderate fall weather. Held in the historic district, the family fun includes live entertainment, spin art, clothesline art, hands-on crafts, a midway of foods, and children's games and activities.

SUPERIOR PECAN COMPANY (ages 6 to 12)

303 Britt Street, Eufaula 36027; (334) 687–2031 or (800) 628–2350. Open October through mid-February. Admission is **Free**.

Your kids should get a kick out of watching this pre–World War II Southern pecan processing and packaging plant operation. The retail area includes pecan specialties, gift packages, and other edibles. This is a great stop if you want a Southern product to take home to those who missed the trip.

Where to Eat

Lakepoint Resort Restaurant. *Alabama 431 North (mail: Box 267), 36072; (334) 687–8011.* Your family will enjoy the view of Lake Eufaula as they savor hearty meals at affordable prices. $–$$

Where to Stay

Best Western. *Highway 431 North, Eufaula 36027; (334) 687–3900 or (800) 528–1234.* **Free** continental breakfast and a swimming pool. $

Kendall Manor Inn. *534 West Broad, Eufaula 36027; (334) 687–8847.* The columned home allows children only age 14 and older. Welcome beverage and breakfast included. All 6 guest rooms have private baths. $$–$$$

Jameson Inn. *136 Towne Center Boulevard, Eufaula 36072; (334) 687–7747 or (800) 541–3268.* You'll enjoy the savings from a **Free** continental breakfast, and your kids will enjoy the pool. $

Lakepoint State Park Resort. *Highway 431 North, Eufaula 36027; (334) 687–8011 or (800) 544–5253.* Under a canopy of shade trees, the resort has 101 units, reasonable rates, lots of creature comforts, and views of the lake. $

For More Information

Eufaula–Barbour County Chamber of Commerce. *102 North Orange Avenue (Box 697), Eufaula 36072–0697; (334) 687–6664 or (800) 524–7529; Fax (334) 687–5240; Web site www.ebchamber.org.*

Historic Chattahoochee Commission. *211 North Eufaula Avenue, Eufaula 36027; (334) 687–9755; Fax (334) 687–6631; Web site www.hcc-al-ga.org.*

A Fullman Family Adventure When people know how much we have traipsed over Alabama, they often ask about our favorite places. Always on the top of the list is Eufaula, a place we've visited many times. Its moss-draped trees, slow pace, and columned homes make it so distinctive, so very Southern, and so appealing when the bustle of big-city life needs diluting.

The town is dear to Christine, who especially loves stately, old homes. For Milton and his cameras, the city of majestic homes is a workplace of joy.

Union Springs

Union Springs is small enough that your family can do much of their exploring on foot. Park downtown and from that vantage point cover a several-block radius as you search out historic homes and buildings. You can pick up a walking-tour brochure from City Hall or across the street at Main Drug Store (302 North Prairie Street), in what was the first brick building erected on Prairie Street. Dating from 1867, it was originally a mercantile store with a saloon in the basement.

A major focus in Union Springs is field dogs, often called pointers, which are so revered that a monument to them has been erected on downtown's main street.

A nnual Event Annually on February 22 Union Springs holds the nation's largest amateur field-dog trials. Townspeople call the trials **"Bullock County's Mardi Gras"** because parties and revelry are abundant.

BIRD DOG STATUE (all ages)

Prairie Street, Union Springs. Available around the clock. Admission is **Free**.

The bronze statue is a life-size pointer atop a 7-foot granite base engraved with the names of eleven Bullock County men in the Bird Dog Hall of Fame.

 ### BULLOCK COUNTY JAIL (ages 6 to 12)

West Hardaway (mail: Box 5236), Union Springs 36089; (334) 738–TOUR or 738–3582. Open by appointment only. Admission is **Free**.

The old Bullock County Jail is just the place a kid needs to round out a good day's trip. With its dark exterior, turrets, and old stone, the jail no longer houses the corrupt. Instead it is a museum and community gathering place. Yet your youngsters will want to see it; there's something about a still-working gallows and a young boy's imagination that clicks. The second-floor gallows and trapdoor allowed executed prisoners to conveniently drop to within toting distance of the jail's front entrance.

Built in 1897, the old jail never was glamorous nor was it meant to be. At present it adds a new attraction to a small town that tourists otherwise might bypass.

BULLOCK COUNTY COURTHOUSE (all ages)

Prairie Street (mail: Box 5236), Union Springs 36089; (334) 738–3582 or 738–TOUR. Open Monday through Friday from 8:00 A.M. to 4:30 P.M. Admission is **Free**.

The astute members of your family may notice that the Bullock County Courthouse is a replica of the executive building in Washington, D.C.

 ### LOG CABIN MUSEUM AND CONFEDERATE CEMETERY (all ages)

Highway 82 West, Union Springs 36089; (334) 738–3582 or 738–TOUR. Cabin hours vary, so call first. Cemetery is available daily. Admission is **Free**.

You can visit a real 1850 log cabin and have a tour given by a descendant of its original owner. The cemetery includes graves of both Union and Confederate soldiers. Walk among the markers and discuss with your children the price of war, both for the winning side and the losing side.

A Fullman Family Adventure

Union Springs had just begun to restore its old jail when we first discovered this sleepy little town.

By chance on a sunny day, we stopped by a downtown department store and chatted with a store owner who mentioned the jail and the city's plans to salvage it.

When we expressed interest, the merchant quickly reached for his telephone and called local mover and shaker and tourism maven Barbara McLaurine, who actually is tourism director. When she heard we longed for a look inside, she asked us to wait a few minutes until she could meet us. With jail keys in hand, she arrived soon thereafter and gave us a guided tour through the eerie relic.

In the jail's then-raw state, we had no trouble imagining how it must have been when prisoners had been kept there.

In sharp contrast to the dank jail, we noticed outside a patch of green grass and a picnic table.

Even if we had had a lunch basket in tow, we probably would not have had an appetite after hearing about the prisoners, many of whom were executed, by hanging, inside the jail.

Where to Eat

Crispy Chick. *102 South Prairie, Union Springs 36089; (334) 738–3494.* Kid's plate and great fried chicken. $

McKee's Country Grill. *Highway 82 West, Union Springs 36089; (334) 738–2834.* Locally owned with outstanding barbecue. $

Where to Stay

Greenway Inn. *Highway 82 East, Union Springs 36089; (334) 738–4680.* Budget priced. Town's only motel is clean, caters to hunters. $

The Merriott Bed & Breakfast. *106 Hunter Avenue, Union Springs 36089; (334) 738–3746.* This Victorian-style, antique-filled house is within walking distance of downtown. The owner is a kindergarten teacher, so she welcomes your children. $

Special Events On the first Saturday and Sunday of May, Union Springs hosts a **pilgrimage** and **historic home tours.**

Another popular event is the **Chunnenuggee Fair** held the first Saturday in May. Sited in the business district, it includes arts and crafts from local and regional vendors.

For More Information

Union Springs/Bullock County Tourism Council. *106 East Conecuh Street (Box 5236), Union Springs 36089; (334) 738–TOUR; Fax (334) 738–5068; E–mail macl@ustconline.net.*

Historic Chattahoochee Commission. *211 North Eufaula Avenue, Eufaula 36027; (334) 687–9755; Fax (334) 687–6631; Web site www.hcc-al-ga.org.*

Tuskegee

Your children will learn about peanuts, sweet potatoes, and an ex-slave's ambition when you visit Tuskegee.

The town's focal point is the campus of Tuskegee University. A prestigious college, it traces its start to humble beginnings in the late 1800s, a time when African Americans—particularly those living in the South—did not have much opportunity for higher education. The school, which originally held classes in a dilapidated church and shanty, now is internationally recognized.

 GEORGE WASHINGTON CARVER MUSEUM (all ages)
1212 Old Montgomery Road (Drawer 10), Tuskegee Institute 36088; (334) 727–3200; www.tuin@nps.gov. Open daily from 9:00 A.M. to 5:00 P.M. Closed on some major holidays. Admission is **Free**.

The logical starting point for a visit to Tuskegee Institute is the George Washington Carver Museum, which doubles as the campus's visitors center. Films explain the lives of educator and Tuskegee Institute founder Booker T. Washington and scientist George Washington Carver.

Be sure that your children note the vegetable specimens and samples of Carver's most important crops—peanuts and sweet potatoes—which he used to develop hundreds of other by-products. His work, which came before the turn of the century, is credited with encouraging Southern farmers to grow more than just cotton. His nudge opened up new agri-industries in the area. Be sure your children understand that Carver began his life as a slave but went on to earn a master's degree and to become a noted leader in agricultural research.

THE OAKS (all ages)

1212 Old Montgomery Road (Drawer 10), Tuskegee Institute 36088; (334) 727–3200. Open daily from 9:00 A.M. to 5:00 P.M. Closed on some major holidays. **Free** *admission.*

After you've seen the George Washington Carver museum, walk or drive up the hill to tour The Oaks, the former home of Booker T. Washington, who served as the first principal of Tuskegee State Normal School. Built by university students, the house, with two levels and fifteen rooms, is where the educator lived until his death in 1915.

Washington is memorialized with a center-of-campus monument that shows him lifting the veil of ignorance from fellow blacks. Adjacent to the statue is a park where your family might rest or snack before continuing.

TUSKEGEE INSTITUTE NATIONAL HISTORIC SITE (ages 8 to 12)

Drawer 10, Tuskegee 36087–0010; (334) 727–6390. Open daily from 9:00 A.M. to 5:00 P.M. Admission is **Free**.

Don't overlook the chance for a driving tour of the campus, which includes 165 buildings, including twenty-seven with historical significance. If you want specifics on these, get a self-guide brochure at the Carver Museum.

Music Makers Matched in Tuskegee

The original members of the Commodores—Thomas McClary, Lionel Richie, Milan Williams, Walter Orange, William King, and Ronald LaPread—met as freshmen at Tuskegee Institute and began the group that grew from a hit regional act to a worldwide phenomenon.

The group's first big hit was an instrumental called "Machine Gun." That was followed with a string of twenty-two gold records, six platinum, two double-platinum, and three triple-platinum albums, selling close to forty million records. Among the group's hits were "Three Times A Lady," "Sail On," and "Still."

TUSKEGEE NATIONAL FOREST (all ages)

125 National Forest Road 949, Tuskegee 36083; (334) 727–0295. Open daily from dawn to dusk. Admission is **Free**.

· In the forest your family can camp, picnic, hike, fish, and go horse-back riding. The area has a replica of the cabin where famous African-American educator Booker T. Washington was born. The Bartram Trail commemorates naturalist William Bartram, who identified many species of native plants and trees. Bold Destiny/Bedford V. Cash Memorial Trail has horse and hiking trails that wind 14 miles through the northern half of the forest.

Where to Stay

Tuskegee University Kellogg Conference Center. *East Campus Avenue at Nurses' Home Road (Box 1242), Tuskegee 36088; (334) 727–3000 or (800) 949–6161.* The center has 110 rooms, a restaurant, an indoor swimming pool, and exercise equipment. Kids under 19 stay **Free** with their parents. $–$$

For More Information

Tuskegee Area Chamber of Commerce. *121 South Main Street, Tuskegee 36087; (334) 727–6619; Fax (334) 727–5600.*

Alabama Bureau of Tourism and Travel. *401 Adams Avenue (Box 4927), Montgomery 36103; (334) 242–4545 or (800) ALABAMA.* When calling the State of Alabama, ask for a **Free** copy of the *Black Heritage Guide to Alabama.* The book outlines more than 250 sites with links to black history.

Opelika

Not far from the Auburn University campus, Opelika has several appeals, including a charming and restored downtown, factory-outlet shopping, and a museum that showcases the region's history.

MUSEUM OF EAST ALABAMA (all ages)

121 South Ninth Street, Opelika 36801; (334) 749–2751. Open Tuesday through Friday from 10:00 A.M. to 4:00 P.M. and Saturday from 2:00 to 4:00 P.M. Admission is **Free**.

Thousands of items—ranging from old typewriters and old toys to tools—give glimpses of what life was like years ago in this region.

 LEE COUNTY COURTHOUSE (all ages)
215 South Ninth Street (Box 666), Opelika 36803; (334) 887–8747 or (800) 321–8880. Open weekdays from 8:30 A.M. to 4:30 P.M. Admission is **Free**.
Within walking distance of the Museum of East Alabama is the city's landmark, Lee County Courthouse, which is listed in the National Register of Historic Places. The columned building dates from 1896 and is worth a walk-through to see the marble floors and arched windows.

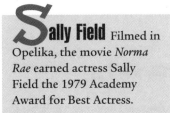

Sally Field Filmed in Opelika, the movie *Norma Rae* earned actress Sally Field the 1979 Academy Award for Best Actress.

Where to Shop

USA Factory Stores. *1220 Fox Run Parkway (Drawer 2523), Opelika 36803; (334) 749–0561. Open Monday through Saturday from 9:00 A.M. to 9:00 P.M. and Sunday from noon to 6:00 P.M. (Winter hours vary, so call first.) Admission is* **Free**. Have a shopper in your bunch? Then don't miss USA Factory Stores, off Interstate 85, where bargains range from clocks and cookware to shoes and paper in some two dozen stores.

Where to Eat

Provino's. *3903-B Pepperell Parkway, Opelika 36801; (334) 742–0340.* Italian atmosphere and memorable Italian food. Save with the early-bird dinner special. $–$$$

Warehouse Bistro. *105 Rocket Avenue, Opelika 36801; (334) 745–6353.* Fine dining. $$–$$$$

Where to Stay

Days Inn. *1014 Anand Avenue, Opelika 36804; (334) 749–5080 or (800) DAYS–INN.* **Free** breakfast, in-room coffee, and a swimming pool. Kids under 12 stay **Free**. $–$$

Shoney's Inn. *1520 Columbus Parkway, Opelika 36804; (334) 742–0270 or (800) 222–2222.* **Free** breakfast. $

For More Information

Auburn-Opelika Convention and Visitors Bureau. *714 East Glenn Avenue, Auburn 36830 (mail: Box 2216, Auburn 36831–2216); (334) 887–8747 or (800) 321–8880; Fax (334) 821–5500; Web site www.auburn-opelika.com.*

Auburn

If your bunch plans to visit Auburn, they better first practice yelling, "war eagle," the football battle cry that grows more intense on game days in this college town that is nicknamed "The Plains."

The name was inspired by the Oliver Goldsmith poem, "The Deserted Village," which includes the line, "Sweet Auburn, loveliest village on the plain." And lovely it is, whether on fall weekends when football fever is rampant or on hot summer days when a water park offers relief.

War Eagle Several stories have circulated about the origins of Auburn's famous "War Eagle" cheer. One of the oldest stories dates from 1892, when Auburn was playing Georgia. In the stands that day was a Civil War veteran, who had with him an eagle he had found years earlier on the battlefield. According to legend the eagle broke free and began majestically circling the playing field. As the eagle soared, Auburn began a steady march toward the Georgia end zone for a thrilling victory. Delighted with the flight and impending victory, fans began yelling, "War Eagle!" At game's end the eagle plunged suddenly to the ground and died, imbuing Auburn students forever with his spirit.

SURFSIDE WATER PARK (all ages)
2780 South College Street, Auburn 36832; (334) 821–7873. Open daily Memorial Day through Labor Day from 10:00 a.m. to 7:00 p.m. Open on May weekends before Memorial Day. Cost is $15.00 for adults and kids 48 inches or taller and $10.70 for kids "walking to under 48 inches." Grandparents who bring their grandchildren are admitted Free, *but be sure to ask for that discount.*

If you arrive on a blistering day, you'll have little choice but to head first to Surfside Water Park. Just off exit 51 of Interstate 85, the park has plenty of places to dunk, soak, float, and cool, whether on gentle waves, sandy beaches, a lazy river, a body flume, or a speed slide.

With a snack bar, volleyball courts, a video arcade, and a children's pool and play area, the park truly is a family kind of place. Be aware, however, that despite the appealing picnic areas inside the park, visitors are not allowed to take in their own refreshments. Instead, they can buy some from the park's snack bar.

RV campsites adjacent to the water park have power, water and sewer hookups, and cable TV connections. Also available for campers are ice machines, a laundry room, vending machines, and a bathhouse with showers. Tent camping is permitted.

CHEWACLA STATE PARK (all ages)

124 Shell Toomer Parkway, Auburn 36830; (334) 887–5621 or (800) ALA–PARK. Open daylight hours. Park admission is $1.00 for adults, fifty cents for ages 6 to 11, and **Free** *to younger children. Rental rates for rustic cabins range from $44.10 to $58.50, including tax; improved campground sites are $13.00; and primitive sites are $9.00.*

Is your family looking for outdoor activities? Then don't miss Chewacla State Park, which sits across from Surfside Water Park and has several hundred acres, a sprawling lake, picnic tables and shelters, a playground, a lakefront beach, swimming (without a lifeguard), fishing, trailer and tent campsites, and cabins. The park's limited number of cabins book quickly, so you should make your reservations well in advance. Keep in mind, too, that there is a two-night minimum stay on weekends and a three-night requirement on holidays. Fishing boats, canoes, and paddleboats may be rented by the hour. Once you've explored this corner of Auburn, head back to town.

TOOMER'S DRUG STORE (all ages)

100 North College Street (U.S. Highway 29), Auburn 36830; (334) 887–3488. Admission is **Free***.*

If you need a boost before plunging into your trek, you'll find cool refreshment at Toomer's Drugstore, Auburn's oldest business. Diagonally across the street from the main entrance to the university's campus, the drugstore is known for its lemonade, made from juice you can watch being squeezed by hand. You'll find traditional drugstore needs here, also.

TIGER TRAIL OF AUBURN

College Street and East Magnolia Avenue at Toomer's Corner, Auburn; (334) 887–7011. Open daily. Admission is **Free***.*

As your family traipses through the Uptown Auburn area, look down at the sidewalks. You'll see plaques embedded with the names of athletes who have brought recognition to Auburn. Among the inductees are basketball star Charles Barkley, Olympic swimming medalist Rowdy Gaines, and baseball great Bo Jackson. There's also a coaches' corner where names of coaching greats are immortalized.

Special Events On the last weekend in April, Auburn University hosts **Fan Day,** allowing fans to visit with coaches and players of the upcoming season. These visits make big memories for little visitors.

Football is the reason for another Auburn event, **Homecoming,** which takes place on a Saturday in late October. The tradition, complete with Friday-night pep rally and outdoor concert, dates back to the early 1900s.

JONATHAN BELL LOVELACE ATHLETIC MUSEUM AND HALL OF HONOR (all ages)

Auburn University Athletic Complex, Auburn 36831; (334) 844–4570. Open Monday through Friday from 8:00 A.M. to 4:30 P.M. and Saturday from 9:00 A.M. to 4:30 P.M. Admission is **Free**.

With high-tech, interactive exhibits, life-size talking dioramas, and traditional displays, the museum will give your children a chance to relive great Tiger memories and learn about some of America's well-known athletes.

AUBURN UNIVERSITY HISTORIC DISTRICT (all ages)

Auburn University Campus, College Street, Auburn 36830; (334) 844–4080 (campus tours) or (334) 821–5500. Admission is **Free**.

The campus has several interesting buildings, including a chapel that was built in the 1850s. Some people report that a ghost, possibly a Civil War soldier, haunts this Gothic Revival–style church that was used as a hospital during the War Between the States.

Football is the pulse of Auburn, so drive by Jordan-Hare Stadium, home of the Auburn Tigers. With a capacity for some 85,000 fans, the stadium comes to life during games. If you want to attend a gridiron clash, plan ahead to get tickets, because they usually are difficult to find.

On game day drive your kids past the surrounding acreage to let them see the phenomenon of tailgaters who come days in advance, decorate their RVs, dress themselves in Auburn regalia, and take this competition quite seriously, especially when it's against its cross-state rival, the University of Alabama.

Where to Shop

Behind The Glass. *168 East Magnolia Avenue, Auburn 36830; (334) 826–1133.* Unexpected finds in a boutique and gift shop with books and a wide range of crazy, cool, and fun things.

Where to Eat

Cheeburger Cheeburger. *160 North College Street, Auburn 36830; (334) 826–0845.* Great cheeseburgers, fries, and onion loaves. $

Ivy's. *In Auburn University Hotel and Conference Center. 241 South College Street, Auburn 36830; (334) 821–8200 or (800)* *228–2876.* Wide range of choices, including sandwiches, salad, steak, and seafood. Children's menu. $–$$

McAlister's Gourmet Deli of Auburn. *1651 East University Drive, Auburn 36830; (334) 502–0101.* Sandwiches, salads, and spuds. $

Where to Stay

Auburn University Hotel and Conference Center. *241 South College Street, Auburn 36830; (334) 821–8200 or (800) 228–2876.* Fitness center, swimming pool; within walking distance of campus. Ask about special rates and packages. $–$$$

Chewacla State Park. *124 Shell Toomer Parkway, Auburn 36830; (334) 821–2439.* One large and 4 small units. These book well in advance. $–$$

Comfort Inn. *2283 College Street, Auburn 36832; (334) 821–6699.* **Free** continental breakfast and **Free** newspaper, so you'll start out full and informed. $

Hampton Inn. *2430 South College Street, Auburn 36832; (334) 821–4111.* **Free** continental breakfast and swimming pool. $

For More Information

Auburn-Opelika Convention and Visitors Bureau. *714 East Glenn Avenue, Auburn 36830 (mail: Box 2216,* *Auburn 36831–2216); (334) 887–8747 or (800) 321–8880; Fax (334) 821–5500; Web site www.auburn-opelika.com.*

Loachapoka

Don't pass through the tiny town of Loachapoka without pausing for a closer look, especially at the town's historic district. On State Road 14 and several miles west of Auburn, this is a quiet hamlet, where for decades little has changed. Drive around and look for buildings dating back to the mid-1800s.

LEE COUNTY HISTORICAL MUSEUM (all ages)
6500 Stage Road, Loachapoka 36865; (334) 887–5560 or 887–3007. Open by appointment. **Free**.

If there's a special event going on, you can get inside the Lee County Historical Society Museum, which holds artifacts and memorabilia pertaining to the county. Even if the complex is closed, you can look through the fence to see a restored log cabin, blacksmith shop, cookhouse, and large building filled with old farm tools.

Annual Event Loachapoka on a late October weekend annually hosts **Syrup Soppin' Days**. This is the chance for your children to learn traditional farming techniques, to watch syrup being made and sugar cane being converted to syrup. They'll also learn the best way to eat syrup: by poking a hole in the biscuit's center and filling it with syrup.

For More Information

Auburn-Opelika Convention and Visitors Bureau. *714 East Glenn Avenue, Auburn 36830 (mail: Box 2216, Auburn 36831–2216); (334) 887–8747 or (800) 321–8880; Fax (334) 821–5500; Web site www.auburn-opelika.com.*

Prattville

North of Montgomery in Prattville, you'll find restored nineteenth-century houses and buildings, including the old Mims Hotel, which in 1867 was the home to poet Sidney Lanier, who was teaching in the area. (The hotel has since been moved to a new location and is used as an office and a business space, but the front is the same as when Lanier lived there.) While you're visiting, ask your children if they can name any of Lanier's works. Here's a hint to jog your memory: "The Marshes of Glynn" and "Tiger-Lilies," an account of Lanier's Civil War experiences as a soldier and prisoner.

PRATTAUGAN MUSEUM (ages 8 to 12)

102 East Main Street, Prattville 36067; (334) 361–0961. Open Monday through Friday from 10:00 A.M. to 4:00 P.M. Admission is **Free**.

The downtown Prattville museum is filled with historic documents and memorabilia from the city's early years. The collection gives you a chance to expose your children to history and to talk about how life has changed.

 ### WILDERNESS PARK (all ages)

Upper Kingston Road (mail: Parks and Recreation Department, 101 West Main Street, Prattville 36067); (334) 361–3640. Open dawn to dusk. Admission is **Free**.

Within the city limits of Prattville is Wilderness Park, a natural forest with a 1,500-foot trail that's a good place to stretch your legs. Don't be deceived by the park's subtle beginnings; once you hike back a short distance you will feel you have landed in a tropical jungle, thanks to the abundance of bamboo trees. (There are no rest-room facilities here, so plan a stop before going.)

 ### PRATT PARK: A CHILD'S PLACE (all ages)

Doster Road, Prattville 36067; (334) 361–3640. Open daily, daylight hours. Admission is **Free**.

Kids will love this place, with lots of wooden things to climb on and swing from.

Where to Eat

Catfish House. *3011 Cobbs Ford Road, Millbrook 35054; (334) 285–7225.* Dinner only, but good food and a kid's menu. $

Fantail. *2060 Downing (Interstate 65, exit 179), Millbrook 36054; (334) 285–7255.* Dinner only, seafood buffet, Tuesday through Sunday 5:00 to 9:00 P.M. $$

Jeanette's BBQ & Kountry Cafe. *1675 Highway 31 North, Prattville 36067; (334) 358–1123.* Nice place for families. $

Jim's Restaurant. *1504 South Memorial Drive, Prattville 36067; (334) 365–7231.* Longtime tradition with meats and veggies. $

Where to Stay

Days Inn. *Interstate 65 North, at exit 186 (Box 680388), Prattville 36068; (334) 365–3311 or (800) DAYS–INN.* The 100-unit property has a restaurant, a swimming pool, and room service, if you feel like luxuriating. $

Hampton Inn. *2585 Cobb's Hill Place, Prattville 36066; (334) 285–6767 or (800) 426–7866.* 𝐅𝐫𝐞𝐞 continental breakfast and a swimming pool. $

Jameson Inn. *104 Jameson Court, Prattville 36067; (334) 361–6463.* Kids under 18 stay 𝐅𝐫𝐞𝐞. Swimming pool, fitness center, and 𝐅𝐫𝐞𝐞 deluxe continental breakfast. $

For More Information

Prattville Chamber of Commerce. *1002 East Main Street, Prattville 36066; (334) 365–7392; Fax (334) 361–1314;* *E-mail chamber@prattville.com; Web site www.prattville.com.*

Montgomery

In addition to making history as the birthplace of the Civil War and the civil rights movement, Montgomery has seen many other milestones. The country's first electric streetcar system began operating in Montgomery in 1886. And, in 1910, the Wright Brothers brought their daring aviation deeds to Alabama's capital city, establishing the nation's first school for powered flight.

At present Montgomery combines the qualities of a leading cultural and recreational center with such assets as world-class theater, museums, history, family activities, and irresistible, down-home Southern food. Get your hiking shoes ready when you arrive in the state capital because there's loads to do in Montgomery.

Annual Event On Memorial Day weekend, Montgomery hosts **Jubilee Cityfest**, which includes concerts, military displays, arts and crafts activities, fireworks, and children's activities.

STATE CAPITOL (all ages)

600 Dexter Avenue (mail: Alabama Historical Commission, Capitol Operations, 468 South Perry Street, Montgomery 36130); (334) 242–3750 or (334) 242–3935 (tours). Open Monday through Friday from 9:00 A.M. to 5:00 P.M. and Saturday from 9:00 A.M. to 4:00 P.M. Admission is Free.

A logical beginning is at the most visible attraction: the capitol building, which was renovated in the early 1990s and is open for tours. At this domed building former Governor George Wallace made his "Segregation today, segregation tomorrow, and segregation forever" speech that focused the world's attention on the civil rights struggle in Alabama. Be sure your children notice the bronze star on the steps, signifying where Jefferson Davis took the oath to become the Confederacy's president. You can tour the building using a self-guided brochure, available in the lobby.

FIRST WHITE HOUSE OF THE CONFEDERACY (all ages)

644 Washington Avenue, Montgomery 36104; (334) 242–1861. Open Monday through Friday 8:00 A.M. to 4:30 P.M. Admission is Free.

After touring the impressive capitol building, walk across the street to tour the First White House of the Confederacy, where Jefferson Davis, the Confederacy's only president, lived briefly with his family before moving to Richmond, Virginia. The house stood at Bibb and Lee Streets when the Davises lived in it but was moved in 1921 to prevent its razing. The house is filled with period antiques and many items that formerly belonged to the Davis family. Tours are self-guided, but docents are available to answer questions.

DEXTER AVENUE KING MEMORIAL BAPTIST CHURCH (ages 6 to 12)

454 Dexter Avenue, Montgomery 36104; (334) 263–3970; Fax (334) 263–3910. Tours are Monday through Thursday at 10:00 A.M. and 2:00 P.M. and Friday at 10:00 A.M. Admission is Free.

Just outside the capitol is Dexter Avenue King Memorial Baptist Church, where the late Dr. Martin Luther King, Jr., at one time was pastor. Here African Americans organized their 1955 bus boycott, which helped start the civil rights movement. Recognizing the church's significant role in history, the congregation offers tours, which begin on the lower level, where a mural chronicles the civil rights struggle. The tour ends upstairs in the sanctuary.

CIVIL RIGHTS MEMORIAL (all ages)

400 Washington Avenue (Box 348, Montgomery 36101–0548). (334) 264–0286; Fax (334) 264–0629; www.splcenter.org. Available daily. Admission is **Free**.

Visitors are a constant at the Civil Rights Memorial, in front of the Southern Poverty Law Center and not far from the capitol. Designed by Maya Lin, who also designed the Vietnam Memorial in Washington, D.C., the black-granite memorial commerates key civil rights events. Youngsters may run their fingers through the steady trickle of water that spills over the names of those who played major roles in the struggle.

OLD ALABAMA TOWN (all ages)

301 Columbus Street, Montgomery 36104; (334) 240–4500 or (888) 240–1850; Fax (334) 240–4519; www.mindspring.com/~olatown. Open Monday through Saturday from 9:00 A.M. to 3:00 P.M. Admission is $7.00 for adults, $3.00 for children 6 to 12, and **Free** *for younger children.*

Less sobering are several Montgomery spots created with children in mind. For starters, and while you're downtown, head 4 blocks north to Old Alabama Town, a re-creation of houses and landscapes detailing how people lived in central Alabama from 1800 to 1900. Your family should begin a tour at Loeb Center, where early residents gathered. The re-created town covers 3 easily walked blocks and includes more than three dozen authentic structures. Save time to walk through a barn, see a cotton gin, and go inside a log cabin; then scope out the one-room schoolhouse and watch craft demonstrations. \

ALABAMA SCIENCE CENTER (ages 6 to 12)

244 Dexter Avenue, Montgomery 36104; (334) 832–3902 or (800) 554–6328. Open Tuesday through Friday from 9:00 A.M. to 4:00 P.M. Admission is **Free**.

Housed in the Alabama Power Building, the center is a hands-on facility with exhibits, touch-screen interactive computer programs, and other activities. There are more than fifty exhibits, so plan to stay a while as your children race from one place to another place and learn about science.

ALABAMA CATTLEMAN'S ASSOCIATION MOOSEUM (all ages)

201 South Bainbridge, Montgomery 36104; (334) 265–1867. Open Monday through Friday from 9:00 A.M. to noon and from 1:00 to 4:00 P.M. Admission is Free.

Your kids will have a blast in this place where an electronic host, Adam Bainbridge, helps kids understand the past, present, and future of Alabama cattle. There are plenty of places to play.

Annual Event In early May the Montgomery Museum of Fine Arts hosts **Art in the Park/Flimp Festival**, which offers a chance for children to create street "paintings" (with chalk), artists demonstrating their techniques, a treasure hunt through exhibits in search of clues and answers to riddles, paper making, sand painting, water colors, face and fingernail painting, tethered balloon rides, and a parade of well-dressed pets (bring your own cat, dog, llama, or whatever). Your young children will find a place to build sand castles, crawl through colorful tubes, or create big bubbles. Plus there always are the sounds of music, from jazz to soft rock and country. You'll want to take blankets or lawn chairs; coolers aren't allowed.

 MONTGOMERY MUSEUM OF FINE ARTS (all ages)

1 Museum Drive, Montgomery 36117; (334) 244–5700; Fax (334) 244–5774. Open Tuesday, Wednesday, Friday, and Saturday from 10:00 A.M. to 5:00 P.M. Open Thursday from 10:00 A.M. to 9:00 P.M. Open Sunday from noon to 5:00 P.M. Admission is Free.

Another must-do for kids is found at the Montgomery Museum of Fine Arts. The museum has nineteenth- and twentieth-century paintings, European and American works on paper, plus drawings, etchings, engravings, and other graphics. What your kids will probably like the best is Artwork, an area designed just for them. A hands-on gallery and art studio gives youngsters a chance to touch and to create their own art.

 ALABAMA SHAKESPEARE FESTIVAL (ages 8 to 12)

1 Festival Drive, Montgomery 36117; (334) 277–2273 or (334) 271–5353. Call for schedule. Tickets range typically from $15 to $25.

Across from the museum is the Alabama Shakespeare Festival multi-million-dollar theater complex, which offers both tours and performances. The festival is staged by the fifth-largest Shakespeare company in the world. World-class theater productions include not only works by William Shakespeare but also by the best contemporary playwrights.

MONTGOMERY ZOO (all ages)

2301 Coliseum Parkway, Montgomery 36110; (334) 240–4900. Open daily from 9:00 A.M. to 5:00 P.M. Admission is $4.50 for adults, $2.50 for children 4 to 12, and $2.00 for seniors 65+.

There's no question that your kids will want to see the Montgomery Zoo. Its residents include many rare and endangered species clustered by their native continents and allowed to roam with a minimum of barri-

> **Annual Event** Each February or March the Montgomery Zoo hosts **Zoo Weekend,** with animal shows, games, and crafts.

ers. The best way to get an overview here is to travel aboard the zoo's miniature train, which laces through the complex. Overlook Cafe is the place to find hot dogs, hamburgers, popcorn, ice cream—and a great view of the zoo.

HANK WILLIAMS MUSEUM (all ages)

300 Water Street, Montgomery 36104; (334) 262–3600. Open Monday through Saturday from 9:00 A.M. to 5:00 P.M. and Sunday from 1:00 to 4:00 P.M. Admission is $5.00 for adults and $1.00 for children 12 and younger.

Housed in Union Station, the museum holds memorabilia of the country-music great. Included is the 1952 blue Cadillac in which he died. The gift shop is a fun place.

F. SCOTT FITZGERALD MUSEUM (ages 6 to 12)

919 Felder Avenue, Montgomery 36101; (334) 264–4222. Open Wednesday through Friday from 10:00 A.M. to 2:00 P.M. and on weekends from 1:00 to 3:00 P.M. Admission is **Free***.*

If there's a wordsmith with you, spin by the F. Scott Fitzgerald Museum, said to be the world's only museum devoted to the writer. The Fitzgeralds' roots here are shallow—they rented the house briefly—but the collection of related items is impressive, including Zelda's artwork and letters traded by the couple who came to represent the jazz age.

W. A. GAYLE PLANETARIUM (ages 6 to 12)

1010 Forest Avenue, Montgomery 36106; (334) 241–4799 or 241–4798; Fax (334) 240–4309; www.tsum.edu. Public shows are Monday through Thursday at 3:00 P.M. and Sunday at 2:00 P.M. Admission is $3.00 per person.

Considered one of the country's major planetariums, it features an auditorium designed especially for simulating the natural sky by projecting images of the sun, moon, planets, stars, and other celestial objects on a 50-foot-high domed ceiling.

FORT TOULOUSE/JACKSON PARK NATIONAL HISTORIC LANDMARK (all ages)

2521 West Fort Toulouse Road, Wetumpka 36093; (334) 567–3002; Fax (334) 514–6625. Open daily from dawn to dusk. Admission is $2.00 for adults and $1.00 for children ages 6 to 12.

Hernando De Soto visited this site in 1540, and the French established Fort Toulouse in 1717. Later, in 1814, Andrew Jackson built his namesake fort, marking the end of the Creek Indian War. If your kids don't care about the history of this 165-acre place, they'll at least like the re-created fort, museum, and walking trails.

JASMINE HILL GARDENS (all ages)

3001 Jasmine Hill Road, Wetumpka (mail: Box 210792, Montgomery 36121); (334) 567–6463; Fax (334) 567–6466; www.jasminehill.org. Open Tuesday through Sunday from 9:00 A.M. to 5:00 P.M. and open Monday only on holidays. Closed Thanksgiving Day, December 25, and New Year's Day. Admission is $5.00 for adults, $4.50 for seniors 55+, $3.00 for children 6 to 12, and free for children under 6. Walking tours are self-guided.

Before you arrive at Jasmine Hill Gardens in Wetumpka, ask your children how they think a wonderland of gardens and statues could have come to be on a mountaintop. When they abandon their own speculations, tell them a love story, the tale of a man and a woman who picnicked on the grounds, saw an old cabin, and later, after marrying, returned to this stretch of woodland in the Appalachian Mountains.

Under the direction of Mary Mapes Fitzpatrick, a dozen acres became the heart of Jasmine Hill Gardens, where something always is in bloom. Having traveled to Greece more than a dozen times, Mary and Ben Fitzpatrick collected reproductions of statues that they had shipped home. By the time of Ben's death in 1969, the couple had gathered forty statues, a full-size replica of the Temple of Hera, a wrought-iron fence, and wall plaques copied from the Italian sculptor Della Robbia.

Both children and adults stand in awe of the exact copy of what remains of the Temple of Hera in Greece. The original temple, leveled by an earthquake, later was buried by floodwaters under silt and debris.

The site includes an Olympic visitors' center, a multimedia orientation room, a gift shop, and an exhibition hall displaying new copies of ancient Greek statues. Inclusion of Greek studies in the sixth-grade curriculum in Alabama has brought students from all over the state here to experience Greek architecture, sculpture, art, literature, poetry, history, and drama.

The Fitzpatricks are gone but their garden lives on. Overseen by new owners Jim and Elmore Inscoe, the attraction is a grand place to picnic surrounded by flowers in a garden made from love.

Where to Eat

Chris' Hot Dog Stand. *138 Dexter Avenue, Montgomery 36104; (334) 265–6850.* A tradition for more than eighty years with booths, old-fashioned lunch counters, and Chris' famous sauce. No credit cards accepted. $

Corsino's. *911 South Court Street, Montgomery 36104; (334) 263–9752.* Try the hand-tossed New York–style pizza or share a foot-long Italian sandwich. No credit cards. Closed weekends. $–$$$

Farmer's Market Cafeteria. *315 North McDonough Street, Montgomery 36104; (334) 262–9163.* You won't write home about the setting—a downtown industrial building—but you'll savor the Southern-style cooking. Notice the photos of athletes on the walls. Bountiful breakfast. $

Martin's Restaurant. *1796 Carter Hill Road, Montgomery 36106; (334) 265–1767.* You'll find downhome cooking such as fried chicken, fried catfish, and corn-bread muffins. No frills but comfortable. $

Sassafras Tearoom. *532 Clay Street, Montgomery 36104; (334) 265–7277.* Near Old Alabama Town, it has a Southern tearoom atmosphere and updated takes on Southern foods. Chicken salad is a favorite. Lunch only. $

Capital Count Even though Montgomery has been Alabama's capital since 1846, it was not the state's first. Earlier capitals were in St. Stephens (1817–1819), Huntsville (1819–1820), Cahawba (1820–1826), and Tuscaloosa (1826–1846).

Where to Stay

Comfort Inn-Montgomery South.
1035 South Boulevard, Montgomery 36105; (334) 281–5090 or (800) 228–5150. **Free** continental breakfast and a swimming pool. $

Courtyard by Marriott. *555 Carmichael Road, Montgomery 36117; (334) 272–5533.* Guest laundry, **Free** crib, in-room coffee. Kids under 18 stay **Free**. $$

Holiday Inn East Holidome. *1185 East Boulevard, Montgomery 36117; (334) 272–0370 or (800) HOLIDAY.* Indoor swimiming pool, game area for kids, and a restaurant. $$

Holiday Inn Hotel and Suites. *1100 West South Boulevard, Montgomery 36104; (334) 264–2231 or (800) 611–5868.* **Free** continental breakfast, swimming pool, and a restaurant. $–$$

Key West Inn. *4225 U.S. Highway 231, Wetumpka 36092; (334) 567–2227 or (800) 833–0555.* **Free** continental breakfast. $

La Quinta Inn. *1280 East Boulevard, Montgomery 36117–2231; (334) 271–1620 or (800) NU–ROOMS; Web site www.laquinta.com.* Featuring upscale amenities not typically found at mid-priced hotels. You'll like the 25-inch televisions with Nintendo game systems, in-room coffeemaker, **Free** local telephone calls, and **Free** breakfast. Children under 18 stay **Free** with parents. $

Red Bluff Cottage. *551 Clay Street, Montgomery 36101; (334) 264–0056; Fax (334) 263–3054.* Bright and cheerful with a special room for kids. $–$$

Author's Top Picks

- Water World, Dothan (334–793–0297)

- AdventureLand Theme Park, Dothan (334–793–9100)

- Pike Pioneer Museum, Troy (334–566–3597)

- Tom Mann's Fish World Aquariums, Eufaula (334–687–3655)

- George Washington Carver Museum, Tuskegee (334–727–3200)

- Surfside Water Park, Auburn (334–821–7873)

- Alabama Cattleman's Association MOOseum, Montgomery (334–265–1867)

- Old Alabama Town, Montgomery (334–240–4500 or 888–240–1850)

- F. Scott Fitzgerald Museum, Montgomery (334–264–4222)

- Montgomery Zoo, Montgomery (334–240–4900)

For More Information

Montgomery Area Chamber of Commerce. *(Box 79, Montgomery 36101); (334) 261–1100 or (800) 240–9452; (334) 262–0013* *(visitors center); Fax (334) 261–1111; E-mail tourism@montgomerychamber.org; Web site www.montgomeryal.us.*

Index

explore the south

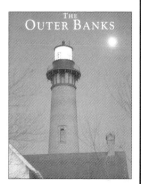

Hiking South Carolina Trails
North Carolina Is My Home
North Carolina Curiosities
Fun with the Family™ in North Carolina
Short Bike Rides® in North Carolina
Outerbanks
Romantic Days & Nights® Savannah
Romantic Days & Nights® Atlanta
Quick Escapes® Atlanta
Georgia: Off the Beaten Path®
Romantic Days & Nights® New Orleans
Quick Escapes® Florida
Fun with the Family™ in Florida
Choose Florida for Retirement: Discoveries for Every Budget
Guide to Sea Kayaking in Southern Florida
Great Family Vacations: South
Recommended Country Inns®: South
Southeastern Lighthouses
Gulf Coast Lighthouses
Choose the South: Retirement Discoveries for Every Budget
Best Bike Rides® in the South
Dixie: A Traveler's Guide

And an *Off the Beaten Path®* guide for every state in the South!